RAILWAYS IN THE VICTORIAN ECONOMY

Railways in the Victorian Economy

Studies in Finance and Economic Growth

Edited by

M. C. REED

DAVID & CHARLES : NEWTON ABBOT

7153 4323 8

*Printed in Great Britain by
Latimer Trend & Company Limited
for David & Charles (Publishers) Limited
South Devon House Railway Station
Newton Abbot Devon*

Contents

Preface

The importance of railways in the British economy was recognised almost as soon as the railway system was established, and has been stressed in virtually every work on the economic history of the Victorian age. But, in general, detailed studies of the impact of railways on certain sectors of the economy, or accounts of the economic history of railways themselves, have not been given so much prominence in the writing of economic history in Britain as has been the case in America, and while a number of local studies have paid full attention to the interaction of railway development and economic growth in various regions, the detailed study of the British railway system has on the whole been divorced from the mainstream of British economic history.

Part of this is no doubt due to the comparatively recent establishment by British Railways of organised archives to preserve and make available for research the mass of material inherited from the pre-nationalisation companies. The collections of the British Transport Historical Records offices must form one of the richest sources of manuscript material for the economic history of modern Britain, and will no doubt be increasingly used in future if their permanence and accessibility are properly guaranteed.

The purpose of this book is to bring together a number of studies in nineteenth century economic history which have made use of material from the British Transport Historical Records, either as part of a larger study, or as a piece of specific research. A number of the pieces included have been reprinted from earlier publications, and some of the articles reprinted in this way were among the first to be based on material from the Transport Archives. Three of the articles included in this volume have not previously been published, and are products of current research into various aspects of the nineteenth century railway system.

The articles included in the present volume concentrate on two main themes: the role of the railway in economic growth (with, conversely, a study of railway policy and its results in economic depression); and the question of railway finance. The first topic, the part played by the railway in promoting economic growth, is obviously a central question in economic history, and one which has been keenly debated in the United States. It is hoped that the studies presented here, while necessarily limited in scope, will point to some spheres where British railway building and operation stimulated growth and affected the development of the economy.

The question of finance is of course one much more peculiar to the development of the railways themselves, though even in this sphere the railways, by virtue of their heavy capital demands, influenced economic development. The financial and commercial sides of railway development provided an example for an increasingly wide range of companies as the century progressed: indeed, many of the problems of railway accountancy discussed by Mr Pollins are still faced by modern companies, and in this sphere as in many others the railways were the first large-scale commercial organisations to have to work out solutions to the problems they faced.

This volume, therefore, does not concern itself solely with railways: its purpose is to present some studies dealing with a very few aspects of the interrelation of railway development and economic questions in what is generally accepted to have been 'the Railway Age'. Necessarily, no completeness can be claimed for the book as a whole, and indeed many of the conclusions put forward in the various papers are put forward by their authors as tentative conclusions only. The present volume should be regarded more as a progress report than as a complete survey in even a limited field, and it is hoped that it will serve to stimulate further discussion and research within the broad theme of its title.

M. C. REED

Acknowledgments

We are indebted to the following for permission to reprint material incorporated in this volume:

The editors of the *Economic History Review*, for material incorporated in S. A. Broadbridge's article 'The Sources of Railway Share Capital', originally published in his article 'The Early Capital Market: the Lancashire and Yorkshire Railway', *Ec Hist Rev*, 2nd series, VIII (1955–6), 200–12.

The editor of the *Journal of Economic History*; for B. R. Mitchell's article, 'The coming of the Railway and United Kingdom Economic Growth', *J Ec Hist*, XXIV (1964), 315–36.

Leicester University Press, for Harold Pollins's article, 'Railway Contractors and the Finance of Railway Development in Britain', *J Trans Hist*, III (1957–8), 41–51, 103–10.

Messrs Sweet & Maxwell, for Mr Pollins's chapter 'Aspects of Railway Accounting before 1868'; from A. C. Littleton and B. S. Yamey (editors), *Studies in the History of Accounting* (1956), pp 332–55.

The editor of the *University of Birmingham Historical Journal*, for D. E. C. Eversley's article, 'The Great Western Railway and the Swindon Works in the Great Depression', *UBHJ*, 5 (1955–6), 167–90.

Standard References and Abbreviations

Throughout this volume the following references have been used:

BTHR	Material held at the British Transport Historical Records Office, Porchester Road, London W1. (Material is referred to by class and piece number.)
BTHR (S) BTHR (Y)	Material from the British Transport Historical Records deposited at Edinburgh and York respectively.
PP	Parliamentary Papers (followed by year and volume number.)
SC	Select Committee.

The place of publication is not given when reference is made to books published in London.

The Coming of the Railway and United Kingdom Economic Growth

by B. R. MITCHELL

According to W. W. Rostow, 'the introduction of the railroad has been historically the most powerful single initiator of take-offs', having 'three major kinds of impact on economic growth during the take-off period', namely, lowering transport costs and bringing new areas and products into the market; developing a major new export sector; and leading on to the development of modern coal, iron, and engineering industries.[1] But though all these three can be traced in mid nineteenth century Britain, the railways are not accorded the role of initiator in that country since, in the Rostow *schema*, the take-off had already occurred before the invention of the locomotive. The size of the investment in Britain's railways is such, however, that it is worth examining their impact, even if this was not so overwhelming as in some other countries.[2]

In considering the influence of railways on the United States economy, L. H. Jenks distinguished three phases or 'moments'—the railroad as an idea, as a construction enterprise, and as a producer of transport services.[3] This provides a useful framework within which to examine railways in the United Kingdom, but a further phase must be added—the railway as a financial enterprise.

> Once railway projects have been conceived and plans for their execution elaborated, it becomes easier for other innovation ideas to be entertained. . . . The first moment of the railroad as an economic force was manifested in a wavelike profusion of new enterprises of many

This paper was first published in *Journal of Economic History*, XXIV (1964), 315–36, and is based on research carried out into long-term capital formation in the United Kingdom, at the University of Cambridge Department of Applied Economics. I should like to acknowledge the help I have received from discussions with my colleagues, especially Miss Phyllis Deane and Dr C. H. Feinstein. Any opinion expressed here is, of course, my own responsibility.

[1] Rostow, *The Process of Economic Growth* (Oxford: Clarendon Press; 2nd ed, 1960), pp 302–3.

[2] I do not wish to imply that I agree with Rostow's reasoning about the impact of new industries. As more than one critic has pointed out, economic growth results from rising productivity, not from newness as such.

[3] L. H. Jenks, 'Railroads as an Economic Force in American Development', *Journal of Economic History*, IV, No 1 (May 1944), 1–20.

sorts. Moreover, its effects in the United States were not exhausted in a decade or so, as they were in England.[1]

At first sight, the speed with which the British trunk railway system was laid down seems to bear out Jenks's statement; apart from the Marylebone line, parts of the St Pancras-Scotland route, and certain extensions at the extremities, the system was complete by 1852. But to accept this is to equate British and American circumstances too closely. In Britain, unlike the United States, railways were not pushing forward into virgin territory, creating new towns and new industries to provide the traffic to justify the original enterprise.[2] From the first, British railways were built with existing traffic very much in mind, as a glance at any of the estimates of revenue in early railway prospectuses will show.[3] These generally showed the size of existing traffic in some detail, though an increase was, of course, always anticipated. Nor were the expectations of the British railway innovators greatly at fault so far as freight traffic was concerned: if anything, they seem to have erred on the side of exaggerating the possibilities rather than underrating them—not surprisingly.[4] The coming of the railway in Britain did not lead to 'a wavelike profusion of new enterprises of many sorts' simply because there were already in existence a great many enterprises with their traffic already flowing in established channels. The railways took over those channels, partially at first, almost entirely in the long run. They provided a better and cheaper service in most cases, or at least compelled existing forms of transport to do so in self-defence, and the benefits of this no doubt affected many industries and ultimately led to the establishment of new enterprises; but they did not to any significant extent simply make possible what had been previously impossible. There is, perhaps, one exception to this statement, namely the industry which stood to gain most from the diffusion of cheaper transport services—coal. The prospect of a new line often led to the sinking of new pits in hitherto untapped parts of the coalfields,[5] and to this extent, the industry felt the impact of the railroad as an idea. But in general, the first of Jenks's phases of railway de-

[1] Jenks, loc cit, pp 2–3.

[2] Paul H. Cootner, 'The Role of the Railroads in American Economic Growth', *Journal of Economic History*, XXIII, No 4 (Dec 1963), 477–521, questions whether this is a correct interpretation of even the American experience.

[3] Many of these are contained in the collections of *Reports and Accounts* at the three offices of the British Transport Commission Historical Records. I am extremely grateful to Mr L. C. Johnson (the former Archivist), Mr Atkinson, and the staff in London, and to Mr R. M. Hogg and Mr E. H. Fowkes and their staffs in Edinburgh and York respectively, for the great help I have received from them.

[4] See, for example, J. Francis, *A History of the English Railway* (2 vols, 1851), I, 203. The tendency to exaggerate was not generally true of the successful promotions of the 1840s.

[5] As in Durham in the 1830s, for instance—see R. C. O. Matthews, *A Study in Trade Cycle History* (Cambridge University Press, 1954), p 212—or in the Rhondda valleys in the 1850s—see J. H. Morris and L. J. Williams, *The South Wales Coal Industry* (Cardiff: University of Wales Press, 1958), p 98.

velopment was hardly experienced in the comparatively mature British economy, and its effects were not 'exhausted within a decade', because they were scarcely felt at all.

To say that the railway as an idea was insignificant in the British economy is not to deny importance to railway capital formation, but to suggest that it lay rather in the direct effects of the construction of lines and in the reduction in the cost of transport services. This is not surprising in a country where commercial relationships were widely established and where the principal centres of industry and trade were already served by existing means of communication. The railways came to supplement and in some cases to supplant those existing means. But it is significant that it was the stage-coaches rather than the canals, the passenger carriers rather than the freight carriers, which were supplanted the earlier and more completely. As the Select Committee on Railways put it as early as 1844,

> . . . from the immense superiority of the locomotive engine, railway companies may be taken, for all practical purposes, to possess a complete monopoly as far as regards the conveyance of passengers. As regards the conveyance of goods, this is not the case to the same extent, since railways are, in many cases, exposed to an effective competition from canals, and since the saving of time does not give such a decided superiority over the old modes of conveyance.[1]

This suggests that, at any rate in their first two decades, the reduction in freight costs brought about by the railways, certainly the reduction in the cost to the economy if not to the individual shipper, was not of overwhelming importance;[2] though one should probably except from this statement the short coal lines, particularly in the North East, where there were no canals. Writing in 1850, Lardner could say:

> The transport of merchandise is the branch of railway business on the due improvement and cultivation of which the ultimate and durable success of these vast enterprises, and the extent of their public utility, will mainly depend; yet it is a branch which has been hitherto comparatively neglected. The brilliant and unexpected results of the business in passenger traffic have not unnaturally dazzled the public, and engrossed the attention of proprietors, directors and managers.[3]

The *Railway Returns* bear out Lardner: in 1842, 12 years after the opening of the Liverpool & Manchester, only a little over 5 million tons of merchandise were carried on the railways of the United Kingdom, or 2,700 tons per mile open. Four million tons of this were coal.[4] Five years later it had risen only to 17 million tons (10 million being coal), or 4,309 tons per

[1] PP 1844, XI, Appendix 2.

[2] See Robert W. Fogel, 'A Quantitative Approach to the Study of Railroads in American Economic Growth: A Report of Some Preliminary Findings', *Journal of Economic History*, XXII, No 2 (June 1962), 163–97, for a controversial analysis which questions the traditional view about the impact of railways on costs in America.

[3] D. Lardner, *Railway Economy* (1850), p 203.

[4] PP 1844, XI, Appendix 2.

mile open.[1] Passengers provided £3·1 million out of total receipts of £4·5 million in 1842-3 and £5·6 million out of £9·8 million in 1848, and their share was not overtaken by freight revenue until 1852.

It is not proposed here to try to follow through the effects of the reduction of transport costs brought about by the railways. To trace these would be an enormous task, perhaps even an impossible one. Suffice it to say now that—while we cannot apply to Britain Jenks's assessment of American experience, that 'there is no convincing evidence that railways have ever carried freight at lower costs either to shippers or to society than canals or waterways'[2]—yet it seems that the reduction in carrying costs brought about in Britain by the coming of the railway did not have an immediately overwhelming impact on industry, and that the effects which it did have operated at least as much through compelling canals to bring their charges down nearer to marginal costs as through the direct attraction of traffic to the new form of transport. In other words, though there were reductions in costs to the shipper, the reductions in costs to society were less marked.

From about the time of the great mania of the 1840s, however, the trunk railways began to pay more attention to their goods traffic; and the effect of this is seen in the faster rate of growth of merchandise receipts than of passenger receipts. There were some reductions made in freight charges, but much more important in causing the expansion of goods traffic was the working out of an elaborate classification of goods by the Railway Clearing House, which got rid of many of the earlier difficulties involved in transferring goods from one railway system to another. The amalgamations of the mid 1840s removed still more completely this obstacle to the full realisation of the benefits of cheaper transport. 'In the early railway age', according to Clapham, the canals' 'real competitive power was strengthened by the slow development of goods traffic—especially of cheap and bulky goods traffic—on many of the railways'.[3] After 1850, however, the same author notes that 'prosperous canals were exceptional, not because of illicit railway devices, though there were such, but because of the sheer superiority of the railway as a means of transport'.[4] The economic impact of the railway as a producer of transport services had been slow in building up to its full effect, but by the time of the Royal Commission of 1867 this had been achieved, as the commission implied in saying:

> In considering the improvement of goods traffic, it is very difficult to institute any comparison with the past, because the introduction of the

[1] Estimated by adding the figures for individual railways in the *Returns* (as published in *Parliamentary Papers*) and making an allowance for omissions.

[2] Jenks, 'Railroads as an Economic Force', p 12.

[3] J. H. Clapham, *An Economic History of Modern Britain* (3 vols; Cambridge University Press, 1926–38), I, 399.

[4] Ibid, II, 199.

> railway system has entirely altered all the conditions of that traffic, and has enabled industry and trade to spring up which, without railways, could have had no existence.[1]

Rostow's widening of the market had at length been achieved, though in a much more gradual fashion than overseas. Perhaps one outstanding example of the slowness of this development may be cited: namely, the carriage of coal by rail to London. The coalfields of south Yorkshire and the east Midlands were linked by rail with the capital by the end of the 1830s, yet it was not until 1845 that any railborne coal reached London, and not until after the opening of the Great Northern that the quantity became significant. Such was its success, however, that, whereas 378,000 tons entered London by rail in 1852 compared with 3,330,000 tons by sea, by 1855 the figures were 1,138,000 tons and 3,017,000 tons respectively, and in 1867 railborne coal exceeded seaborne for the first time, both contributing over 3 million tons.[2] Here is a clear case of traffic- and market-creating opportunities being missed for over a decade.

If, then, the railway as a producer of transport services was not all that much more powerful in its immediate impact on the British economy than the railway as an idea, we are left with two other ways in which the coming of the railway may have had a profound effect—through its actual construction and through its influence on financial institutions and habits. Let us consider these in turn.

The exact place of railway capital formation in the British economy of the mid nineteenth century is shown in Table 1. These statistics are, of course, estimates subject to considerable margins of error, but the proportions shown in Column 3 are probably not very far out. They indicate three things of particular interest: (1) the speed with which railway investment achieved a position of importance in the economy; and (2) coupled with this, the dominance of its position in the second half of the 1840s; (3) the supporting rather than leading nature of the role of railway building in the economic fluctuations of the time. Railway building may have sustained, even at times accelerated, economic growth; but it did not lead it—not, at least, if growth be measured by national income.

Railway capital formation was of little importance nationally in the 1820s, or even in the first half of the following decade,[3] though no doubt it added considerably to effective demand in north-east England and south-

[1] PP 1867, XXXVIII, lxv. It is perhaps worth noting that the social impact of the new form of transport was much more immediately powerful, as the rapid growth of passenger traffic indicates. This would surely repay more study than has yet been made.

[2] B. R. Mitchell and Phyllis Deane, *Abstract of British Historical Statistics* (Cambridge University Press, 1962), p 113.

[3] A table in Gayer, Rostow, and Schwartz, *The Growth and Fluctuation of the British Economy, 1790–1850* (2 vols; Oxford: The Clarendon Press, 1953), I, 254, seems to indicate that it exceeded £10 million in 1833 and 1835, but it is completely misleading. The cost of railways referred to there is the *ultimate* cost of lines authorised in those years.

west Lancashire. In the later 1830s, however, it built up rapidly, at a time when national income at current prices was rising quickly, to nearly 2 per cent of national income. Some idea of the comparative importance of this position is gained by noting that from 1837 to 1842, the value of railway capital formation (excluding purchases of land) was higher than the value of domestic exports to the United States, or that in 1838–40 it was more than double the value of total exports of iron, hardwares, and cutlery. Though sinking back to less than 1 per cent of national income in the early 1840s, railway investment in the second half of the decade leapt ahead to great dominance, taking at its height in 1847 not far short of 7 per cent of national income, which was then at about the same level as at the beginning of the decade.[1] To put it in comparative terms once again, expenditure on railway building was, at its peak, about two thirds of the value of all domestic exports, and half as much again as the value of cotton goods exported; or, to find yet another yardstick, it was over twice as great as the maximum level of the Bank of England's bullion reserve in the decade. Such a level of expenditure, reached in such a comparatively short time, was bound to have an enormous impact on the economy, and it will be our task now to examine this more closely.

The building of railways made a large direct demand on the country's labour force. There were between 40 and 60 men normally employed on each mile of line under construction in the 1850s,[2] and there is no reason to suppose that it was noticeably different before or after. Thus as early as 1839, when there were at least 1,000 miles under construction, the number of men directly employed must have been around 50,000, or 1 per cent of the occupied male population and a seventh of those employed in building and construction[3]—already as great proportionately as those employed in operating the 6,600 miles of line open in 1852. Their total wages for the year must have come to between £2 million and £2·5 million.[4] This is a sizeable sum, and the labour force was a substantial one: already more important than in many old-established industries—paper, glass, pottery, or brickmaking, for example. It was gathered together so quickly and easily largely because of immigration from Ireland and of under-employ-

[1] The large size of this figure seems to call for some comment, though it will come as no surprise to anyone who has read carefully the pages of *The Economist* for the 1840s. The very high temporary expenditure on railway building was achieved partly by a genuine increase in savings (mainly by people who in 1845 had been anxious to be in on what they felt to be a good thing), partly by a falling off in investment in other types of capital formation (probably in inventories more than anything else), and partly by repatriation of funds previously invested overseas.

[2] PP 1857–8, LI. In the immediate aftermath of the great mania, when contractors were trying to keep together their staffs, the average rose above 60 men per mile.

[3] Census *Report*, 1841.

[4] Wage rates for various types of railway construction labourer are given in the *Report* of the Select Committee on Railway Labourers (PP 1846, XIII); in Sir Arthur Helps, *Life and Labours of Mr. Brassey* (1872); and in Earl Brassey, *Work and Wages* (London, 1916).

TABLE 1

UK RAILWAY CAPITAL FORMATION AND NATIONAL INCOME

(£ MILLION)

Year	(1) Gross Expenditure on Railway Capital Formation (excl. land)	(2) National Income	(3) 1 as Percentage of 2
1831	0·2	421	Trace
1832	0·3	417	0·1
1833	0·7	411	0·2
1834	0·9	408	0·2
1835	1·4	404	0·3
1836	2·8	457	0·6
1837	5·2	463	1·1
1838	9·0	492	1·8
1839	9·7	534	1·8
1840	8·7	540	1·6
1841	6·0	550	1·1
1842	4·9	549	0·9
1843	4·0	554	0·7
1844	4·3	568	0·8
1845	13·2	578	2·3
1846	32·7	572	5·7
1847	36·8	550	6·7
1848	26·1	554	4·7
1849	17·1	556	3·1
1850	9·2	565	1·6
1851	7·4	578	1·3
1852	8·3	596	1·4
1853	8·9	610	1·5
1854	11·5	612	1·9
1855	10·1	620	1·6
1856	7·8	656/665	1·2
1857	8·4	636/645	1·3
1858	7·9	624/635	1·2
1859	8·6	647/656	1·3
1860	9·2	684/694	1·3
1861	13·0	717/727	1·8
1862	13·6	741	1·8
1863	16·7	759	2·2
1864	19·5	795	2·5
1865	23·2	822	2·8
1866	20·6	846	2·4
1867	13·7	840	1·6
1868	9·6	836	1·1
1869	8·2	867	0·9

Sources: For Column 1, see Appendix, p 29. For Column 2: Figures up to 1855 and the first ones shown for 1845–61 are estimates by Phyllis Deane, being interpolations between the statistics for benchmark years shown in Phyllis Deane and W. A. Cole, *British Economic Growth, 1688–1959* (Cambridge University Press, 1962). Figures for 1862–9 and the second ones shown for 1856–61 are from C. H. Feinstein, 'Income and Investment in the United Kingdom, 1856–1914', *Economic Journal*, No 282 (June 1961), pp 367–85.

ment in the over-populated countryside of southern England,[1] and though comparatively high wages were paid, it does not appear to have caused other industries any labour problems. One of the first results of the experience in making railways was the emergence of large-scale contractors, who to a great extent replaced, or at any rate subordinated, the mass of small contractors who had built canals and who were used by the early railway companies, often to their dissatisfaction.[2] When the great increase in the labour force began in 1845, it was chiefly these men who were responsible for it.

A House of Commons return[3] gave the numbers employed on lines under construction on 1 May 1847, as 256,509, or approximately 4 per cent of the occupied male population, and this figure can scarcely have been much less in 1846, when their importance and condition was such as to lead to a Select Committee on Railway Labourers. The year 1845 must therefore have been the main time of recruitment of this largely increased labour force; and, even supposing that the bulk of those employed in the late 1830s were retained or recovered, around 200,000 men must have been drawn into the contractors' gangs in the course of only a year or so. Once again, this seems to have been accomplished with considerable ease, and once again the two main sources were the Irish immigrant and the surplus rural population of southern England; while in Scotland the Highlander was at least as important as the Irishman.[4] The wage bill for these men was in the region of £16 million a year, or between 2 and 3 per cent of national income; and since a large part of this represented a net increase in effective demand, it was of some importance to the economy. Since the building of railways was to some degree concentrated geographically, its importance to particular areas must have been large, despite the prevalence of tommy shops, which tended to siphon the multiplier effects away from the places where the navvies were working.

From a quarter of a million men, the railway-building labour force fell within three years to around 50,000, and it stayed at about that level throughout the 1850s until the returns ceased to be made and our information gives out.[5] What happened to the 200,000 men cannot be said with any certainty. Some few doubtless joined the growing numbers employed by the railway to run the lines, but they cannot have been many, since the total increase

[1] Clapham, *Modern Britain*, I, 405–7, summarises most of the published evidence on this question.

[2] The London & Birmingham Company, for example, had great difficulty over its Kilsby tunnel, several contractors failing to fulfill their undertakings.

[3] PP 1847, LXIII.

[4] One witness before the Select Committee on Railway Labourers (PP 1846, XIII) reckoned that there were no recent Irish immigrants on the Caledonian or Hawick lines, but that about two-fifths of the workers were Glasgow–Irish or Edinburgh–Irish (Q 460–62). According to another witness, most of the remainder were Highlanders (Q 73).

[5] *Railway Returns* up to 1860. Allowance has to be made for men employed in completing lines already opened.

from 1847 to 1851 was only 16,000 men. Some went abroad, but again they cannot have constituted a large proportion. Five thousand English navvies were employed on the Paris–Rouen line in the early 1840s—perhaps twice as many went abroad temporarily after 1847 to work on the contracts of Thomas Brassey and others. Some must have been among those who made the 1850s a peak decade for emigration from Britain, not surpassed until the 1880s. Some may have gone into the fast expanding coal mines. Others, perhaps the majority, drifted into general labouring in those parts of the country where the tempo of economic growth was highest. Wherever they went, the rapid disbandment of such a large part of the contractors' gangs does not seem to have caused more than a temporary employment problem.

If the biggest single type of outlay in building railways was on the wages of the men whose main function was, quite simply, to move large quantities of earth, there were other forms of expenditure which were also large, and which in some cases were of much more permanent importance. The chief of these were the great increase brought about in the demand for iron (and, through iron, for coal) and the stimulus given to the previously quite small engineering industry. Here we have the third of Rostow's kinds of impact, and it was as great in Britain as anywhere.[1]

The laying of tracks entailed a large direct demand for iron of a comparatively simple kind—for rails, chairs, and such like, and for bridgework. There was also a considerable amount of iron used in the rolling stock, but that is more conveniently regarded as a demand from the engineering industry. It is possible to make rough estimates of the size of the annual demand for railway iron; and though these are bound to be more often wrong than right for individual years (since renewals could be put off or advanced according to the financial position of the companies), they can be taken as reasonably accurate when aggregated for a number of years. This is done in Table 2 for the various cycles of railway construction in the middle of the nineteenth century, the figures for railway iron being converted to pig-iron equivalent, since this is the type for which national output figures are available.

What stands out from this table, apart from the large and increasing importance of exports of iron (much of which was for railways abroad), is the shortness of the period in which domestic rail demand was of outstanding importance to the British iron industry. According to Clapham, 'The railway demand, direct and indirect, dominated the home market',[2] and though he does not refer to any exact period, we can place the relevance of the statement in the 20–30 years after 1838, with the later 1840s as

[1] Economic growth induced in this way operated mainly through the provision of economies of scale and partly, perhaps, through increased regularity of employment in the coal mines.

[2] Clapham, *Modern Britain*, I, 427.

the peak of dominance. But such was the growth of the export market that it was only for this short time that Clapham's statement is true.

The output of pig iron is estimated to have risen from half a million tons in 1832 to a million tons in 1835 and to one and a half million tons in 1841. The railways, needing about 20,000 tons a year, had scarcely any direct part in bringing about the first part of this increase, which must surely be ascribed chiefly to conditions on the supply side, in particular to the great rise of

TABLE 2

UK PIG IRON OUTPUT AND DEMAND FOR PERMANENT WAY

Years	(1) *Estimated Total Demand for Pig Iron for Permanent Way*	(2) *UK Pig Iron Output*	(3) *Estimated Pig Iron Equivalent Available in UK*	(4) *(1) as Percentage of (2)*	(5) *(1) as Percentage of (3)*
1835–43	795	11,010	8,082	7·2	9·8
1844–51	2,773	15,455	9,690	17·9	28·6
1852–9	2,261	26,253	13,468	8·6	16·8
1860–9	3,611	45,286	23,963	8·0	15·1

Sources and methods of calculation: Column 1: New track laid each year was calculated on assumed ratios between track mileage and geographical mileage (as given in Mitchell and Deane, *Abstract*, pp 225–9). Those ratios were given in *Railway Returns* from 1903 to 1912, during which time they increased at 0·01 per year. This rate has been extrapolated back until a ratio of 2 to 1 is reached in 1877, which ratio has been assumed to hold good for all previous years, it being reckoned that the higher proportion of double track in the early days was offset by the smaller proportion of sidings and of lines with more than two tracks. The weight of iron or steel per mile at various periods, and its conversion ratio from pig iron, was assumed on the basis of I. Lowthian Bell's figures in *The Iron Trade* (1886), pp 30 ff, and of various scattered references in numerous company histories, especially the following: E. T. MacDermot, *History of the Great Western Railway* (3 vols, 1931); G. Dow, *Great Central*, Vol I (1959); W. L. Steel *The History of the London and North Western Railway* (1914); and R. A. Whitehead and F. D. Simpson, *The Story of the Colne Valley* (Brentwood, Essex, 1951). It was assumed that from 1866 to 1869, one quarter of rails laid were of steel. For the purposes of calculating the demand for track renewal, Bell's estimates of the average life of iron rails were used: namely, ten years. His estimates of the loss of weight by wear and tear were also used in calculating the amount of scrap iron to be deducted from gross demand.

Column 2: Estimates and returns reprinted in Mitchell and Deane, *Abstract*, pp 131–2, with interpolations based on pig iron prices for years not mentioned there.

Column 3: The pig iron output figures plus net imports of iron and steel (raised to pig iron equivalent by multiplication by 1·25), minus exports (similarly altered).

Scottish output occasioned by the hot-blast innovation. In the second part of the increase, however, the railways must have been a major stimulus, taking an average of 150,000 to 200,000 tons a year in 1839–41; but they were scarcely the dominant cause, for the deluge of cheap Scottish iron continued to grow.[1] The slackening of railway demand in 1841–3 did, however, affect the iron industry very severely,[2] and though efforts were made to find other markets—exports, for instance, rising from 269,000 tons in 1840 to 450,000 tons in 1843—output fell back to the level of the mid 1830s and prices went much lower.

The upturn in railway demand in 1844 may have had something to do with the revival of the iron industry, but since it was only in the region of 100,000 tons in that year it cannot have been a major cause. In 1845, however, it probably exceeded 250,000 tons, and in 1846 and 1847 together it came to about a million tons. Figures such as these indicate a truly dominant position. Of the increase in pig iron output from 1844 to 1847—some 600,000 tons a year—by far the greater part was absorbed in permanent way in Britain. Exports fell off temporarily in 1845 under the influence of this upsurge of home demand; but such was the rapidity of the extension of productive capacity that in 1847 exports were 100,000 tons higher than in 1844, thus approximately accounting for such part in the increased output as was not absorbed by home rails. The expansion of the industry in Scotland continued, but South Wales grew also, and the stimulus to growth from demand by the railway industry must by that time have been more influential than changes in the conditions of supply—after all, Neilson's invention was by then well into its second decade.

British railways may have drawn the iron industry after them in 1845–7; but the industry continued its expansion steadily thereafter, even though the home railway demand fell back to the more modest level of less than 10 per cent of iron output. There were only three years in the 1850s and 1860s when pig iron output failed to expand—1858, 1861, and 1866. None of these seems to be connected with a reduction in demand from Britain's railways. This demand rose from about the middle of the 1850s, with renewals becoming increasingly important; but the effect was merely to maintain the railway's place in the market for iron as a substantial but not dominant customer, taking in good years only a little over 10 per cent of the make. With the depression in railway construction in 1868–71, even this position was lost, and home railways were never again of great concern to the iron industry.

Though no other industry was quite so strongly affected by the coming of the railway as was iron, mechanical engineering came close. There is no way of measuring the effects of this industry except by regarding expendi-

[1] H. Hamilton, *The Industrial Revolution in Scotland* (Oxford: Clarendon Press, 1932), p 184.

[2] H. Scrivenor, *A History of the Iron Trade* (1854), pp 290–1.

ture on rolling stock as an indicator. This does not seem to be unreasonable, and annual estimates of such expenditure, based on the accounts of a sample group of companies,[1] are shown in Table 3, together with figures of outlays on maintenance and renewal.[2]

TABLE 3

UK EXPENDITURE ON RAILWAY ROLLING STOCK

(£ MILLION)

Years	*Capital Account*	*Maintenance and Renewals*
1835–43	4·0	1·0
1844–51	15·3	5·2
1852–9	10·0	15·5
1860–9	20·0	33·2

Though not especially great in relation to national income, these figures argue that the coming of the railway in Britain gave a substantial fillip to the engineering industry. In the later 1840s, its gross output must have been only in the region of £5 to £10 million[3] at a time when railway expenditure on rolling stock was running at about £2·5 million a year. Over half this expenditure was undoubtedly for the products of the engineering industry; or, in other words, about a fifth of that industry's output went to home railways. We cannot say whether the same was true at the height of the boom of the 1830s, but it seems quite likely that the proportion was not a great deal less. The engineering industry was then substantially smaller, and while the railways spent rather less than £1 million a year, the gross engineering output was almost certainly less than £5 million. The railways, however, did not greatly expand the existing engineering industry but rather, through their specialised demand, created a new section of it, drawing in some older firms and setting up some new ones[4] and eventually leading to the establishment of their own workshops by the bigger railway

[1] The sample consists of all the large and several small companies in Great Britain. The annual expenditure of these was multiplied by a factor based (up to 1861) on their proportion of total expenditure on rolling stock to December 1857 (as given in PP 1857–8, LI) or (after 1861) on their proportionate contribution to the annual increase in the total number of vehicles, allowing for amalgamations (as given in *Railway Returns*). The figure for 1835–43 is taken from PP 1847, LXIII (return of 14 April 1847) corrected for omissions.

[2] Also based on the accounts of a sample group of companies up to 1860, when figures first appeared in *Railway Returns*.

[3] Approximately 50,000 workers were employed at an average wage of £1 a week. This gives a wage bill of roughly £2·5 million. If the proportion of wages to gross output in the engineering trades at the 1907 *Census of Production* is assumed to hold good for the mid nineteenth century, namely 1 to 3, a figure for gross output of £7·5 million is obtained.

[4] See Clapham, *Modern Britain*, I, 447–8.

companies. When that time came, the independent firms found their principal market overseas, and by the 1860s, when home railway demand on the engineering industry was running at £3 million or more a year, almost £1 million of locomotives alone were exported annually.

Of course the building of the railways had direct effects on all sorts of other industries besides iron and engineering, but it is impossible to suggest any sort of exact measure. Bricks and timber were the two commodities, besides iron, which were most called for in railway construction, and the demand for both must have been sharply increased; but as both figure much more prominently in the production of the building industry, it is practically impossible to disentangle the impact of the railways. The greater part of the wood used in the United Kingdom had to be imported; consequently the effects of railway building were, in that case, largely felt abroad. Bricks, on the other hand, were entirely home produced and, thanks to the excise and the work of Shannon, we have statistics on their production up to 1849, the national total of which is given here.[1] Various local statistics were also examined by Shannon, and it was from these that he was able to draw his conclusion that 'except for the first group of textile towns, bricks and building pass through the thirties relatively unmarked by the more purely industrial and financial troubles associated with 1836–9, but do in general show the railway-building of the late thirties'.[2] If one were to hazard a guess at the quantity of bricks needed for the railways, perhaps the difference between the 1837 and 1840 outputs might give a rough order of magnitude for the maximum annual amount—that is, about 200 million. In the boom of the 1840s this figure must have been greatly exceeded. The peak of activity for the building industry was in 1845,[3] and by 1847 there had been a marked decline. Brick output, however, continued to rise, and was over 370 million higher in 1847 than in 1845. Perhaps the railways in the latter year used more than twice this figure.

In considering the figures of railway capital formation in relation to national income in Table 1, the supporting rather than leading nature of railway construction in British economic fluctuations was noted. It is time to examine this proposition more closely.

In the first decade of major railway building, the main peak of economic activity, reflected in the steepest annual increase in national income and amply attested in other ways,[4] was in 1836. This was the year when the promotion of railway schemes reached a height, but the actual expenditure of money on capital formation did not become of much importance until

[1] From H. A. Shannon, 'Bricks—A Trade Index, 1785–1849', *Economica*, New Series, No 1 (Aug 1934), 300–18.

[2] Ibid, p 309.

[3] See E. W. Cooney, 'Long Waves in Building in the British Economy of the Nineteenth Century', *Economic History Review*, 2nd Series, XIII, No 2 (Dec 1960), 257–69, and the comment on it by A. R. Hall in ibid, XIV, No 2 (Dec 1961), 330–2.

[4] For example, Gayer, Rostow, and Schwartz, *Growth and Fluctuation*, I, 242–76.

the following three or four years, when, according to Matthews, it 'constituted the chief inflationary element in the economy'.[1] The pattern was repeated almost exactly in the great mania of the 1840s. The promotion phase coincided with the upswing of the trade cycle to its peak in 1845 (though, thanks to delays in the mechanism of securing parliamentary authority, 1846 was easily the most important year for railway Acts). It is worth noting, however, that Tooke reckoned that it was not until 'the restored prosperity of trade was no longer doubtful, and the rate of interest had for about a year and a half been under 3 per cent', that 'the attention of the public was strongly attracted to the favourable results of the investments made in the principal lines of railway then in operation'.[2] Expenditure on capital formation continued to build up after the promotion bubble had burst and reached a maximum in 1847, a year of crisis in the money market and of depression in many industries, and it continued at a high level in 1848 and 1849. The effects of the depression must, therefore, have been partially cushioned by the continuation of heavy outlays by the railway companies. This pattern of railway capital formation running behind the spurts of economic growth but sustaining the economy when other elements flagged was continued into the 1850s, though on a much muted scale.[3]

TABLE 4

BRICKS CHARGED WITH DUTY

(MILLIONS)

1832	972	1837	1,478	1842	1,272	1846	2,040
1833	1,011	1838	1,427	1843	1,159	1847	2,194
1834	1,152	1839	1,569	1844	1,421	1848	1,461
1835	1,349	1840	1,678	1845	1,821	1849	1,463
1836	1,606	1841	1,424				

Railway construction may not have led the fluctuations of the British economy, but there is one respect in which railways were the leaders—namely, the development of the capital market. According to Shannon, 'it was the railways that won the acceptance of general limited liability',[4] an event of some significance at the time but of still greater importance later. Moreover, it was in the mania of the 1840s that the Stock Exchange first 'dealt seriously in joint stock shares as opposed to bonds; and, in fact, be-

[1] R. C. O. Matthews, *A Study in Trade Cycle History* (Cambridge University Press, 1954), p 212.

[2] T. Tooke, *A History of Prices*, IV (1848), 63–4.

[3] J. R. T. Hughes, *Fluctuations in Trade, Industry and Finance, 1850–1860* (Oxford: Clarendon Press, 1960), p 206.

[4] H. A. Shannon, 'The Coming of General Limited Liability', in E. M. Carus-Wilson, ed; *Essays in Economic History*, I (1954), 376.

came heavily involved in the machinery of their flotation'.[1] Then again, it was the railways which brought about the very rapid growth in provincial stock exchanges in the 1840s,[2] a development which eventually helped to direct the surplus profits of established British industries into a variety of different channels. Yet perhaps most important of all was 'the addition of railway securities to the traditional media of investment, the creation of a much broadened base of equities for the purchaser of income'.[3] A special part of this addition was the very great expansion in preference shares brought about by the railway companies. This type of share 'grew out of the financial embarrassments of the early transportation companies',[4] but in the 1840s its use was developed by some concerns to enable them to extend their lines and equipment and to further schemes of amalgamation. The great expansion in equities quoted on the Stock Exchange can be illustrated by referring to Spackman's oft-quoted figures. According to him, £224 million was invested in equities dealt in on the London Stock Exchange in 1843, of which £57·5 million was in railways.[5] A decade later, £273 million had been paid up on railway shares (of which £43·5 million was in preference shares), and a further £64·5 million had been lent to railway companies.[6] A class of property had thus been, if not created, then vastly expanded—a class which attracted investors wanting comparative security coupled with a higher return than was offered by bonds.

According to Phyllis Deane, 'By the 1820s and early 1830s, in effect before the beginning of the main railway age, the economy had left behind its pre-industrial levels of capital formation', even though 'it had taken over a century for the average to rise from not much more than 3 per cent of national income to something less than 10 per cent'.[7] Reckoning roughly on the basis of her suggested figures for various sectors, it would seem that around the early 1830s the proportion was, in fact, a good deal less than 10 per cent—perhaps, indeed, only 6 or 7 per cent. Yet by the mid 1850s it had risen permanently to 10 per cent or more.[8] The connection between this increase and the coming of the railways, with their influence on the Stock Exchange and on the employment of savings, seems inescapable. New classes of people were encouraged to invest via the Stock Exchange instead of hiding their savings in the mattress or leaving them idle in a variety of other ways. As *The Economist* put it: 'Railway property is a new

[1] Gayer *et al*, *Growth and Fluctuation*, I, 409.

[2] B. C. Hunt, *The Development of the Business Corporation in England, 1800–1867* (Cambridge, Mass, 1936), p 107–8.

[3] G. H. Evans, *British Corporation Finance*, 1775–1850 (Baltimore, 1936), p 149

[4] Hunt, *Business Corporation*, p 106.

[5] W. F. Spackman, *Statistical Tables of the United Kingdom and its Dependencies* (1843), p 157.

[6] PP 1854–5, XLVIII ('Report of Railway Department', xvii).

[7] Phyllis Deane, 'Capital Formation in Britain before the Railway Age', *Economic Development and Cultural Change*, IX, No 3 (Apr 1961), 368.

[8] Feinstein, 'Income and Investment' (cited in Table 1).

feature in England's social economy which has introduced commercial feelings to the firesides of thousands.'[1] And Disraeli, with a certain metropolitan arrogance, noted that 'all seemed to come from the provinces, and from unknown people in the provinces'.[2] Unknown to the politicians and financiers of London they may have been, but among them were found many substantial businessmen, and the greater part of the money required to build Britain's railways came from this class rather than from the small investor.[3] Businessmen found in the railways a more rewarding way of employing their surplus profits than in the funds or simply in leaving them on deposit at a bank. Thus new habits of employing savings were encouraged, not only among professional men, small traders, widows, and others in the nascent rentier class, but also among large merchants and industrialists.

These new habits of saving were mainly stimulated in the promotion booms, when they were directed principally into ordinary shares. But they were not lost in succeeding depression, for though ordinary shares went temporarily into disfavour, calls had to be met on shares already bought; and in order to finish their lines, many companies had to get more money than anticipated and so took to issuing preference shares and various forms of loan stock, for which there was a ready market. Indeed, up to the 1870s at any rate, it was these, rather than ordinary shares, which made railway stock, in Clapham's phrase, 'a universal family investment for all families which had anything to invest'.[4] Ordinary shares tended to remain something of a speculator's buy, except in one or two periods (notably the mid 1840s and the mid 1860s), until the last quarter of the nineteenth century. But railway preference shares and debentures offered a large field for those with the rentier outlook or for entrepreneurs seeking greater security for part of their wealth. When home rails could no longer provide sufficient outlets for these people, they tended to look for the same qualities in other securities, and the record of overseas investment suggests that, on the whole, it was in public utilities overseas that they found them most easily.[5] Thus it seems likely that the coming of the railway not only was largely instrumental in raising the country's savings level above 10 per cent of national income but it also helped to determine the channels into which those savings were directed long after home rails had ceased to be a major recipient. It appears that the British rentier—and, perhaps equally important, the institutions of the capital market—had come to like public utility securities, and when the home supply was insufficient they sought

[1] *The Economist* (1845), 310.

[2] *Endymion* (London, 1881), ch lviii.

[3] This statement is based on analysis of some of the (comparatively few) surviving shareholders' registers at British Transport Historical Records.

[4] Clapham, *Modern Britain*, II, 357.

[5] See L. H. Jenks, *The Migration of British Capital to 1875* (New York, 1927), especially ch v.

them overseas rather than turn their attention strongly to other types at home. Perhaps these propositions can never be established completely; but they would surely repay further study.

Whatever its influence in other countries, the introduction of railways in Britain did not have a very great immediate impact on the economy, the main effects not being felt until during and after the great mania of the 1840s. The direct effects of the construction of railways were then, for a time, very great—especially in providing employment for unskilled labourers and in stimulating the iron and engineering industries. Moreover, it was from this time onward that the active development of freight traffic was vigorously pursued by the companies, with important consequences for many British industries. But probably the major influence of the coming of the railway was on the development of the capital market and on the level of savings. The growth of what M. M. Postan has called 'the new class of "pure" investors, the people who had learned to put their money into profitable use, and to decide that use by the sole criterion of interest'[1] received an enormous fillip from the railways. The not-quite-so-'pure' investor, whose *alter ego* was an entrepreneur anxious to diversify his investments, was equally stimulated. Once the habits of saving and of employing savings had been changed, the investors did not revert to the old situation when the outlets offered by home rails declined, but the money was diverted into new channels offering yields and security similar to those to which home rails had accustomed them.

APPENDIX

ANNUAL STATISTICS OF RAILWAY CAPITAL FORMATION, 1831–1919

The annual statistics of gross capital formation in railways, which are given in Table 1 of this article, are taken from a series of estimates made in the course of the long-term capital formation inquiry referred to in the footnote at the beginning. The full estimates are of annual figures for gross and net capital formation at current and constant prices, and they distinguish outlays on rolling stock, on the main ancillary businesses, on land, and on permanent way and buildings. It is hoped to publish these eventually in a monograph on United Kingdom Capital Formation since 1830. Meanwhile, the full series to 1919 for gross capital formation in railways at current prices is shown here.

A full account of the methods by which these figures were estimated may be had from the University of Cambridge Department of Applied Economics. They may be briefly described as follows. Those railway company accounts which have survived and are kept at the British Transport Historical Record offices in London, Edinburgh, and York were examined, and the statistics of expenditure on capital account were extracted and adjusted to make them fit a uniform defini-

[1] Postan, 'Recent Trends in the Accumulation of Capital', *Economic History Review* VI (Oct 1935), 1–12.

tion of capital expenditure. This covered a large proportion of all railways, varying from those with half the total paid-up capital in the 1830s to those with nearly all the paid-up capital in 1913. The expenditure of the remaining companies, whose accounts have not survived, was then estimated on the basis of the known expenditure of the others. After 1843, when the *Railway Returns* (published annually in the *Sessional Papers* of Parliament) show the paid-up capital of each company, it was assumed that the expenditure of the 'unknown' group of companies was in the same proportion to the expenditure of the 'known' group of companies as were their respective paid-up capitals. Before 1843, the proportion was based on capital authorised, which provides the only recorded annual statistics for that period.

Authorisations were assumed to have been spent over a period of years in accordance with the experience of the companies whose accounts have survived.

In addition to expenditure on capital account, gross capital formation must include expenditures on renewals. These were estimated by taking a proportion of the recorded outlays on repairs and renewals combined, as given in the *Railway Returns* for track and buildings from 1854 and for carriages and wagons from 1860. For earlier years, and for outlays on engines throughout, the accounts of a sample group of companies were used as the basis of estimation.

Appendix Table 1

GROSS UK CAPITAL FORMATION BY RAILWAY COMPANIES, 1831–1919

(IN £ MILLION AT CURRENT PRICES)

Year	(1) *Permanent Way and Works*	(2) *Rolling Stock*	(3) *Ancillary Businesses*[1]	(4) *Land*	(5) *Total Gross Capital Formation*
1831	0·17	0·03	0·02	0·04	0·3
1832	0·26	0·04	0·02	0·06	0·4
1833	0·53	0·08	0·06	0·12	0·8
1834	0·72	0·11	0·07	0·16	1·0
1835	1·17	0·17	0·05	0·25	1·6
1836	2·45	0·34	0·02	0·50	3·3
1837	4·51	0·61	0·04	0·86	6·0
1838	7·88	1·08	0·02	1·69	10·6
1839	8·60	1·12	0·02	1·30	11·1
1840	7·68	0·99	0·04	0·96	9·7
1841	5·28	0·69	0·05	0·51	6·5
1842	4·28	0·57	0·04	0·48	5·3
1843	3·47	0·51	0·03	0·74	4·7
1844	3·67	0·54	0·02	0·73	4·9

[1] The figures in this column are of expenditure on ancillary businesses on capital account only. Expenditure on renewals could be separated from way and works renewals only with difficulty, and the amounts involved are too small to make this worth while.

APPENDIX TABLE 1 (*continued*)

1845[2]	10·42	0·78	0·02	1·84	13·0
1846[2]	23·15	2·47	0·05	4·36	30·2
1847[2]	31·87	4·78	0·12	7·10	43·9
1848[2]	25·15	2·71	0·10	4·97	33·1
1849[2]	18·66	2·34	0·04	3·78	24·9
1850[2]	9·85	1·35	0·04	1·85	13·1
1851[2]	6·68	1·66	0·07	1·51	9·9
1852	6·85	1·28	0·18	1·40	9·7
1853	6·94	1·85	0·07	1·35	10·2
1854	8·49	2·98	0·08	1·19	12·7
1855	7·68	2·27	0·13	1·25	11·3
1856	6·12	1·55	0·13	1·19	9·0
1857	6·76	1·44	0·20	1·26	9·6
1858	6·51	1·20	0·24	1·38	9·3
1859	7·13	1·37	0·15	1·29	9·9
1860	6·91	2·09	0·15	1·79	11·0
1861	10·31	2·51	0·17	1·44	14·4
1862	10·76	2·61	0·25	2·52	16·2
1863	14·33	2·15	0·20	3·27	20·0
1864	15·43	3·83	0·28	3·44	23·0
1865	18·74	4·11	0·40	5·00	28·2
1866	15·93	4·29	0·43	4·92	25·6
1867	10·57	2·90	0·20	3·76	17·5
1868	7·43	1·95	0·19	3·60	13·2
1869	6·32	1·67	0·20	3·32	11·7
1870	5·85	2·47	0·25	3·74	12·3
1871	7·44	3·33	0·25	3·21	14·2
1872	8·86	3·86	0·41	2·87	16·0
1873	10·50	4·80	0·54	3·33	19·2
1874	13·52	4·79	0·62	4·48	23·7
1875	14·08	4·51	0·79	4·18	23·7
1876	14·05	3·63	0·59	4·28	22·6
1877	12·78	3·03	0·48	4·12	20·4
1878	12·11	2·16	0·83	4·09	19·1
1879	9·61	2·05	0·71	2·89	15·3
1880	9·05	2·71	0·91	2·45	14·9
1881	10·70	3·06	0·80	2·66	17·3
1882	10·47	3·23	1·36	3·82	18·9
1883	10·88	4·42	1·24	3·92	20·4

[2] All the annual figures in this table relate to the periods when expenditure was incorporated into the companies' accounts, not to the periods in which the services paid for were actually performed. In general, this does not seem to have had much effect on the figures except in the late 1840s. No alteration has been made in this table to the estimates derived from the companies' accounts; but it seems clear that some adjustment ought to be made when they are to be used for cyclical analysis. An approach to the capital expenditure total by way of estimated cost of materials used and the wage bill suggests that the figures for these years are in error by the following amounts: 1845—£2 million too low; 1846—£7 million too low; 1847—correct; 1848—£2 million too high; 1849—£4 million too high; 1850—£2 million too high; and 1851—£1 million too high.

APPENDIX TABLE 1 (*continued*)

1884	13·80	3·63	0·99	3·53	21·9
1885	10·57	3·34	0·69	2·58	17·2
1886	9·30	2·17	0·61	2·17	14·2
1887	8·08	2·36	0·65	1·90	13·0
1888	7·66	2·71	0·64	1·77	12·8
1889	7·90	3·36	0·71	2·37	14·3
1890	8·74	4·27	0·58	2·27	16·0
1891	10·45	5·10	0·50	2·65	18·7
1892	10·35	4·73	0·44	2·33	18·0
1893	10·01	3·56	0·44	1·85	15·9
1894	10·25	3·22	0·60	2·18	16·4
1895	11·17	3·18	0·48	2·37	17·3
1896	11·39	3·91	0·59	2·55	18·6
1897	12·07	4·72	0·80	2·85	20·6
1898	13·98	4·88	1·00	2·87	22·9
1899	13·47	7·15	1·10	3·68	25·5
1900	14·19	6·83	1·76	4·00	26·9
1901	13·54	6·32	1·49	3·48	24·9
1902	13·09	4·83	1·65	2·48	22·2
1903	14·96	4·28	1·88	3·88	25·1
1904	14·97	3·74	1·78	2·13	22·8
1905	12·53	4·70	1·77	2·10	21·2
1906	12·12	5·02	1·59	1·71	20·5
1907	9·47	5·12	1·51	1·62	17·9
1908	7·38	3·48	1·29	1·13	13·3
1909	6·18	3·18	0·82	0·93	11·2
1910	5·91	2·88	1·11	0·62	10·5
1911	5·96	3·29	0·81	0·90	11·0
1912	6·01	4·54	0·82	0·75	12·2
1913	8·47	5·22	1·05	1·14	15·8
1914[3]	9·23	3·76	0·83	0·69	14·5
1915[3]	6·78	2·64	0·34	0·53	10·3
1916[3]	4·20	2·75	0·32	0·24	7·5
1917[3]	4·34	3·16	0·28	0·07	7·8
1918[3]	3·70	3·73	0·13	0·03	7·6
1919	5·70	5·26	0·46	0·20	12·2

[3] Figures of expenditure on repairs and renewals are not available for these years, since they were omitted from company accounts during the war years on Board of Trade authority. The renewal element in the figures given here has been estimated with the help of a paper showing monthly maintenance and renewal figures in 1919. Adjustments to current prices of the war years were made by an index of rolling stock prices, constructed for the purpose of expressing the capital formation estimates in constant prices.

The Railways and the Iron Industry: A Study of their Relationship in Scotland

By Wray Vamplew

During the nineteenth century, especially in the last three decades, the fortunes of the Scottish economy became increasingly dependent upon the activity of the heavy industries which by 1900 employed 15 per cent of the total Scottish labour force.[1] The iron and, towards the end of the century, the steel industry occupied key positions in the economy because they possessed important backward linkages with coalmining and forward linkages with engineering and shipbuilding. Moreover, they were significant heavy industries in their own right for in 1848 26 per cent of British pig iron was made in Scotland and between 1881 and 1889 Scotland was the leading regional producer of open hearth steel.[2] Thus to establish the part played by the railways in Scottish economic growth it is necessary to examine their impact upon the development of the iron and steel industries by considering the railways' demand for ferrous products, their service as a means of transport and their influence on determining the location of the industries.

I

The significance of Scottish railway demand to the indigenous iron industry can be determined only by knowing the size of that demand in relation to the output of the industry. However, even the producers of Scottish iron had no idea of the composition of their market. The president of the West of Scotland Iron & Steel Institute in the early 1890s 'did not feel capable of giving a reliable computation of demand' outside ship-

I am indebted to the staff of the British Transport Commission's historical records in Waterloo Place, Edinburgh for their willingness to search for and place at my disposal innumerable records. I am also grateful to Professor S. B. Saul, Dr P. L. Payne, Messrs D. L. Smith and K. Warren and especially Professor R. H. Campbell for helpful advice.

[1] T. J. Byres, 'Entrepreneurship in the Scottish Heavy Industries, 1870–1900' in P. J. Payne (edit), *Studies in Scottish Business History* (Cass, 1967), p 250.

[2] A. D. Gayer, W. W. Rostow and A. J. S. Schwartz, *The Growth and Fluctuation of the British Economy 1790–1850* (Clarendon Press, Oxford, 1953), p 323.

W. A. Sinclair, 'The Growth of the British Steel Industry in the late nineteenth century', *Scottish Journal of Political Economy*, 1959, 37 (afterwards *ScJPE*).

building.[1] Yet, although aggregate data is not readily available, a model can be constructed which utilises scattered information to produce an estimate of the railways' demand for iron used both in laying the permanent way and in building rolling stock.[2] An editorial in *Herapath's Railway Journal* over a century ago disposes of any claims that one facet of the model might have of representing the actual position.

> How men can believe that anyone can, six or eight years beforehand, tell when a rail will wear out, and a sleeper will rot, and still more wonderful how many of them exactly, out of thousands, shall fail in that year, . . . is to us not surprising, but astonishing.[3]

Even with the benefit of hindsight the model cannot hope to be accurate, but it can give some idea of the order of magnitude of the demand.

Basically the model is an attempt to estimate the consumption of iron by the Scottish railways in the nineteenth century. Two major constituents of total demand are dealt with, namely the permanent way and the rolling-stock demands. Each of these is divided into two main categories, those of new demand and of replacement demand. In making an estimate many things have to be assumed and the validity of the estimate as an indication of the order of magnitude of the railway demand rests on the 'realness' of the assumptions. How real some of them are is discussed in the text as is the potential error emanating from their use. A list of main assumptions follows:

Assumptions Used in Calculating Permanent-Way Demand

(1) Companies did not stock materials substantially in advance of use.

(2) The ratio of sidings to track mileage was constant before 1867 and was typified by the ratio on the Caledonian. Between 1867 and 1904 the ratio rose linearly.

(3) The Caledonian was also representative in the age of its rails in 1866–7, in replacing all components of the permanent way at the same time, and in introducing fishplates and longer rails.

(4) The average weight of rails and chairs increased linearly between known points. The companies used in calculating these known points were typical.

(5) The ages of rails quoted by contemporary authorities were realistic.

(6) Renewals were normally distributed around an assumed average age.

[1] *Journal of the West of Scotland Iron and Steel Institute*, 1892/3, 6 (afterwards *JWScI & SInst*).

[2] Some railway company accounts occasionally list the quantities of rails purchased in certain years, but these are too infrequent to render their use worth while and they also suffer from the handicap of being records of orders not deliveries. It must be pointed out that the model is concerned with quantities and not values as speculation in Scottish pig-iron makes it impossible to determine the price received by the producer. For details of this speculation see R. H. Campbell, 'Fluctuations in Stocks: a Nineteenth Century Case Study', *Oxford Economic Papers*, 1957.

[3] *Herapath's Railway Journal* (afterwards *HRJ*), 6 March 1852.

(7) The general pattern of the adoption of steel rails was illustrated by the Glasgow & South Western and the North Eastern railways.
(8) Train miles run reflected the intensity of use of a railway system and affected the general trend of expected life of a rail.

Assumptions Used in Calculating Rolling-stock Demand

(1) Rolling stock of the minor companies bore some relation to train miles run.
(2) Locomotives had a life of 25 years; carriages and wagons lasted 30 years.
(3) Before 1861 all scrapped vehicles were replaced.
(4) In the early days of railway development before 1850 there was some relationship between the numbers of locomotives and the numbers of other rolling stock.
(5) Locomotives and tenders consisted solely of iron and steel.
(6) All carriages were second class and all non-coaching stock were mineral wagons.
(7) Rolling stock built by R. & Y. Pickering was typical of that used on Scottish railways.
(8) Over time the ratio between tare weight and amount of metal used remained constant.

A problem to be faced in the calculation of railway demand for permanent-way material is that official statistics of Scottish railway mileage did not begin until the late 1840s and did not distinguish between track and route mileage before 1860. Moreover, the accuracy of these figures is distorted by lags in the flow of information between the companies and the Board of Trade. To overcome these handicaps various sources were used, primarily Bradshaw and corrected versions of H. G. Lewin's *Early British Railways* and *The Railway Mania and its Aftermath*, to produce an estimate of railway mileage which differs from the official version in chronology, but which shows negligible total error.[1] In estimating track mileage it is difficult to allow for the doubling of a line originally single as this is not recorded in either the official or secondary statistics. However, only 3½ miles are unaccounted for up to 1860 and this was distributed proportionately amongst known construction. From 1860 the official data is reliable if corrected for obvious errors and allowances made for rounding. Lines of more than double track were not listed separately for Scotland before 1893, but at this date such track accounted for less than 0·4 per cent of total mileage. If the railway companies had bought materials in advance and stocked them, for the purposes of the model the mileage figures would have to be backdated, but there is no evidence of this being done on a substantial scale. Contracts were often made in advance to secure advantage

[1] This can be seen in Appendix 1, columns 1 and 2.

of low prices, but generally the rails were to be delivered at a future date when needed.[1] Any error emanating from this assumption would not be perpetuated in the renewals estimate since rails cannot begin to wear out until the railway is brought into operation.

Sidings are not adequately recorded until the turn of the century when the following ratios between track mileage in operation and sidings mileage are obtained; 1904, 1·00: 0·39; 1905, 1·00: 0·41; 1906, 1·00: 0·43.[2] In 1867 a ratio of 1·00: 0·27 was to be found on the Caledonian system and, for the purposes of the model, this was deemed to hold for Scottish railways as a whole.[3] Since railway construction went on in the more isolated regions throughout the remaining years of the century and there was a general, but not explosive, expansion in industrialisation elsewhere there is no strong objection to the assumption of a linear trend in the sidings ratio between 1867 and 1904. Prior to 1867 the ratio of 1·00: 0·27 was assumed to hold in the absence of any evidence to the contrary. Any error will be a once and for all effect as sidings renewals tended to be made from old materials. In addition the fact that sidings were generally less than one-fifth of total demand before 1855 and that this proportion declined thereafter with the rising importance of track renewals will diminish the importance of any error.

The early lines laid relatively light rails, but the increases in both the weight and speed of the traffic rendered necessary a corresponding increase in the weight of the permanent way. In 1830 the Garnkirk & Glasgow had used 28 lb rails (36 lb in some places), but had been relaid with heavier material within seven years. In 1837 both the Arbroath & Forfar and the Dundee & Arbroath opted for a 48 lb rail and by 1840 a 75 lb rail was the choice of the Edinburgh & Glasgow and the Glasgow, Paisley & Greenock.[4] Development was less rapid in the next 60 years, but by the end of the century 90 lb rails were standard on many lines. Chairs and fishplates also increased in weight, but it should be noted that there was no weight relationship between the constituent parts of the permanent way although

[1] eg North British: BTHR(S), RAC(S) 1/1A, 24 March 1859. Slamannan: Mitchell Library, Glasgow, 53154–7, 8 February 1838. North British: *HRJ*, 30 March 1872.

[2] Calculated from the *Railway Returns* of the Board of Trade. Figures exist for earlier years, but are marred by the absence of returns from the major Scottish companies.

[3] Calculated from a comprehensive report made to the Caledonian Shareholders' Inquiry of 1867/8 by John Hawksworth, engineer of the company. BTHR(S) RAC(S) 1/3 (afterwards Hawksworth). It is apparent that no universal relationship holds between track mileage and the mileage of sidings, points and crossings. Sidings are much more intensive in the industrial regions, eg one mile of the Caldeonian's Dalmarnock branch had 5 miles 579 yd of sidings as contrasted with the 3 miles 510 yd existing on the 43 miles of track between Dundee and Perth. The Peebles, an agricultural line, possessed 2·41 miles of sidings to its 18·72 miles of track. Hawksworth, loc cit; *Railway Times*, 21 March 1857.

[4] Mitchell Library 53154–7 (Garnkirk and Glasgow), 1 March 1837. *Select Committee on Railways*, PP 1839, X, p 129. *Accident Reports*, PP 1859, XXVII, p 42. *Railway Times*, 29 December 1838.

heavier chairs came into use with the adoption of the steel rail. Average weights given in Appendix 1 (Colums 7 and 8) were calculated for most years using data extracted from company histories, official accident reports, directors' reports to shareholders and company minute books. For years where no information was available weights were obtained by assuming a linear trend between calculated points. This assumption is justified on the grounds that there was unlikely to be a sudden and universal decision to adopt a heavier rail for all new lines; a linear trend represents the gradual replacement of lighter rails by heavier ones.

Developments in the permanent way such as the use of the fishplate and the increase in the length of rails were taken to follow the pattern of introduction as on the Caledonian. Support for this can be found in the accident and directors' reports.

The major problem in constructing the model is that of estimating renewals. In the early days rails became obsolescent rather than worn out.[1] Estimates of how long the permanent way would last were wildly optimistic. Miller, the engineer of the North British, claimed that 'a period of twenty-five years may be safely assumed as an average over the North British lines' for rails and, although some chairs were occasionally broken, he thought 'they would last for more than double the period of the rails'.[2] However, by the 1880s an iron rail was expected to last but 10 years on main lines and most sections were relaid within 9 to 12 years.[3] Really the duration of rails ought not to be expressed in terms of years as 'the life of rails was entirely a question of tonnage, and of speed and of frequency of trains'.[4] Unfortunately information as to traffic density is available only on a company basis and then only in terms of train miles run, with no mention of ton mileage.[5] However, this data can be used to produce an index of traffic density based on train miles run per mile of track. For Scotland this index rose from 4·65 in 1861 to 9·88 by the end of the century. The reduction in average rail age from 15 to 19 years in 1867 (calculated from Hawksworth's data covering 46 per cent of Scottish railway mileage) to 9 to 12 years in 1886 (given by Sir Lowthian Bell in his study of the British iron trade) was attributed primarily to this increasing wear and tear.[6] These estimated average ages were taken as correct in the sense that a rail

[1] Replacing too light track with heavier materials occurred in the early 1850s on the Dundee, Perth & Aberdeen Junction (*Railway Times*, 20 September 1851), the Monklands (*HRJ*, 30 October 1852) and on the Dundee & Arbroath (*HRJ*, 8 January 1853).

[2] Report of the Committee of Inquiry into the North British Railway, BTHR(S), RAC(S) 1/1A, 26 July 1849, p 4. D. Lardner in his *Railway Economy* (London, 1850), p 51 expected at least a 20 year life for rails.

[3] I. L. Bell, *The Iron Trade of the United Kingdom* (London, 1886), p 34.

[4] *Railway News*, 23 May 1876.

[5] It was in a regression of average length of life of rails on ton miles per mile of road that R. W. Fogel found statistical significance. *Railroads and American Economic Growth* (Johns Hopkins University, 1964), p 172.

[6] The index of traffic density automatically allows for long-term trends in weights of trains and rails etc when used in conjunction with the evidence on ages of rails.

laid between 15 and 19 years before 1867 could be expected to be due for renewal in the year of Hawksworth's report. Estimates of the potential length of life of rails put down in other years were then obtained by assuming that the trend towards a shorter life bore a direct relationship to the trend of the traffic-density index. Allowance was made for the varying intensity of traffic within Scotland at any particular point of time by assuming that renewals of all rails laid in the same year would be distributed normally around the estimated average length of life of those rails.[1] Data in Hawksworth's detailed tables, whilst not exhibiting a completely normal distribution, suggest that such an assumption is not without justification. It would be too long a process to work out renewals for individual companies and so an aggregate renewals table was constructed with the assumption that these rails would be of the same weight as those on new lines each year. This leads to some underestimation of demand in the early 1850s when revelations of excessive capital expenditure led to construction on what was termed the 'cheap principle', involving few heavy works and the use of lighter operating equipment which included the permanent way. However, the error would be at most 2 per cent of total permanent-way demand and this only in certain years.

The increases in the weight and speed of traffic so shortened the life of wrought-iron rails that alternative materials were sought. As early as 1853 the Edinburgh and Glasgow laid some of M. Stirling's hardened iron-top rails in Falkirk tunnel and by the late 1850s these patented, hardened rails were employed on the heavily used parts of the North British.[2] As the quality of iron rails deteriorated[3] the Glasgow and South Western also recognised the 'importance of considering whether a more lasting description of rail, made so by Messrs Dodds and Sons Patent Process, or otherwise, should not, for the future be used'.[4] Despite their apparent success they were not widely adopted, not so much because of cost, but more because it was discovered that the hardening sometimes made the rails brittle.[5] Early attempts to increase the length of active life radically, by the use of double-headed rails which could be turned, failed because the surface of the lower head became indented through long contact with the cast-iron

[1] Fogel, op cit, pp 171–2 also makes this assumption.

[2] BTHR(S), RAC(S), 1/73 and 1/1A. Maurice Stirling's rails were being experimentally manufactured at Dundyvan in 1849. *Railway Chronicle*, 22 September 1849.

[3] *Royal Commission on Railways*, PP 1867, XXXVIII, Q 17039. Professor Rankine's presidential address, *Transactions of the Engineers and Shipbuilders of Scotland*, 1858/9 (afterwards *TESS*). The Glasgow & South Western complained of 'the inferior quality of the rails manufactured now, compared with those furnished at the construction of the railway'. *HRJ*, 16 March 1861. Inferior quality as well as the increasing intensity of traffic may well have been the reason that made 'very few makers . . . disposed to give even a seven year guarantee for iron rails'. *HRJ*, 26 April 1866.

[4] *HRJ*, 16 March 1861.

[5] *Accident Report*, PP 1872, LII, p 39. The cost to the North British was about £1 a ton including the erection of special furnaces and the purchase of the patent. BTHR(S), RAC(S) 1/1A, 26 September 1860 and 22 March 1761.

chairs.[1] Steel was the key to longer life, either to edge iron rails as done by the Glasgow Iron Company,[2] or, more generally in the form of a complete rail. Being harder such rails were less liable to be crushed, and being stronger they were less liable to fracture, both of which meant greater durability.[3]

The switch to steel rails did not follow automatically or rapidly from the granting of Bessemer's patent. The English witnesses to the Royal Commission of 1867 explained their reluctance to adopt the steel rail as being a product of its high price and an unsureness as to the degree of its durability.[4] There is no reason to believe that the Scottish companies would be any more progressive in their adoption. Experiments on the wearing qualities of steel rails and switches were begun in 1861 by James Deas of the North British who found them 'giving great satisfaction' on severely worked sections.[5] However, elsewhere there were complaints of breakages, but this was explained as being because the steel was too hard 'or, what is more likely, the maker has been sailing too close to the wind in his attempt to use Scotch or other common iron along with haematite'.[6] The majority of companies experimented with the new rails, but as late as October 1871 the Great North of Scotland had not used them at all.[7] Even with their greater durability proved (this was not acknowledged by the Caledonian until 1873) the high price of steel rails relative to that of iron delayed their general substitution. With the narrowing of the price differential the steel rail was widely adopted and by 1879 most companies were, like the North British, 'laying down almost nothing but steel rails'.[8] Price would, however, determine only the material for renewals and not their timing as the necessity for safety would allow

[1] K. N. Salkade, *Permanent Way Textbook* (Bombay, 1934), p 134.

[2] *Engineering*, 13 August 1869.

[3] Tests showed that steel could withstand 2¼ times the strain taken by iron of similar section. I. L. Bell, *Memoranda as to the Wear of Rails* (North Eastern Railway, 1896), p 58. However, the strength of steel in fact led to a lessening of the anticipated life of steel rails by allowing heavier axle loads.

[4] *Royal Commission on Railways*, PP 1867, XXXVIII, QQ 16220, 17407 and 17838.

[5] BTHR(S), RAC(S) 1/1A, January 1862. *Engineering*, 5 April 1867.

[6] *Engineering*, 29 June 1866. Though it is now recognised that steel rails are more liable to suddenly fail transversely—'metal fatigue'—than wrought-iron ones. However, they are free from the longitudinal splitting which iron rails are apt to suffer. J. D. Dearden, 'The Centenary of the Steel Rail', *Railway Steel Topics*, Vol 4, No 1, 1957, pp 21–3. See also J. E. Stead, 'Micro-Mechanical Examination of Old Steel Rails and Tyres', *JWScI & SInst* 1896–7, pp 25–36.

[7] *HRJ*, 14 October 1871.

[8] BTHR(S), RAC(S) 1/2, February 1879. In 1864 the price of iron rail was £7 a ton and that of Bessemer steel rails £17 10s a ton. In the next six years steel rails fell in price to £10 a ton whilst iron ones remained around £7. In the next few years prices of both rose, but in the four years from 1873 the price of steel rails relative to that of iron fell some 50 per cent. K. Warren, 'The Sheffield Rail Trade, 1861–1930', *Institute of British Geographers*, Vol 34, 1964, 139. J. C. Carr and W. Taplin, *A History of the British Steel Industry* (Blackwell, Oxford, 1962), p 29.

little margin for postponement.[1] A second factor conditioning the choice of metal was the bottleneck in production of steel rails. With the increased desire to use such rails after 1870 the manufacturers became overwhelmed with orders—'the difficulty now appears to be not to pay for steel rails but to get them'[2]—and the pressure would not be eased until production capacity expanded. For the purposes of the model the rate of supersession of steel over iron shown in Table 1 has been taken from the records of the Glasgow & South Western and from information given by Lowthian Bell on the English North Eastern.

TABLE 1

STEEL RAILS AS A PERCENTAGE OF RAILS LAID

Year	*North Eastern*[1]	*Glasgow & South Western*[2]	*Model*
1870	6·21	?	5
1871	7·90	9·69	10
1872	13·35	17·20	15
1873	10·59	15·46	15
1874	26·44	24·66	25
1875	35·02	62·71	60
1876	33·89	58·39	60
1877	59·80	77·03	80
1878	98·89	79·94	80
1879	98·69	?	100

Notes:

[1] Calculated from I. L. Bell, *Memorandum as to the Wear of Rails*, North Eastern Railway, 1896, p 29.

[2] Calculated from data in company records (BTHR(S), RAC(S) 1/11–12.

As with the first iron rails the early advocates of steel overestimated its potential useful life. One witness to the 1867 Commission thought 40 years not improbable.[3] Again, as with iron, the increasing intensity of traffic rendered such calculations invalid. Bell's reports on the North Eastern in

[1] The cost of permanent-way material could possibly influence a decision as to new construction, eg the Edinburgh & Glasgow delayed making contracts for rails as they anticipated a price fall (*Railway Times*, 7 March 1840), but since rails are one of the last items necessary there is sufficient scope for altering dates of rail purchases without retarding actual construction. Frequently rails were ordered when prices were low although not needed there and then, eg North British (*HRJ*, 30 March 1872), Border Union (BTHR(S), RAC(S) 1/A, 24 March 1857), Highland (*HRJ*, 1 May 1880). The reason was not simply to cut costs, but also to make a profit on their eventual sale as scrap.

Safety factors prevent the postponement of relaying, but low prices may well advance it. However, it has been pointed out that price fluctuations do not normally affect replacements of rails. W. Hoffman, *British Industry 1700–1950* (Blackwell, Oxford, 1965), p 246.

[2] *HRJ*, 18 March 1871.

[3] *Royal Commission on Railways*, PP 1867, XXXVIII, QQ 17404–5.

1896 and 1900 show an average age in the region of 15 to 17 years.[1] In the mid 1920s the average length of life was given as 21½ years, but the increase may be due simply to the realisation that rails had previously been taken up too soon.[2] Another contributory reason was that steel rails were made softer when it was appreciated that hard rails were apt to wear more.[3] A similar procedure to that used in calculating the renewals of iron rails was adopted for steel.

In general, line renewals were made with new rails and although some branches were relaid with old rails, as was the Wilsontown branch of the Edinburgh & Glasgow in 1857, such work was not significant.[4] Repairs made with old materials were a more frequent occurrence, but again were not of statistical importance. Sidings renewals, however, were generally effected with old rails and chairs.[5] There would be plenty of these available as usually whole stretches of line would be relaid at a time not all of which would be equally worn.

Finally, although chairs and spikes might be expected to have longer lives than the rails which come into contact with the traffic, it was the general practice that 'whenever renewals are made, the old road is wholly replaced by new rails, chairs, sleepers and fastenings'.[6]

The results found in Appendix 1 and Column 9 and summarised in Table 2 must be checked against data not used in the construction of the model to test their statistical validity. The aggregate figures cannot be tested as there are no independent estimates available, but some indication as to the validity of trends and fluctuations can perhaps be obtained from isolated information given by individual companies in their annual reports and from data contained in old materials books. Such information as exists is insufficient to 'prove' that the results are correct but gives no indication that they are wildly inaccurate. The model was applied to the Glasgow & South Western Railway and the estimated renewals checked against figures for actual renewals given by the company engineer in his half-yearly reports.[7] Error was commonly less than $\pm$ 10 per cent, which does not suggest that a model aggregating all Scottish railways would be highly unrealistic. Confirmation that the Caledonian was not atypical in having the greater part of its renewals concentrated 15 to 19 years after

[1] I. L. Bell, *Memoranda as to the Wear of Rails*, 1896, p 27. I. L. Bell, *Memoranda as to the Wear of Rails*, 1900, p 76.

[2] W. V. Wood & Sir Josiah Stamp, *Railways* (1928), p 48. Bell in his preface to the *Memoranda of 1900* wrote of 'the impossibility of predicting the life of a rail, which in my opinion cannot be ascertained until it is actually removed from the line'.

[3] PP 1900, LXXVI (part one), Cd 174, p 108. H. J. Skelton, *Economics of Iron and Steel* (1894), p 241.

[4] BTHR(S), RAC(S) 1/73. See also *HRJ*, 26 March 1864.

[5] Hawksworth, op cit, p 19. Bell, *Memoranda* (1896), p 31. Bell, *Iron Trade* (1886), p 41.

[6] Hawksworth, op cit, p 19.

[7] BTHR(S), RAC(S) 1/11–12

being laid was sought in the records of the sales of old North British permanent-way material.[1] These showed a peak slightly later than might have been expected, but as this company was following a penny-pinching policy in the early 1860s in an effort to maintain dividends it can be hazarded that they might delay renewals to the maximum that safety would allow.[2] However, before discussing the significance of the results it is necessary to compute an estimate of the iron used for other railway purposes.

II

The other major railway demand for iron was for that used in rolling stock. Early railway bridges were mainly of timber or stone partly because of fears about the safety of iron castings when subject to tensile forces when employed in railway underbridging.[3] Iron came more into use towards the end of the century and steel made a spectacular debut in the bridging of the Firth of Forth, but the quantities used were probably small. However, figures exist for the metal content of the Tay and Forth bridges and these have been taken into account. Stations were built primarily of wood or stone (and later brick) and their demand for iron must have been relatively slight.

Rolling-stock demand for iron can only be estimated if the totals of rolling stock are known. These can be built up from figures given in company accounts and scattered references in company histories and specialist railway journals. The major companies are fairly well covered and allowance has been made for missing entries on the assumption that their total stock would bear the same ratio to train miles run (goods and passenger) as that of known companies. The quantitative dominance of the major companies renders error from this assumption slight. Renewals were taken as replacements to existing stock and do not include engines which underwent 'heavy' repairs, although rebuilds, a fairly elastic term generally inferring the complete modernisation of an engine, have been counted. Conversions of wagons and carriages, of which there were relatively few, have been ignored. Totals of renewals for companies where records were incomplete or unobtainable were estimated by assuming an average life of 25 years for locomotives and tenders and 30 years for carriages and wagons. If anything these assumptions (based on details available in shareholders' inquiries, data as to dates of scrapping in company histories and a comparison of scrapping figures with those of earlier additions to stock) err on

[1] BTHR(S), NBR 4/46–7, Sales and Receipts of Old Materials.

[2] See the Report of the Committee of Inquiry into the North British Railway 1866. BTHR(S) RAC(S) 1/1B.

[3] *Royal Commission on the Application of Iron to Railway Structures*, PP 1849, XXIX, p xvii. J. Mitchell, Paper to the British Association on the Highland Railway, quoted in *Engineering*, 13 September 1867, 205–7. *TESS*, 1890–1, 141.

the low side. However, the great majority of renewals are accurate figures obtained from locomotive superintendents' reports.

Quantification is not facilitated when one of the major companies, the North British, admits that 'a considerable difference exists between the actual and reported stocks',[1] but such errors (when known) can be corrected and confidence can be placed in the estimates, shown in Appendix 2, after 1850. The figures before this date for locomotives are fairly reliable although no allowance could be made for a few missing minor companies. The main difficulty arises with the coaching and wagon stock as the companies did not generally publish figures before 1850. Total stock in 1850 was therefore estimated by deducting additions since that date from the total given in the Railway Returns of 1861 assuming that there was a renewal of all scrapped vehicles. This figure was then distributed between the years 1840 to 1850 in the same proportion as was locomotive stock. At a later date there does not appear to be a relationship, either in aggregate or on a company basis, between the buying of locomotive and other stock, but this may not be so of the initial purchases before railways began operations.

The problem of private wagons is virtually impossible to solve.[2] Undoubtedly such wagons were part of railway demand for if traders had not provided them the railway companies would have had to, but unfortunately there is no means of estimating their numbers with any degree of accuracy. That they were considerable is not open to question; the Royal Commission on Railways in 1867 reported that it was 'a common case on many lines for traders to provide their own wagons' and in 1898 when the Caledonian owned 63,000 wagons it was reckoned that a further 33,000 traders' vehicles were in use on that system.[3] In both the early 1870s and early 1890s the Caledonian bought large numbers of wagons from the traders in efforts to improve the efficiency of its service and so it is of little use to attempt to derive a trend from the figures of traders and company stock given in the shareholders' inquiry of 1867–8.[4] In any event there is no justification for assuming that the traders would buy wagons in the same years as the railway companies. In fact it is arguable that they might take advantage of lower prices available when railway demand was not putting pressure on the capacity of the manufacturers. Complaints of colliery owners, the major owners of private vehicles, as to a deficiency of the

[1] Committee on North British, 1866, op cit, p 9.

[2] Although a principal coalowner put a locomotive and 60 wagons on to the Glasgow, Paisley & Greenock in 1842 (*Railway Times*, 9 July 1842), private locomotives were generally confined to the sidings and yards of their owners and would not have had to be provided by the railways in default of the industrialist or colliery proprietor. The real problem is that of private wagons not locomotives.

[3] *Royal Commission on Railways*, PP 1867, XXXVIII, p lxix. *Edinburgh Evening Dispatch*, 19 February 1898.

[4] BTHR(S), RAC(S) 1/3–5, *passim*.

wagon supply by the railways suggests that the traders were unwilling to make purchases themselves at instances not of their own choosing.[1] The difficulties referred to above make it impossible to include estimates of the numbers of privately owned wagons in the calculations. The error from this exclusion could possibly amount to some 6,000 tons of iron in certain years.

In estimating the amounts of iron used in the construction of rolling stock more assumptions have to be made, but again it is emphasised that all that is being sought is some idea of the order of magnitude of the demand without any claims being made as to its exactitude. Locomotives were taken to consist solely of iron and steel, as were tenders, their weights being calculated from references in company records and accident reports, but primarily from the works of the Stephenson Locomotive Society. In the second half of the century their weights doubled, that of locomotives rising from below 23 tons to around 45 tons and that of tenders increasing to well over 30 tons from 15 tons.[2] Wastage in their construction may have been high, but the employment of Bell's figures in calculating pig-iron equivalents makes some allowance for wastage. It is also probable that much of the metal was capable of re-use. All carriages were taken as standard second class and all non-coaching stock as the standard mineral wagon then in operation. As mineral wagons dominated the numbers of stock, error emanating from this assumption will not be significant. The amount of metal used in these vehicles in the late nineteenth century was computed primarily from data in the design book of Messrs R. & Y. Pickering, carriage and wagon builders of Wishaw, who supplied much Scottish rolling stock.[3] For earlier dates the ratio between metal and tare weight in the later vehicles was assumed to hold. The weight of metal in carriages trebled to about 6 tons between 1850 and 1900 as the companies increased the passenger capacity of their vehicles, but there was scarcely any increase in the metal content of mineral wagons as those of 8 tons capacity soon became standard.

Total demand for rolling-stock iron expressed in terms of pig-iron equivalent is summarised in Table 2 together with permanent-way demand. There is a rising trend from an average annual demand of under 6,000 tons in the 1850s to nearly 33,000 by the last decade of the century. It must be borne in mind that substantial error may have arisen from the ignoring of traders' wagons. If these were of the same magnitude and dimensions as those of the railway companies a further 6,000 tons of iron might have gone for railway purposes in some years during the last quarter

[1] *Scotsman*, 24 March; 7 May; 11 October 1873; *Colliery Guardian*, 5 June 1861; *Railway Times*, 27 December 1851; *HRJ*, 29 October 1853.

[2] See Appendix 3.

[3] The records of this company are kept in the Scottish Business Records Archives, Adam Smith Building, University of Glasgow.

of the nineteenth century.[1] However, total railway demand for pig iron is dominated by permanent-way requirements which rose from averaging 25,000 tons each year to over 90,000 in the same period.

III

These estimates of potential railway consumption of the products of the Scottish iron industry were probably nowhere near achieved for much of the permanent-way material was purchased in England and Wales. In 1827 the Ballochney obtained patent malleable-iron rails from the Bedlington Iron Company of Northumberland and re-ordered from the same firm when relaying with heavier rails ten years later.[2] The preference of the early Scottish railways for English rails is understandable since the Scottish iron industry was relatively undeveloped, lacking both the experience and expertise in rail making which the English companies had acquired by virtue of the earlier railway development south of the border. Scotland's ironmasters made attempts to enter what was at times a highly lucrative market, but the tendency to purchase outside Scotland remained as strong as ever. The Aberdeen company bought rails for the whole of its line from Messrs Scholefield of Rotherham and the New British Iron Company gained the Caledonian contract. The Great North of Scotland obtained its rails from Bolckow & Vaughan of Middlesbrough and the same firm was chosen by the Edinburgh, Perth & Dundee, who also had dealings with Morrissey, Jansen & Company of Newcastle and the short-lived East of Scotland Malleable Iron Company.[3] It was not only this Scottish company that tried to break into the rail market. Two other specialist firms, the West of Scotland and the Ayrshire Malleable Iron companies, also tried and failed.[4] At least one established ironmaster also made the attempt. John Wilson of Dundyvan shared the first contracts of the North British with Cargill, Morrissey & Company of Newcastle and Sir John Guest of Dowlais, but many of his rails proved defective and in April 1849 he was paid £2,000 for the cancellation of a contract for 1,000 tons of rails.[5] As the railways stretched to the north of Scotland and the era of the iron rail drew to a close it was still English firms that supplied Scotland with rails.[6]

[1] Although at first there was a wide diversity in practice, by the 1880s private wagons were generally conforming to railway company standards and specifications. J. Reid, *TESS*, 1882–3, p 11, and the *Minutes of the Fifeshire Main Collieries*, GD 58/25/1, p 225, Scottish Record Office, Edinburgh.

[2] Mitchell Library 53154–7, Ballochney, 28 May 1827, 7 February 1837.

[3] *Scottish Railway Gazette*, 30 August 1845. *National Library of Scotland*, Mss 6355, pp 38–9. BTHR(S), GNS 1/1, p 47 and EPD 1/3, pp 10, 288, 295, 476.

[4] R. H. Campbell, 'Early Malleable Iron Production in Scotland', *Business History*, Vol 4, No 1, 1961, 23–33.

[5] BTHR(S), NBR 1/4, 19 April 1849. Wilson also gained a contract from the Glasgow Dumfries & Carlisle, but 'as an inducement for for-going certain claims of damages which he had preferred against the individual directors of the time'. *HRJ*, 13 April 1850.

[6] Eg for the Sutherland. *Engineering*, 6 March 1868.

The extent of non-Scottish supplies of rails can be judged from an inquiry into rails broken on the Caledonian between November 1871 and March 1872. Of 81 rails examined the suppliers were as follows:

26	Darlington Iron Company
20	Bolckow and Vaughan, Middlesbrough
7	North Yorkshire Iron Company
4	Stockton Rail Mill Company
3	Mersey Steel Company
2	J. Brown's Steel Company, Sheffield
2	Ebbw Vale Steel Company
1	Dowlais
1	Glasgow Iron Company
15	Unknown[1]

A combination of factors explains the failure of the Scots to obtain a share of the market for rails. The introduction of puddling was delayed until about 1836 as Scotland had no reserves of skilled labour and English and Welsh workmen had to be brought in to instruct the Scots in the art.[2] Even then the finished product was not of a high enough standard to seriously challenge that of the established manufacturers south of the border. The main reason for this was the 1 per cent phosphorus content of ordinary Scotch pig which increased the fluidity of the metal thus improving it for foundry purposes, but raising a problem for the malleable-iron producers akin to that later to face the Bessemer steel manufacturers in Scotland in that the metal produced was too brittle. This would not have been a great handicap if the Scots had been willing to mix with other brands for it was well known that mixing produced better iron and such a procedure was adopted, for example, in South Wales.[3] However, in the early days at least, the Scottish ironmasters would not follow such a practice.[4] Most of them did not even attempt to produce malleable iron, being satisfied with the substantial profits from their pig iron. Serious efforts to breach the walls of the rail market came when the pig-iron sector was relatively depressed and a desire grew to augment declining profits by the making of malleable iron which was in demand. In the late forties three companies were set up specifically to enter this trade, but unfortunately the application of the decision to invest coincided with high costs of con-

[1] *Accident Reports*, PP 1872, LII, p 39. (These breakages were the result of a defective locomotive, rather than faults in the rails.)

[2] *Colliery Guardian*, 4 April 1868. J. H. Clapham, *An Economic History of Modern Britain: The Early Railway Age* (Cambridge University Press, 1930), p 426. A. Miller, *The Rise and Progress of Coatbridge* (1864), p 171. I am grateful to Mr Kenneth Warren for this reference and also for p 59 (1).

[3] *Railway Magazine and the Annals of Science*, Vol 3, 1838, pp 401–2. *Royal Commission on Application of Iron, PP* 1849, XXIX, QQ 519, 1389 and p 265.

[4] One exception was the Blaikie Brothers of Aberdeen who used three-quarters best hot-blast Scotch pig iron with one-quarter Welch pig. Ibid, p 142.

struction, thus saddling the emergent companies with high capital expenditure, whilst production did not start until prices for rails were on a downward trend. All three companies failed and with their failure ended the large-scale attempts of the Scots to emulate the malleable-iron producers of England and Wales.[1] The superior skills of the latter allowed them to take advantage of cheapening transport costs which, although enabling the export trade of Scotch pig to develop, also meant that Welsh rail makers could employ such iron, delivering it back in a finished form in Glasgow at prices which the Scots could not hope to compete with.[2]

In the late 1860s the Scots began to mix their local iron with Cleveland iron in order to meet competition from that district in the production of plate for shipbuilding. Over 70,000 tons was imported from Cleveland in 1867, but malleable iron production remained comparatively small, accounting for 142,000 tons of a total of Scottish iron make of some 1,031,000 tons in that year.[3]

IV

The change to steel rails made little difference to the nationality of the supplier. Sheffield had the first two regular makers of such rails, the trade being latched on to their existing quality work in railway iron. In the 1860s half the Bessemer rails made in Britain originated in Sheffield. The Welsh manufacturers lagged a little in switching to the new product and had to overcome a declining reputation as makers of iron rails whilst the other areas to achieve fame in the steel rail trade had still to establish a name for quality work.[4] To 1865 only one Scottish company, that of Rowan of Glasgow, had entered the steel rail business and the pressure of other orders, coupled with a lack of demand, led to a suspension of their

[1] R. H. Campbell, 'Early Malleable Iron Production in Scotland', op cit.
The decision to invest in malleable iron plant was taken when the price of *all* iron was high, but the pig-iron trade, although still profitable in the 1840s, was relatively depressed compared with the extremely profitable 1830s. One reason being that in Lanarkshire the better fields were being worked out and higher royalties were being demanded for the remainder thus resulting in increased costs. Many ironmasters were aware that their pig was being taken over the border, made into malleable iron and shipped back, and hoped that the development of malleable iron production in Scotland would enable them to keep some of the profits of that branch of the industry at home. See R. H. Campbell, 'The Growth and Fluctuations of the Scottish Pig Iron Trade 1828–73' (Aberdeen Univ PhD thesis, 1956), pp 127–37, 209; and *Ayrshire Advertiser*, 14 January 1847.

[2] W. Truran, *The Iron Trade of Great Britain* (1855), p 169.

[3] D. Bremner, *The Industries of Scotland* (Edinburgh, 1869), pp 33–5. *The Economist*, 14 March 1868, remarked that the 'comparatively high price of Scotch appears to be favouring the introduction of the cheap North of England brands into the Scotch foundries and malleable iron works'. See also *Monthly Circular of William Connal*, pig iron storekeeper of Glasgow, for December 1859 and December 1874 kept in Mitchell Library. The famous Scottish forges of Parkhead and Lancefield founded their reputation in skill rather than the cheapness of their products. R. H. Campbell, op cit, p 137.

[4] K. Warren, loc cit, 131.

Bessemer rail work which although later revived found only limited success.[1] The next serious attempt came when the Steel Company of Scotland was formed in 1871 as the first large new company set up especially to utilise the Siemens' process, erecting open hearth furnaces at their Hallside works for this purpose in 1873. The original intention was to specialise in the manufacture of steel rails, but the general expansion in rail-making capacity operated against profitable production and the company adopted a policy of diversification, successfully producing steel for constructional work and shipbuilding.[2] Of eight Scottish firms possessing Siemens' plant in 1884 only the Steel Company of Scotland and David Colville & Sons of the Dalzell Works, Motherwell manufactured rails and the last-named firm did not feature rails in the advertisement of its products.[3]

It must have been difficult for the Steel Company of Scotland to make headway in the steel rail market in view of the general expansion of capacity and the reputation of established suppliers. The North British gave its contracts in 1893–4 to the Moss Bay Company of Workington and to Cammell & Company of Sheffield; 10,000 tons were purchased from Cammells after the Steel Company of Scotland had been refused a further contract. The newer railways would not even give the Scottish firm a trial. The Edinburgh Suburban & Southside obtained its rails from the Moss Bay Company and the Glasgow Central Underground opted for Cammell & Company.[4]

Several factors account for the failure of the Scottish ironmasters to grasp what was a second chance to break into the rail trade. One was obviously that their first failure meant that they had few links with the market. A second factor operating in the short run was that the late 1870s were generally a period of low prices which strengthened the reluctance of the ironmasters to venture from a still fairly stable position into a new enterprise. This reluctance to change was a product of the structure of an industry concerned primarily with the making and marketing of pig iron. There was no strong incentive for them to take up the manufacture of

[1] K. Warren, loc cit, p 135. F. Kohn, *Iron and Steel Manufacture* (London, 1869), p 84. I. F. Gibson, 'The Establishment of the Scottish Steel Industry', *ScJPE*, Vol 5, 1958, 24–5.

[2] Carr & Taplin, op cit, p 35; Gibson, op cit, pp 28–9. The directors' report for October 1879 speaks of a 'growing demand in this direction (ship and bridge building)' and that for August 1880 states that production was 'chiefly steel for ship and boiler purposes'. The report for October 1881 suggests that by then major fluctuations in sales were produced by shipbuilding and constructional demand with rails playing only a minor role. See also a list of the products of the company in the *Scottish News*, 11 May 1886.

[3] H. W. Griffiths, *Iron and Steel Manufacturers of Great Britain* (London, 1884), pp 66–71, 140. A point of interest here is that letters between Dübs, the famous locomotive builder, and Anderson, the secretary of the Callander & Oban, suggest that Dübs might have been considering entering the rail trade, but probably the explanation is that he was acting on behalf of the Steel Company of Scotland, of which he was a director, but was using his works address. BTHR(S), COB 8/14 letters for May 1875.

[4] BTHR(S), NBR 1/40, 22 June, 21 December 1893, 26 April, 17 August 1894. BTHR(S), ESS 1/1, p 34. *Railway World*, Vol 3, August 1894, p 270.

steel; the persons who had to find new markets for their product or, alternatively, adopt the new steelmaking processes were the manufacturers of malleable iron who were a minority of the Scottish ironmasters. Not until the early 1880s was there anything that could be termed a Scottish steel industry and this came as the growing demand for shipbuilding caused firstly the makers of malleable iron and secondly a few, but only a few, of the iron smelters to change to the manufacture of steel.[1] Development, however, was rapid and by the 1880s Scotland was the leading open-hearth steel-producing region in Britain.[2]

There was also a strong technical obstacle to change in that the phosphorus content of Scottish ore (hence pig) rendered it unsuitable for both the Bessemer and Siemens' processes until the development of the Gilchrist-Thomas technique. Early attempts by Thomas Jackson and William Dixon, the latter under the personal supervision of Henry Bessemer, had proved failures because of this. Rowan, who succeeded, had used Cumberland pig.[3] The Steel Company of Scotland, in making an attempt at the large-scale production of steel, was hoping to utilise 'Blue Billy', the residue after the copper and silver have been extracted from iron pyrites, which was at that time becoming the raw material of the Scottish sulphuric acid industry. Although the costs proved to be too high it was this hope that 'Blue Billy' would solve the problem of suitable ore supplies that encouraged the attempt to make steel where the established ironmasters stood aloof. As local Scottish ore reserves were worked out Scottish smelting plants became increasingly dependent on imported ores with which they produced supplies of pig suitable for the manufacture of acid steel thus easing the transition to the steel age.[4]

Permanent-way iron in the form of chairs and spikes came from the Scottish iron companies. The early minute books of the North British list contracts with George Mushett of Dalkeith, W. Scott of Inverleithing, a Mr Whitelaw of Aberdeen and Tod and Sons of Edinburgh. The only order outside Scotland was for 2,800 tons of chairs from Fox Henderson of Birmingham.[5] These forms of railway iron were products of the foundry for which Scottish pig was eminently suited. With the change to

[1] R. H. Campbell, *Scotland Since 1707* (Blackwell, Oxford, 1965), pp 232–4. *HRJ*, 27 January 1883 commented on the 'limited area of steel manufacture in Scotland'.

The change of the malleable iron-makers would be necessitated by their main market, the shipyards, adopting steel as a constructional material. The relatively late development of the malleable sector of the iron industry in Scotland had coincided with the rise of iron shipbuilding on the Clyde which in the 1860s and 1870s absorbed between 65 and 70 per cent of total Scottish malleable production. Gibson, op cit, p 33; Sinclair, op cit, p 35.

[2] Gibson, op cit, p 29; Sinclair, op cit, p 37.

[3] Carr & Taplin, op cit, p 28; Campbell, *Scotland Since 1707*, p 232.

[4] Campbell, *Scotland Since 1707*, pp 233–4; Gibson, op cit, p 32.

[5] BTHR(S), NBR 1/1–6 *passim.* See also EPD 1/3, p 48. GNS 1/1, p 477. SCR 1/19, p 36. (Edinburgh & Northern) *Scottish Railway Gazette*, 28 February 1846. (Aberdeen) *HRJ*, 19 October 1850.

steel, however, some orders began to be placed with English manufacturers.

The Phoenix Foundry, Glasgow, obtained the exclusive right of manufacture in Scotland of Griffin's patent iron sleepers. However, there is no evidence of their use on Scottish railways and presumably, as with the iron sleepers produced by the Anderston Foundry and Messrs P. & W. McLellan, their market lay abroad.[1]

Little metal was used in the early railway bridges and in any case Scottish hot-blast iron was regarded as inferior for the purposes of large castings by many engineers.[2] At a later date iron and steel came more into use, but at first external suppliers were still resorted to. The cast-iron columns for the first Tay bridge came from the Falkirk iron works, but most of the girder work originated in Cardiff. However, its successor was built with the products of the Dalmarnock Iron Works and the Steel Company of Scotland and the latter firm with Colvilles also secured part of the contract for the construction of the Forth bridge, although 12,000 of the 55,000 tons were to come from the Landore Works, Swansea.[3]

When railways went underground Scotland once again did not supply all her own railway metal. Although the steel for the Glasgow Central came from the Steel Company of Scotland and the Glasgow Iron & Steel Company, Wishaw, the contract for the iron work and girders had to be shared by David Colville & Sons with Goodwin, Jardine & Company and Dorman, Long & Company, both of Middlesbrough, the latter company with Moor Iron & Steel Company of Stockton on Tees providing the plates.[4]

The majority, but not all, rolling-stock iron probably originated in Scotland. It would be expected that the locomotives, carriages and wagons purchased in England, of which there were quite a number before the railways set up their own workshops and the Scottish private manufacturers became established,[5] would utilise English materials, especially when even a Scot declared that Scottish iron was 'quite unfit for wheel-making'.[6] In addition throughout the century large quantities of best quality Yorkshire iron were used everywhere in the manufacture of crank and other axles, often being preferred to steel.[7] On the other hand Krupps of Germany had introduced steel tyres to Scotland via the Great North of Scotland about

[1] J. Mayer, *Engineering and Shipbuilding Industries of Glasgow and the Clyde* (British Association, 1876), p 103.

[2] *Royal Commission on the Application of Iron*, PP 1849, XXIX, Q 230—'the custom in Scotland has been to care nothing about the quality'; p 381, 'not adapted for making bridges or heavy machinery'.

[3] *HRJ*, 26 October 1872. *Engineering*, 28 February 1890.

[4] *Railway World*, Vol 3, August 1894, 270.

[5] Up to 1849 English builders supplied at least 207 of the 383 locomotives known to be in use on Scottish railways.

[6] W. Neilson, *TESS*, 1857–8, 120.

[7] H. Skelton, op cit, p 69. *Moores Monthly Magazine*, May 1896, 39. Dübs & Co, *Orders outward*. Scottish Business Records Archives.

1860, but by 1863 Rowan & Company of Glasgow were producing Bessemer steel tyres, axles and forgings of the highest quality.[1] At first a lack of demand restricted their output of steel to 40 tons a month, but in 1871 the firm was fully engaged on general steel forgings and production of high-class steel tyres for railway use. The latter link with railways was consolidated in 1872 when the firm undertook limited liability and one of the new directors was a representative of Neilson & Company, the locomotive builders.[2] The Steel Company of Scotland also manufactured rolling-stock components, but the Scottish companies by no means monopolised their native railways' contracts. At the end of the century the Caledonian was splitting its orders for engine tyres equally between H. Bessemer & Company and the Steel Company of Scotland, the latter also sharing the wagon-tyre contract with an English firm. In addition wagon drawbars were supplied by Cammell & Company of Sheffield.[3]

The private rolling-stock manufacturers also sub-contracted outside Scotland. In the 1890s Dübs obtained crucible cast steels from Cammells, some cast-steel tyres from Krupps and frequently other locomotive fittings such as bearing springs, and copper pipes and tubes from English firms. The chief manufacturer of wagons in Scotland, R. & Y. Pickering & Company purchased wagon brasses and rolled knee bars from the Sandwell Iron & Axle Company, Smethwick, and nuts and bolts from another Smethwick firm, the Patent Rivet Company. However, the bulk of their metal requirements were met within Scotland. Steel plates for Dübs came from the Steel Company of Scotland, Neilson & Maxwell and P. & W. McLellan, the latter firm also supplying many of the tyres and axles. Alexander Rowan provided the spark arresters and J. Wilson & Son the wrought-iron pipes and furnace lubricators. For Pickerings wagon castings came from Pott, Cassels & Williamson, engineers of Motherwell, and the Ardeer Foundry, Stevenson. Wilson Baird of Glasgow supplied bar iron, knee bars, steel tyres and axles and 'Siemen-Martin' steel plates, while wrought-iron buffer forgings were made by Miller, Russell & Company, Overton Forge Ltd, Wishaw.[4]

By the end of the century many Scottish engineering firms were making their own castings mainly from Scots metal, but in the late 1860s it was 'contrary to the usual practice of mechanical engineering works in Scotland to make their castings on the spot' although the demand was still for Scottish metal 'from the numerous and well-fitted foundries in the neighbourhood'.[5]

[1] E. L. Ahrons, *The British Steam Locomotive* (1927), pp 163–5. Stephenson Locomotive Society, *The Great North of Scotland Railway* (1954), p 303. Kohn, op cit, p 84.

[2] Carr & Taplin, op cit, p 28; Gibson, op cit, p 25.

[3] BTHR(S), CAL 1/40, 14 December 1897.

[4] Dübs & Company, *Orders Outwards*; R. & Y. Pickering, *Contract Book No. 1*; Scottish Business Records Archives.

[5] *Engineering*, 18 October 1867.

TABLE 2

RAILWAY DEMAND FOR IRON

Period	*Demand for Permanent-way Iron*	*Demand for Rolling-stock Iron*	*Production of Scottish Pig*
1840–9	38·8	5·5	454
1850–9	25·3	5·5	815
1860–9	62·3	11·6	1083
1870–9	86·3	24·2	1022
1880–9	80·4	26·3	1034
1890–9	91·4	32·8	935

Notes:

All measured in '000 tons of pig iron per annum.

For sources and fuller details see Appendixes 1 to 4.

V

With the aid of a calculating machine and numerous assumptions it has been possible to make an estimate of Scottish railway demand for iron. As is shown in Table 2 this demand exhibited an upward trend except in the decade 1850–9 when the wounds of the mania were being licked and replacement demand was not yet heavy, and in the decade 1880–9 when the use of steel rails cut replacement demand for a while. Demand in the 1840s totalled some 44,000 tons and in successive decades 31,000 tons, 74,000 tons, 111,000 tons, and 107,000, reaching 124,000 tons in the last decade of the century. Many problems have emerged in the computation of these estimates, but have been overcome (some more successfully, or more convincingly, than others) by the use of assumptions based on evidence available. However, in trying to determine the importance of the railway demand, a further difficulty arises in the statistics of Scottish iron production. The early 'Mineral Statistics' tend to reiterate the errors of the secondary sources on which their Scottish figures are based. However, a reliable set of statistics can be produced from the records of William Connal & Company, storekeepers of pig iron in Glasgow. They are especially useful in that they register not only production, but also sales of the iron, which is valuable information as stock movements were often in the order of ±10 per cent of total sales.[1]

Annual production of pig iron averaged 450,000 tons in the 1840s and maintained a high rate of growth throughout the next decade before attaining a peak of 1,083,000 tons per annum in the 1860s. There followed a period of stagnation and eventual decline, but as pig-iron manufacture

[1] R. H. Campbell, 'Statistics of the Scottish Pig Iron Trade 1830–65', *JWScI & S*, Vol 64, 1956–7. Monthly Circulars of William Connal and Co, Mitchell Library.

fell away so that of steel began to increase, rising from 50,000 tons in 1879 to 245,000 by 1886. Information as to the production of malleable iron, from which rails were made, is not available in a comprehensive series for Scotland, although it is clear that this sector of the iron industry did not achieve a position of any significance until the late 1850s at the earliest. Between 1864 and 1880 malleable-iron production averaged 200,000 tons per annum. Its rate of decline in the face of the overwhelming superiority of steel was much slower than in England, but this was a sign of conservatism, not of strength, as technical progress within the industry was non-existent.[1]

Of course, not all new rails need be a new demand upon the iron industry, or even upon the railmaking section of that industry. The committee inquiring into the affairs of the North British in 1849 were informed 'that when the rails are so far bruised and injured as to be unfit for service, they can be rerolled, and the deficiency in quantity supplied at about £2 10s. per ton, so that replacing the rails will not be so serious an expense as many persons may suppose'. Moreover, as the company's engineer pointed out, they 'will not be greatly diminished in weight'.[2] How much iron rails lost in weight through abrasion in use and waste in rerolling is difficult to say, but for steel the comparable figures were up to 20 per cent in use and 7½ per cent in remanufacture.[3] However, it is doubtful if much rerolling went on because of the costs involved in shipping the rails to English and Welsh railmakers especially when a local market existed for scrap.[4] The Glasgow & South Western had not formed any decided opinion as to the cost/durability ratio of the rerolled rails it was using in 1858, but the resident engineer thought it might 'be for the interest of the Company to convert all their old rails, by rerolling, into new ones, if this can be effected at moderate cost'. The absence of further statements suggests that costs were too high if it is remembered that the North British sold most, if not all, of its old rails as scrap and would be unlikely to miss the opportunity of rerolling if it were at all profitable.[5]

[1] Carr & Taplin, op cit, p 108. Gibson, op cit, p 37. Byres, op cit, p 256.

[2] Committee of Inquiry into the North British Railway, 1849, p 2.

[3] I. L. Bell, *The Iron Trade of the United Kingdom*, pp 37, 41.

[4] The companies did not reroll their own rails. In fact the London & North Western was unique amongst British railways because of its policy of rolling its own rails. C. E. R. Sherrington, *The Economics of Rail Transport in Great Britain* (London, 1928), p 83. It is also fair to argue that not enough renewals were needed to stimulate the rise of a rerolling trade within Scotland especially in view of the fact that the malleable iron industry, possessors of potential rerolling equipment, was virtually non-existent in Scotland until (say) 1860 and thus could not take up rerolling as a profitable sideline. Thus the bulk of rerolling if it was to be done on a substantial scale would have to be done by specialist railmakers south of the border.

[5] BTHR(S), RAC(S) 1/11, 20 August 1858. BTHR(S), NBR 4/46 4/47, Sales and Receipts of Old Materials.

The railways seem to have missed few opportunities to sell old materials. The Caledonian was a relatively prosperous company in 1897, but still sold, amongst other items,

What then can be said about the role played by her railways in the development of Scotland's iron and steel industries? If all the iron used by the railways had originated as Scottish pig, only on rare occasions before 1875 would it have accounted for 10 per cent of total Scottish sales or production of pig iron. The average potential level of consumption between 1840 and 1870 was below 7 per cent as is shown in Table 2. Following the fall in demand after the completion of the post-mania construction the proportion was less than 5 per cent, but it began to increase during the 1860s as further building and the replacement of worn-out equipment took place. However, most rails (totalling perhaps half of the permanent-way demand by weight), were supplied by English manufacturers. Even allowing for English use of 50 per cent Scotch pig in their rail manufacture this further reduces the importance of the railway demand.[1] On these assumptions, and if all rolling-stock iron was Scottish, it is arguable that without that demand Scottish pig-iron production would have achieved over 95 per cent of the growth attained between 1840–4 and 1865–9.

It is more difficult to ascertain quantitatively the part of the railways in the expansion of the malleable-iron and cast-iron sectors of the industry. No Scottish ironmaster managed to successfully break into the market for rails and those firms founded deliberately to exploit the railway demand for wrought iron failed to prosper. The rise of the Scottish malleable-iron industry owed little to the railways. No production figures are available for cast iron, but if all Scottish pig domestically consumed—some 173,000 tons per annum in the 1840s and 283,000 tons in the following decade—is taken as being in the making of cast iron then the railways required at the most between 7 per cent and 10 per cent. The lower figure is counting non-rail permanent-way demand only, and the higher total includes rolling-stock demand. For the 1860s computation is made more difficult because of the growth of the malleable-iron sector which consumed a proportion of the pig iron. If Bremner's figure of 142,000 tons in 1867 is typical of malleable-iron production of the decade then by a similar calculation as above between 10 per cent and 15 per cent of cast-iron production went to meet railway requirements.[2]

Two factors were operating on the demand side to make the railway's needs of more importance to the Scottish iron and steel industry in the last quarter of the nineteenth century. Firstly, equipment was getting heavier. Between 1860 and 1900 the average weight of rails rose 26 per cent, of chairs 75 per cent, and of locomotives 58 per cent.[3] Secondly, renewals

coach trimmers' rags, old axle grease, old tickets and waste cinders. The proceeds from these sales were not inconsiderable; in two months in 1895 the North British obtained £7,588. BTHR(S), CAL 1/41, 14 December 1897; NBR 1/40, 20 July 1895.

[1] No English witness to the Royal Commission on the Application of Iron to Railway Structures quoted a ratio above this.

[2] Bremner, op cit, p 33.

[3] See Appendix 1, Columns 7 and 8, and Appendix 3, Column 1.

began to exercise a strong influence upon demand, as is indicated in Appendix 1. Not only does renewal demand exhibit less fluctuation from year to year than new mileage demand; it also, except in years of unusual constructional activity, dominates absolutely total demand for permanent-way iron. In only 7 years in the last quarter of the century did new track opened exceed 25 per cent of total track renewed.

The proportion of total pig-iron production potentially absorbed by the railways rose from about 10 per cent to 15 per cent by the end of the century with occasional fluctuations at least as high as 20 per cent. Again much permanent-way material came from south of the border and less Scottish metal would be used in its preparation than previously.[1] For the purposes of the model the increase in rail production within Scotland was considered as being cancelled out by this diminished use of Scottish pig in England. On the same assumptions as before a rate of growth in the order of 90 per cent of that actually achieved by the pig-iron industry between 1870–4 and 1895–9 could have been expected if there had been no railway demand. However, allowance must be made for the increased use of English pig by the Scottish steelmakers. Imports, primarily from Cleveland rose from 72,000 tons in 1867 to average 300,000 tons per annum during the period 1875–80 and over 425,000 tons between 1885 and 1890.[2] If railway steel produced in Scotland contained as much English pig as did Scottish steel in general, then the absence of railway demand would have cut the rate of growth by only about 5 per cent.

In fact, as pig-iron production remained stagnant at slightly over 1,020,000 tons per annum during the 1870s and 1880s before declining to 935,000 tons in the following decade, it can be argued that railway demand via the other sectors of the industry had an important part in maintaining the level of output and the use of existing capacity as the demand for coastwise and foreign shipments fell away. Furthermore, although the Scottish steel industry was reliant on the shipyards, the major steel producer was originally set up to tap the railway demand for rails, albeit not just Scottish railways. The Steel Company of Scotland might have developed anyhow when the Clyde shipbuilders turned to steel, but the existence of the company may have encouraged that switch by having the material on hand; moreover, who is to say what lessons may have been learned from ten years' experience?[3]

It has been suggested that in the aggregate the Scottish iron and steel industries did not need indigenous railway markets to ensure growth, al-

[1] See pp 59 and 64.

[2] See Appendix 4, Column 10.

[3] Dr P. L. Payne informs me that the Steel Company of Scotland made great play in its advertising of the ship *Rotomahana* which was built of steel and which was involved in an accident from which an iron-hulled ship would have sunk. Dr Payne feels that the widespread publicity given to this encouraged the shipowners to purchase steel from the Scottish company and converted them from their previous use of iron.

though one section of that industry, the pig-iron trade, may have been grateful for their stabilising influence towards the close of the century. Individual firms may have been more dependent for their fortunes upon railway demand, but this is unlikely in view of the tremendous influence which external markets exerted on the industry as a whole. The evidence that exists suggests that the engineering firms which supplied the home railways with equipment generally diversified their output to various markets at home and abroad thus reducing the significance of Scottish railway demand for iron through this channel.

At times the railways in Scotland may have been more a backward linkage of the Scottish iron industry than the reverse. Rolling-stock scrap was estimated by multiplying the various quantities of scrapped vehicles by the average weight of each category an average life ago. These average lives were the same as those used in calculating renewals. Few vehicles were scrapped before 1860. After that date totals for scrapped vehicles were obtained by a comparison of total existing stock (as given in the Railway Returns) with the figures for renewals and additions to stock as estimated from the railway company records. From 1870 these are reliable, but for the previous decade it is probably best to assume that the number of scrapped stock was the same as the stock renewed. Expressed in terms of pig-iron equivalent, scrapped rolling stock produced about 2,000 tons of material each year in the 1860s. As the railway network expanded, heavier vehicles and a great volume of scrapping increased this to around 15,000 tons by the late 1890s.[1]

As for the permanent way, rerolling of rails does not appear to have been the prevalent practice. Most companies followed the policy of the Caledonian, whose old materials were 'either sold or applied to incidental repairs on portions of the line which do not require to be renewed, or in the construction of additional sidings and branches'.[2] How much was sold and how much relaid is difficult to determine. In the absence of information for any Scottish company it must be accepted that the figure for those re-employed lies somewhere between one third and two thirds. The former was the estimate of the storekeeper of the North Eastern regarding rails taken from main lines and branches, and the latter estimate is of rails taken from main lines only, which were found to 'have a further useful life in sidings and branches, where traffic is light'.[3] Ultimately all rails would become scrap, but the time-lag might be extensive. As late as 1923, 70 years after the opening of the line, some of the original Great North of Scotland rails were to be found in odd sidings.[4]

Some old rails were sold to other companies; the Fordell purchased

[1] See Appendix 5.
[2] Hawksworth, op cit, p 19.
[3] I. L. Bell, *Memoranda* (1896), p 31. Wood & Stamp, op cit, p 48.
[4] Stephenson Locomotive Society, *Great North of Scotland*, p 303.

second-hand rails from the North British as did the Selkirk Peebles. The major buyers of scrap iron were, however, the engineers and ironmasters. As early as 1836 the Ballochney sold 6½ tons of old rails to the Dundyvan Iron Company.[1]

With the change to steel, problems were raised. Questions about the utility of used steel rails featured predominantly in the discussion of a paper on 'The Maintenance and Renewal of Permanent Way' given to the Institution of Civil Engineers in 1866. Wrought-iron rails could be cut up, piled, forged or rolled down into something useful, but was this as true of the more durable and practically unbreakable steel ones? In fact C. W. Siemens' recently introduced open-hearth furnace meant that they could be reworked. Not only were they 'capable of ready conversion', but they were 'worth nearly or quite as much, ton for ton, and irrespective of the extent to which they may have been worn, as Bessemer ingots themselves'.[2] Furthermore, Scotland had little integration between her iron and steel making which meant that the steel producers lacked supplies of molten iron. This handicap was overcome by their expert use of large quantities of steel scrap obtained mainly from the shipyards, but presumably also from the railways.[3]

However, the chief customer for railway scrap, if the sales of the North British are at all typical, was the engineering industry. Most of the old materials were purchased by Scottish companies although occasionally, as in 1879, London firms would tender successfully for large amounts. It was not just the larger companies that bought the scrap, for frequently small firms, who were willing to pick up odd amounts at points over the system, would obtain contracts. The bulk of the scrap metal, however, would be taken by one or two of the large engineering firms and this became increasingly true as steel, which needed special facilities for reconversion, increased its proportion of total railway scrap metal towards the end of the century. In the case of the North British Messrs P. & W. McLellan, who possessed such facilities, dominated the sales by the early 1890s, taking 49 per cent in 1892 and 66 per cent in 1896.[4]

These difficulties make it impossible to estimate accurately how much scrap was coming on to the market, but with a few assumptions it is possible to hazard a guess. If half the rails lifted from main lines and sidings were immediately sold for scrap and the rest had a further active life of (say) ten years, then towards the end of the century perhaps 70,000 tons of used railway material was being sold each year.[5] This was equal to 6 per cent

[1] G. Dott, *Early Scottish Colliery Wagonways* (St Margaret's Technical Press, 1947), p 7. Mitchell Library, 53154–7, Ballochney, 2 February 1836.

[2] *Proceedings ICE*, 20 March 1866. *Engineer*, 20 April 1866.

[3] K. Warren, 'Locational Problems of the Scottish Iron and Steel Industry since 1760', *Scottish Geographical Magazine*, April 1965, 26.

[4] BTHR(S), NBR 4/46, 4/47, Sales and Receipts of Old Materials.

[5] See Appendix 5.

of total pig-iron production and over 80 per cent of railway demands for Scottish pig. In the aggregate the railways were almost meeting their own requirements, though of course purchasers of the old materials and suppliers of the new were generally not one and the same.

VI

The advent of railways in Britain could have had disastrous results for the Scottish iron industry. Before their coming the high cost of carriage and the remoteness of Scottish industrial location protected it, but as the efficiency of bulk transport improved a decline in its fortunes might have occurred due to English and Welsh competition, had not the application of the hot blast cut production costs so drastically.

It is arguable, however, that it was shipping and not the railways that carried the Anglo-Scottish trade of the iron industry. Ironically in the immediate post-mania construction boom the absence of through railway communication enforced the use of coastal shipping to deliver rails from south of the border. The *Perthshire Advertiser* commented on the fact that 'since Saturday no fewer than three vessels have arrived at Perth, loaded with rails, from Wales for the Scottish Central Railway'.[1] Even when a railway link had been established contracts frequently specified delivery at various ports along the line.[2] Presumably cheaper shipping rates held sway as they did regarding the shipment of Scottish pig iron to England.[3] A further factor making for the employment of sea rather than rail transport would be the links already established with the shippers. In the decade from 1836 the Scottish iron industry was commercially dependent on the English and overseas markets, and on the easy access to tide water which helped cheapen supply costs. Clapham estimated that not less than three-quarters of the Scottish make was shipped down the Clyde in 1846.[4] In the mid century two leading Scottish foundries, the Carron Company and the Albion Works of Andrew McLaren at Alloa shipped goods direct from their works to London wharves.[5] The railways' share of Scottish pig taken to England remained meagre, accounting for only 36,000 tons in the years

[1] Quoted in *HRJ*, 15 November 1845.

[2] eg The Portpatrick contract with Bailey Brothers & Co of Liverpool. *HRJ*, 16 April 1859.

[3] In 1883 the rate for Scottish pig by sea from Ardrossan to Runcorn was 3s a ton, (Minutes of Evidence for Manchester Ship Canal Bill—quoted in K. Warren, *Rail Trade*, op cit, p 155.)

Railway charges on the Caledonian for such merchandise were from 5d a ton for 1 mile, 3s 8½d for 25 miles, 5s 3½d for 50 miles and 7s 4d for 100 miles. (BTHR(S), HRP(S) 51, p 274.)

[4] Clapham, op cit, p 426. The figures in Appendix 4 suggest that two thirds would be more appropriate.

[5] R. H. Campbell, *Carron Company* (Oliver and Boyd, 1961), p 213. Carron Company Records GD 58/18/78. Circular to Shipping Agents (undated) S.R.O. S. Griffiths, *Guide to the Iron Trade of Great Britain* (1873), p 168.

1888–90 compared with the 561,000 tons sent by sea.[1] It was the facility for shipment that undoubtedly helped maintain Scots pig-iron exports in the face of growing competition, for both the Forth and Clyde 'may be reached at a cost of about one-tenth of the railway carriage payable on English pig irons made in the Midlands, before the latter can reach equally good shipping ports'.[2]

Was this where the railways made their contribution? Even within Scotland the railways do not appear to have monopolised the iron traffic. Lack of data makes it impossible to express this statement adequately in quantitative terms. Generally the official traffic returns failed to distinguish iron ore from other minerals and this is especially true of the two major companies serving the iron-producing districts. Thus the role of the railways has to be assessed on the basis of qualitative statements rather than on statistical evidence. The Monkland and the Forth & Clyde canals in the West of Scotland preceded the development of the trade in 'hot blast' iron and greatly assisted in its growth, though the coming of the railways allowed even more territory to be opened up. For instance, the Wishaw & Coltness line made possible the use of a large field of ironstone found in the coal measures some time previously, but which had been before the construction of the railway 'an object scarcely worthy of attention'.[3] Further south, the Dalmellington Iron Company was not unduly hampered by the delayed construction of railway links forcing it to cart all its pig iron several miles to Ayr. It was making a profit from 1853 and producing 27,000 tons when a railway connection eventually came four years later.[4] In 1846 most of the iron manufactured in the Airdrie district went out by canal in both directions and elsewhere the famous ironmaster dynasty, the Bairds, had a canal running through the centre of their works on which 'a great proportion of the manufactured iron is sent out'.[5]

However, gradually the railways began to secure the traffic. Despite the existence of an east-west canal system, plenty of pig iron and coal was being transported by rail from the West of Scotland to Leith Docks in 1867; and when haematite ore began to be brought into Scotland from north-west England the Solway railway viaduct was built with the specific intention of obtaining this trade.[6] Yet it was not until the last decades of the century that the railways really began to tap the iron traffic of the canals. One reason for this delay was that the canals in the industrial areas were railway-owned and the companies saw no sense in siphoning off the traffic

[1] Calculated from figures in an unnamed newspaper cutting found in the volumes of *Connal's Monthly Circulars.*

[2] Skelton, op cit, p 29.

[3] R. H. Campbell, thesis cited, pp 3, 210.

[4] D. L. Smith, *The Dalmellington Iron Company* (David and Charles, Newton Abbot, 1967), pp 19–27.

[5] *Select Committee on Railway and Canal Amalgamations*, PP 1846, XIII, Q 915. Bremner, op cit, p 37.

[6] *Royal Commission on Railways*, PP 1867, XXXVIII, Q 9468.

until the customers demanded railway accommodation.[1] Moreover, the railways had few outstanding advantages over canals. Their speed is not so essential in the short-distance haulage of bulk goods unless the transport mode is stretched to full capacity. Regularity of service was assured as on the Forth-Clyde canal system stoppages through bad weather were rare and holdups for repairs averaged less than a day and a half a year.[2] Where the railways scored was that the use of canals involved cartage costs and transhipment expenses between the works and the canals, a factor of increasing importance as the location of sectors of the industry shifted. The malleable-iron industry, for example, moved away from the canals and out of the Coatbridge area.[3]

It might be argued that on the basis of financial evidence the Scottish ironmasters showed little interest in obtaining railway facilities before 1850. The Houldsworths were willing to invest £31,000 in an attempt to obtain a railway connection from Ayr to their Dalmellington Iron Works, but generally Scottish ironmasters participated only to a limited extent in railway investment in the first half of the century. John Houldsworth, John Wilson of Dundyvan and the Baird dynasty subscribed £89,000, £63,000 and £30,000 respectively in 1846 (actual investment was well below these figures—perhaps less than 50 per cent), but the vast majority of ironmasters seem to have preferred a less active role in railway promotion.[4] However, this cannot really be attributed to a lack of interest for at a later date ironmasters were often prominent on the boards of railway companies. The probable reason for their lack of financial support is that the rapid expansion of capacity in the Scottish iron industry required most of their available funds.[5] It may be significant that William Baird, later to become chairman of the company, did not join the Caledonian board until 1852.[6]

The performance of the railways was by no means satisfactory to the ironmasters. Complaints that rates were too high were frequent, especially when the Scottish producers were feeling the pinch of English competition. The president of the West of Scotland Iron & Steel Institute maintained that English west-coast makers could deliver into the lower reaches of the Clyde by winter at the same cost as railways took local iron there, and that English east-coast producers could deliver by sea to Aberdeen and Dundee

[1] *Royal Commission on Canals and Waterways*, PP 1907, XXXIII, Appendix 39, especially p 146.

[2] Ibid, Appendix 39, p 140. The stopping of the canal linking Glasgow to Greenock in 1801 by frost caused the manager of the Muirkirk Iron Company to favourably view a scheme for a railway between those towns which he considered might 'help off the pigs well'. 'Early Scottish Railways', *The Three Banks Review*, No 74, June 1967, 30.

[3] *Royal Commission on Canals and Waterways*, PP 1907, XXXIII, Appendix 39, p 146. K. Warren, 'Locational Problems', loc cit, p 23.

[4] D. L. Smith, op cit, p 27, *PP* 1846, XXXVIII, *Railway Subscriptions*.

[5] R. H. Campbell, 'Investment in the Scottish Pig Iron Trade 1830–43', *ScJPE*, October 1954.

[6] Bradshaw, 1852, p 241, BTHR(S), RAC(S) 1/3 March, 1853.

at less than the railways charged from Lanarkshire. This, he argued, was not in the interests of the railway companies as they would eventually lose business, and so they should reduce rates to allow the Scottish industry to become competitive.[1] No mention was made of whether the railways could afford to do this as a short-run gamble on a long-term success. In fact the railways had served the industry well in the depression of the late seventies, giving the ironmasters a drawback of 15 per cent from their ordinary charges.[2]

The efficiency of railway service was hampered by the use of too small wagons. The Caledonian had experimented with a 50-ton vehicle for use in the iron trade, but little came of it and responsibility for this lay primarily with the ironmasters whose existing equipment provided a serious obstacle to any changes on the part of the railway companies.[3] Even at the beginning of the twentieth century it could be claimed that 'there is not, at the present time, a single shipping port, iron and steel work, or gaswork, or any work in Scotland, capable of dealing with a wagon of a carrying capacity of 30 or even 20 tons. . . .'[4] Furthermore, the firms frequently possessed inadequate tracks for marshalling trucks quickly which did not facilitate railway efficiency, nor did the use of railway wagons as storage points. Privately owned wagons also prevented the railways from making the best use of existing capacity.[5]

It was also claimed that not all areas were adequately served. Bremner maintained that Messrs Rigby & Beardmore would have obtained a greater share of government contracts for armour plating had their Parkhead forge been nearer to a railway.[6] Again there is no mention of whether it would have been in the railway companies' interests to spend money in accommodating the firm. If the railway connection was to have such beneficial results then there is no reason why the firm should not have paid for its construction. Overall it is fair to conclude that unsatisfactory railway service was not solely the fault of the providers of that service.

The railways also had a role in determining the location of the iron and steel industries, but once again their importance did not achieve its greatest significance until the steel age. The high input to output ratio of the early iron industry led to a choice of an interior location for smelting in preference to a coastal site, and primarily these works were situated on the Monkland Canal or its cuts. The coming of the railway accentuated the choice of an interior site by further opening up large fields of raw materials.

[1] *JWScI & SInst*, 1897, 10.
[2] *Scotsman*, 31 March 1880.
[3] *Engineering*, 12 February 1892. *Locomotive Magazine*, 1899, 108.
[4] G. Paish, 'The British Railway Position', 1902, p 117, quoted in D. Aldcroft, 'The Entrepreneur and the British Economy 1870–1914', *Economic History Review*, 2nd ser, XVII (1964), 129.
[5] D. L. Burn, *Economic History of Steel-Making* (CUP, 1940), p 167.
[6] D. Bremner, *op cit*, p 55.

Such was the importance of the supplies of coal available from the deep seams in the central part of the Lanarkshire coalfield that the pig-iron industry remained in the Coatbridge area, in preference to the coast (and shipping ports to its major markets), even when ores were having to be brought to the district after local resources became exhausted.[1] Railways (existing and potential) were probably the determining factor in the location of the Ayrshire industry which developed in the 1840s as Lanarkshire entrepreneurs feared the exhaustion of blackband deposits.[2]

The first malleable-iron works also chose sites around the Monkland Canal, but in 1840 the Mossend works were erected alongside the Wishaw & Coltness railway and the ill-fated West of Scotland Malleable Iron Company picked the same railway a few years later. Later the malleable-iron industry tended to shift away from the Coatbridge area and Motherwell and Wishaw became centres of the industry especially after 1870 Lack of space around Coatbridge may have been one cause of the shift, but railway connections from these new centres to their markets must have helped determine the new locations.[3]

Coalfield location was of less importance to the steel industry as fuel comprised a smaller proportion of the cost of manufacture than in pig iron.[4] Here the railways played a decisive part. One necessity of the site chosen by the Steel Company of Scotland was that it should have 'good railway connections with coal and iron districts' and the decision must have been influenced by the Caledonian's willingness to conclude a favourable traffic agreement.[5] Canals were no longer considered as locational determinants and all new steel works relied on the railways as transport agencies. Hallside (1871), Wishaw (1885), Dalzell (1881), Clydebridge (1888) and Hemington (1890) were all along the Caledonian line from Glasgow to Wishaw.[6]

The laying out of railways may have aided the iron industry by leading to the discovery of new deposits of ore. Frequently the possibility of a railway being constructed led to a geological survey of the district involved. Occasionally this resulted in the discovery of a new mineral field as in Ayrshire, or about the Denny line in the Stirling area, or in various parts of Aberdeenshire and Banffshire. However, this aspect of the role of the railways should not be exaggerated in the case of the iron

[1] G. Thomson (ed), *The County of Lanark* (*The Third Statistical Account of Scotland*, Vol VIII, 1960), p 30. K. Warren, 'Locational Problems', loc cit, 21.

[2] Ibid. D. L. Smith, op cit, p 19.

[3] Thomson, *Lanark*, p 30. K. Warren, 'Locational Problems', loc cit, 23.

[4] In the early 1890s 1 ton of pig iron would require 1·54 tons of coal in its making but only 1·25 tons in its conversion to steel. Calculated from quantities given in *JWScI & SInst*, 1892–3, 3.

[5] Steel Company of Scotland letterbooks—quoted in Gibson, op cit, p 27. BTHR(S), CAL 1/19 item 983.

[6] Thomson, *Lanark*, p 30.

industry as it was of far more importance as regards the discovery of coal deposits.[1]

Clearly the Scottish railways were of much more importance to the native iron and steel industry in providing transport facilities than in consuming the products of the industry. However, it is not apparent that they played a significant role before 1850—the 'take-off' years of the iron industry. Coastal shipping took most of the Anglo-Scottish traffic and not until the last 30 years of the century did railways come to supersede canals in the domestic ferrous trade. As a determinant of the location of the industry the railways were of significance at an earlier date, but did not attain their greatest importance until the steel age.

VII

Finally, as the role cannot be assigned to the railways, it may be of interest to examine the factors promoting the expansion of the Scottish iron industry. It is clear that transport services in the 'take-off' years were primarily provided by the canals and coastal shipping, but these were in existence before that period and probably acted more as permissive factors in aiding and allowing the expansion than actually stimulating it. The growth of the industry stemmed directly from the introduction of the hot blast in the late 1820s which had a twofold effect in allowing the inferior coke of Scotland to be replaced by uncoked coal and also in enabling the high temperatures necessary for the reduction of the blackband ironstone to be attained economically. The ready availability of minerals, the cheap labour supply and small mineral royalties all combined to boost the Scottish pig-iron industry on the basis of low-cost production. Although some engineers held that hot-blast iron was insufficiently strong, especially for large castings, and some specifications, including government ordnance, excluded its use, the comparative cost advantage secured by the Scottish industry generally allowed markets to be easily obtained, with the result that Scotland's share of total British pig-iron production rose from 5 per cent in 1825 to 17 per cent in 1840 and 26 per cent in 1848.

The high profitability of the industry encouraged the native ironmasters to maintain a high rate of investment, despite the gradual decline into depression, because of the lingering optimistic expectations engendered by the boom of 1836 and the technological developments with the industry.[2]

[1] *Scottish Railway Gazette*, 7 March 1846. *Railway Times*, 19 July 1856. *HRJ*, 24 September 1864.

[2] Campbell, *Scotland Since 1707*, pp 117–23. Gayer, Rostow & Schwartz, op cit, p 323. Coke had been obtained from Lanarkshire splint coal, but 55 per cent had been lost in the process of conversion. At the Clyde Iron Works 1 ton of cast iron had required:

	Tons	*Cwt*	*Qtr*	
in 1829 using coke and cold air	8	1	1	of coal
in 1830 using coke and heated air	5	3	1	of coal
in 1833 using coal and heated air	2	5	1	of coal

This continued investment meant that when British demand for railway iron surged upwards the Scottish industry possessed the capacity necessary to absorb it. The railway mania 'gave a great stimulus to the iron trade'[1] and nowhere more than in Scotland, where pig-iron production rapidly increased in order to meet the requirements of rail makers in England and Wales who supplied the growing mania demand in Scotland, England and Wales.

Although demand from her own railways was slight, the production of pig to be made into rails in England and increasingly abroad was an important factor in the expansion of the Scottish iron industry in the 30 years preceding the formation of the Steel Company of Scotland.[2]

The viability of the pig-iron industry was in fact dependent on sales to external markets. Between 1846 and 1870 29 per cent of production was exported directly to foreign countries and 32 per cent to England and Wales.[3] Henry Bessemer's presidential address to the Iron & Steel Institute contained the significant remark that 'wherever civilisation had advanced Scotch pig had found its way'.[4] The development of the Cleveland iron industry with its cheaper product, together with the discoveries of iron fields in Lincolnshire and Northamptonshire, depreciated the general selling position of Scotch pig iron in English markets. However, the qualities of the Scottish metal, especially the mixing abilities of No 1 pig, and the facilities for shipment helped maintain Scotland's foreign markets.[5]

Yet consumption within Scotland must have made an important contribution as it averaged about two fifths of total sales of Scottish pig. Undoubtedly some of this also went abroad in the form of finished products. By the mid 1860s shipbuilding was a major consumer of Scottish pig, taking around 15 per cent of annual production, although the development of cheaper iron production in north-east England, coincident with the rise of iron shipbuilding on the Clyde, prevented the Scottish ironmasters from monopolising this market. The revival of pig-iron production in 1879 was attributed directly to steamship contracts made with the Clyde yards.[6] It is also clear that the malleable-iron industry owed its existence to shipyard

This had 'a great effect on the increase of the manufacture in Scotland', but in England and Wales the reduction in costs was not so great as less coal had been needed originally.

H. Scrivenor, *History of the Iron Trade* (1854), pp 259–61. Campbell, 'Investment in the Scottish Pig Iron Trade', loc cit, 248–9.

[1] Scrivenor, op cit, p 286.

[2] Fogel, op cit, pp 193–5. P. Temin, *Iron and Steel in Nineteenth Century America* (M.I.T. Press, 1964), p 21. T. Brassey, *Work and Wages* (1872), p 191.

[3] Calculated from Appendix 4, Columns 5, 7 and 8.

[4] *Transactions of the Iron and Steel Institute*, 1872, 5.

[5] Scotland achieved the cheapest production in Britain in 1855 at which point her reserves of blackband ironstone had dwindled.

Carr & Taplin, op cit, p 81. S. Griffiths, op cit, pp 27–8.

[6] *Connal's Circular* for December 1879, p 4. For an estimate of shipyard demand for iron, see Appendix 4 ,Column 4.

demand. Shipbuilding contributed a great deal, too, to the growth and prosperity of the Scottish steel industry. In fact, as one steelmaker recalled in 1911, it was fair to conclude 'that when the Clyde is busy trade generally, and especially the iron and steel trade . . . is also busy. That has been I believe, the universal experience of the past.'[1]

Overall, it is fair to say that there was an independence in the development of the Scottish pig-iron trade, though not of the malleable iron and steel industries, and the development of her heavy industries. Even the most important home consumer, the Clyde shipyards, gained their reputation first as engineers, only progressing to shipbuilding at a later stage; and even then the reliance on the Scottish iron industry was not complete, although growth might have been slower without the readily available local supplies. The iron trade of Scotland was predominantly a pig-iron producing trade not dependent for its prosperity on the further manufacture of iron within Scotland or on the heavy industries of Scotland in general. However, with the rise of the Scottish steel industry, based upon open-hearth production for the shipyards, Scotland began to consume more of her domestically produced pig, the proportion growing from 23 per cent in 1882–3 to 50 per cent in the early 1890s and 59 per cent in 1902.[2]

Both as carriers of raw materials and finished products and as determinants of the location of the iron and steel industry, railways, functioning as transport agencies, became more important in the last three decades of the century, though they had previously aided the siting of the iron industry by allowing the exploitation of local mineral deposits. When consumption of the products of the industry is also considered—the support to the stagnating pig-iron sector, the establishment of a rail-making company which diversified into other products, and the prestige which the steel industry as a whole must have received from the construction of the Forth bridge—the indications are more than ever that the Scottish railways only became of significance to the industry as it shifted from its traditional form of a pig-iron trade to one of steel production.

[1] Quoted in Byres, op cit, p 251.

[2] Skelton, op cit, p 28. Warren, 'Locational Problems', loc cit, 25. The estimates in Appendix 4 do not agree precisely, but the same trend is apparent.

APPENDIX 1

SCOTTISH RAILWAYS: DEMAND FOR PERMANENT-WAY IRON, 1840–1900

Year	(1)	(2)	(3)	(4)	(5)	(6)	(7)	(8)	(9)
1840	—	199	106	27	—	133	—	—	28·7
1841	—	225	51	14	—	65	—	—	13·9
1842	—	271	93	25	—	118	74·60	—	25·5
1843	—	282	11	2	—	14	74·14	—	3·0
1844	—	282	0	0	—	0	—	—	0
1845	—	292	19	5	—	24	73·14	—	5·0
1846	—	357	126	34	1	161	72·72	—	34·0
1847	—	465	206	56	28	289	72·30	25·55	61·0
1848	—	758	589	159	33	781	72·09	25·10	164·5
1849	763	872	187	50	13	251	71·88	24·65	52·5
1850	892	971	164	44	14	222	71·59	24·10	46·2
1851	961	976	9	3	15	27	70·06	23·65	5·5
1852	978	998	29	8	19	56	68·52	23·20	11·2
1853	996	1012	14	4	23	41	68·68	22·10	7·8
1854	1043	1062	60	16	32	108	68·84	21·00	21·3
1855	1091	1121	75	20	34	130	69·00	22·00	25·7
1856	1205	1217	125	34	43	201	69·29	23·00	40·1
1857	1250	1256	40	11	48	99	69·58	24·00	20·0
1858	1353	1342	99	27	60	185	70·23	24·77	38·2
1859	1428	1418	82	22	73	178	70·88	25·54	37·1
1860	1486	1471	62	17	82	160	71·52	26·31	33·8
1861	—	—	154	41	85	280	71·92	27·10	62·3
1862	—	—	169	46	116	330	72·33	27·58	73·1
1863	—	—	252	68	124	444	72·72	28·06	99·1
1864	—	—	118	32	141	293	73·11	28·52	65·7
1865	—	—	113	31	155	289	73·51	28·98	65·4
1866	—	—	45	12	169	226	73·73	29·49	51·7
1867	—	—	57	15	165	237	73·95	30·00	54·4
1868	—	—	92	40	151	283	74·17	30·62	65·4
1869	—	—	70	30	126	226	74·39	31·24	52·6
1870	—	—	153	54	179	387	74·63	31·86	90·7
1871	—	—	22	18	209	249	74·73	32·48	58·3
1872	—	—	43	24	238	305	74·82	33·10	74·6
1873	—	—	36	23	268	326	74·93	33·40	84·0
1874	—	—	88	38	285	410	75·02	33·70	95·7
1875	—	—	33	22	314	400	75·13	34·00	90·2
1876	—	—	8	15	291	314	75·24	35·37	71·7
1877	—	—	55	29	337	421	75·36	36·74	95·5
1878	—	—	109	46	353	508	75·99	38·11	117·7
1879	—	—	25	21	320	366	76·52	39·48	85·1
1880	—	—	59	32	309	400	77·07	40·85	93·1
1881	—	—	26	22	290	338	78·03	40·39	79·0
1882	—	—	20	20	271	311	78·99	39·93	73·0
1883	—	—	30	30	254	313	79·95	39·47	73·9
1884	—	—	49	23	232	304	80·91	39·00	71·9
1885	—	—	28	23	203	254	81·87	38·73	61·7*
1886	—	—	54	32	168	254	82·83	38·17	77·3*
1887	—	—	37	26	147	210	83·81	37·66	72·4*
1888	—	—	40	28	128	196	84·31	38·92	77·5*
1889	—	—	28	24	125	125	84·81	40·18	54·6*
1890	—	—	97	48	132	276	85·21	41·44	69·3*

APPENDIX 1 (*continued*)

Year	(1)	(2)	(3)	(4)	(5)	(6)	(7)	(8)	(9)
1891	—	—	10	19	157	186	85·72	42·70	47·3
1892	—	—	21	22	188	231	86·23	43·52	58·8
1893	—	—	43	30	229	308	86·84	44·36	78·8
1894	—	—	134	64	266	463	87·35	45·18	120·6
1895	—	—	41	27	304	373	87·86	46·00	97·3
1896	—	—	82	46	321	449	88·37	46·00	118·7
1897	—	—	80	44	345	469	88·90	46·00	124·7
1898	—	—	41	31	335	407	89·41	46·00	108·1
1899	—	—	9	20	314	343	89·93	46·00	91·8
1900	—	—	17	23	288	328	90·35	46·00	88·2

Notes and Sources:

(1) Official route mileage figures taken from *Railway Returns.*

(2) Estimated route mileage derived from H. G. Lewin's *Early British Railways* (1925) and *Mania and its Aftermath* (1936), E. Carter's *An Historical Geography of the Railways of the British Isles* (1959) and contemporary editions of Bradshaw's *Railway Shareholder's Manual.* The official returns do not include lines built in England, but later taken over by Scottish companies, until the date of the takeover, whilst the estimates include these on opening if they were constructed only nominally independent of the Scottish line.

(3) New track mileage (estimated until 1860, official from 1860).

(4) New siding mileage; for source see text.

(5) Track mileage of renewals; for source see text.

(6) Total miles of track laid in the year.

(7) Average weight (in pounds per yard) of rails; for source see text.

(8) Average weight (in pounds) of chairs, source as (7). Fishplates were taken as increasing linearly in weight from 20 lb in 1860 to 26 lb in 1900. Spikes were considered to weigh 1 lb throughout the century.

(9) Total amount of iron estimated to have been used by Scottish railways on their permanent way; measured in '000 tons and converted to pig-iron equivalent by use of the conversion ratios given by I. L. Bell in *The Iron Trade of the United Kingdom*, London, 1886, p 36.

* Signifies a total including iron used in the Tay and Forth bridges.

Appendix 2

ROLLING STOCK OF THE SCOTTISH RAILWAYS, 1840–1900

Year	(1) *Additions*				(2) *Renewals*				(3) *Total New Stock*			
	E	*T*	*C*	*W*	*E*	*T*	*C*	*W*	*E*	*T*	*C*	*W*
1840	32	32	128	1472	—	—	—	—	32	32	128	1472
1841	13	13	52	598	—	—	—	—	13	13	52	598
1842	3	3	12	138	—	—	—	—	3	3	12	138
1843	5	5	20	230	—	—	—	—	5	5	20	230
1844	14	14	56	644	—	—	—	—	14	14	56	644
1845	38	38	152	1748	—	—	—	—	38	38	152	1748
1846	45	45	180	2070	—	—	—	—	45	45	180	2070
1847	46	46	184	2116	—	—	—	—	46	46	184	2116
1848	131	131	524	6026	—	—	—	—	131	131	524	6026
1849	32	32	128	1472	—	—	—	—	32	32	128	1472
1850	14	11	35	929	—	—	—	—	14	11	35	929
1851	26	16	23	691	—	—	34	99	26	16	57	790
1852	20	20	3	778	—	—	7	23	20	20	10	801
1853	13	13	20	1151	3	3	27	116	16	16	47	1267
1854	40	38?	62	1408	2	2	9	103	42	40?	71	1511
1855	58	52	72	1320	4	4	39	224	62	56	111	1544
1856	35	34	21	409	3	3	NK	NK	38	37	21+	409+
1857	48	47	76	1028	3	3	85	667	51	50	161	1695
1858	18	17	74	371	8	8	71	805	26	25	145	1176
1859	28	24	39	700	11	11	50	813	39	35	89	1513
1860	40	38	55	907	13	13	59	578	53	51	114	1485
1861	60	51	52	3979	16	16	47	696	76	67	99	4675
1862	29	24	23	548	8	8	50	293	37	32	73	841
1863	50	48	111	2184	6	4	40	226	56	52	151	2410
1864	83	79	236	2691	7	4	49	436	90	83	285	3127
1865	49	47	76	2003	10	5	30	211	59	52	106	2214
1866	90	33+	205	2696	4	4	17	228	94	37+	222	2924
1867	65	38+	26	579	29	3	14	594	94	41+	40	1173
1868	26	26	75	435	41	18	41	1158	67	44	116	1593
1869	21	12	86	1780	31	15	94	1004	52	27	180	2784
1870	22	16	134	2826	76	63	46	1416	98	79	180	4242
1871	46	43	230	4626	51	36	98	1269	97	78	328	6385
1872	33	32	230	5116*	76	63	46	1416	109	95	276	6532
1873	55	49	168	5663	55	43	77	1673	110	92	245	7336
1874	49	41	156	2377	64	43	42	1760	113	83	198	4133
1875	35	29	53	1266	45	34	46	1663	80	63	99	2929
1876	40	36	74	4036	55	43	55	1858	95	79	129	5894
1877	60	59	136	7660	48	27	63	3116	108	86	199	10776
1878	25	23	176	1138	54	43	165	2092	79	66	331	3230
1879	20	15	27	306	49	33	139	2366	69	48	166	2672
1880	6	6	56	2721	58	37	135	3017	64	43	191	5738
1881	29	24	35	2743	70	49	157	3500	99	73	192	6243
1882	9	14	33	1614	47	38	138	3187	56	52	171	4801
1883	31	30	16	2076	52	51	164	3972	83	81	180	6048
1884	24	17	170	396	76	54	180	3998	100	71	350	4394
1885	5	4	112	951	76	52	153	4422	81	56	265	5373
1886	21	9	84	70	74	48	204	4196	95	57	288	4266
1887	7	1	143	841	65	37	150	3932	72	38	293	4773

APPENDIX 2 (*continued*)

Year	(1) *Additions*				(2) *Renewals*				(3) *Total New Stock*			
	E	*T*	*C*	*W*	*E*	*T*	*C*	*W*	*E*	*T*	*C*	*W*
1888	15	8	127	5267	64	25	132	3524	79	33	259	8791
1889	28	20	117	5438	58	37	151	3212	86	57	268	8650
1890	25	25	75	4893	62	19	194	3218	87	44	269	8111
1891	29	33	135	5781*	63	33	189	2908	92	66	324	8689
1892	44	42	178	4777	61	42	160	3128	105	84	338	7905
1893	47	26	208	1262	58	25	134	3327	105	51	342	4589
1894	28	28	58	2401	59	36	122	2804	87	64	180	5205
1895	32	31	69	3034	70	29	141	3273	102	60	210	6307
1896	60	59	102	6214	70	41	165	3520	130	100	267	9734
1897	46	46	226	1954	73	32	141	3274	119	78	367	5228
1898	63	33+	31	4750	80	39	124	3465	143	72+	155	8315
1899	87	79	181	6457	64	33	127	3249	151	112	308	9706
1900	104	97	189	2464	66	28	114	3234	170	125	303	5698

Source:

BTHR(S), RAC(S) 1/1–73.
Railway Returns.

Notes:

E=Engines T=Tenders C=Coaching Stock W=Wagons NK=Not known
* Caledonian also purchased 6772 traders' wagons in 1872 and 1313 in 1891.

The method of obtaining the above figures is to be found in the text. In addition it must be noted that all locomotives before 1850 were assumed to have tenders.

Appendix 3

SCOTTISH RAILWAYS: DEMAND FOR ROLLING-STOCK IRON, 1840–1900

Year	(1)	(2)	(3)	(4)	(5)
1840	15·7	9·8	1·00	1·05	3·0
1841	16·5	10·4	1·25	1·24	1·3
1842	17·3	11·0	1·50	1·43	0·3
1843	18·1	11·7	1·75	1·62	0·6
1844	20·2	13·1	2·00	1·81	1·5
1845	21·0	13·5	2·01	2·00	6·4
1846	21·0	13·5	2·02	2·08	7·5
1847	21·4	13·7	2·03	2·16	7·6
1848	21·8	13·9	2·03	2·25	21·8
1849	22·2	14·1	2·04	2·33	5·3
1850	22·6	14·6	2·04	2·41	3·6
1851	23·1	14·7	2·05	2·48	3·7
1852	20·7	13·3	2·09	2·55	3·4
1853	20·7	13·3	2·13	2·55	4·8
1854	23·4	15·0	2·17	2·55	7·0
1855	24·7	15·4	2·21	2·56	8·2
1856	24·0	15·3	2·25	2·56	3·2
1857	23·8	15·3	2·30	2·56	8·3
1858	26·4	17·6	2·35	2·57	5·6
1859	29·2	15·2	2·40	2·57	7·2
1860	29·1	16·9	2·45	2·57	8·1
1861	26·3	17·9	2·50	2·58	19·2
1862	28·3	17·0	2·55	2·58	4·9
1863	30·0	21·1	2·61	2·58	11·6
1864	30·1	22·5	2·67	2·59	16·6
1865	29·4	20·9	2·74	2·59	10·9
1866	31·3	23·5	2·80	2·59	14·8
1867	32·7	22·0	2·86	2·60	8·8
1868	32·3	21·6	2·92	2·60	9·4
1869	33·2	21·5	2·98	2·60	12·3
1870	31·8	21·2	3·04	2·61	20·1
1871	30·4	20·4	3·10	2·61	27·1
1872	32·6	18·8	3·16	2·61	28·4
1873	33·1	21·5	3·22	2·62	31·2
1874	35·7	25·3	3·28	2·62	21·5
1875	34·4	24·5	3·35	2·62	15·1
1876	35·1	25·4	3·41	2·63	25·9
1877	36·2	24·8	3·48	2·63	42·3
1878	36·4	26·1	3·54	2·63	17·1
1879	41·2	27·2	3·61	2·64	14·2
1880	47·8	27·0	3·68	2·64	24·5
1881	35·4	27·6	3·75	2·64	27·7
1882	41·0	27·7	3·82	2·64	20·8
1883	39·7	27·7	3·80	2·64	27·0
1884	40·6	28·3	3·97	2·65	20·7

APPENDIX 3 (*continued*)

Year	(1)	(2)	(3)	(4)	(5)
1885	40·1	28·9	4·06	2·65	24·7
1886	41·7	30·8	4·15	2·65	22·4
1887	40·4	28·7	4·24	2·65	21·9
1888	40·9	28·9	4·33	2·65	34·7
1889	40·1	28·1	4·41	2·65	35·4
1890	40·6	33·8	4·50	2·65	10·8
1891	42·1	32·0	4·65	2·65	38·4
1892	41·8	31·8	4·80	2·65	37·2
1893	46·8	33·0	4·95	2·65	25·7
1894	49·4	36·9	5·10	2·65	26·7
1895	45·2	33·5	5·25	2·65	30·7
1896	45·3	35·9	5·40	2·65	44·9
1897	43·9	32·8	5·55	2·65	27·2
1898	43·8	33·5	5·70	2·65	39·6
1899	44·7	34·1	5·85	2·65	47·7
1900	46·2	33·8	6·00	2·65	36·2

Notes and Sources:

(1) (2) Average weight of (1) locomotives (2) tenders expressed in tons. Calculated from data in the histories of the Scottish railway companies published by the *Stephenson Locomotive Society*—the Caledonian 1947, the Glasgow and South Western 1950, the Great North of Scotland 1954 and the Highland 1955. No differentiation was made between tank and tender locomotives as this is cancelled out by a similar non-differentiation in the physical quantities table in Appendix 2. To 1852 a constant proportionality was assumed between the weights of engines and tenders. The weights of tenders may be exaggerated by some of them being in 'working order', but the error resulting from this is insignificant.

(3) (4) Amount of iron in (3) carriages and (4) wagons expressed in tons of pig-iron equivalent. Estimated from references in the company histories; the record books of *R & Y Pickering*, wagon builders of Wishaw (kept in the Scottish Business Records Archives, University of Glasgow), *Royal Commission on Coal Supplies*, PP 1904, XXIII, p 282; F. Wishaw, *The Railways of Great Britain and Ireland* (1840), *passim*; D. Lardner, *Railway Economy* (London, 1850), p 105; C. E. R. Sherrington, *The Economics of Rail Transport in Great Britain* (1928), pp 198, 213, 217; *Transactions of the Engineers and Shipbuilders of Scotland*, 1860–1 presidential address, 1866–7, 115; 1882–3, p 10, and from information supplied by Messrs J. Hay and A. MacLean of the North British Railway Group. Linear trends were taken to hold between known points and until the introduction of steel underframes in the 1890s a constant proportion was assumed between the tare weight of a vehicle and the amount of metal used in its construction (with allowances for the use of bogies and experiments in wheel arrangements).

(5) Total estimated demand for rolling stock iron expressed in terms of '000 tons of pig-iron equivalent. Calculated by multiplying the total additions to rolling stock shown in Appendix 2 by the appropriate average weights.

APPENDIX 4

STATISTICS OF THE SCOTTISH PIG-IRON TRADE, 1840–1900

Year	(1)	(2)	(3)	(4)	(5)	(6)	(7)	(8)	(9)	(10)
1840	28·7	3·0	31·7	*	241	*	*	*	*	—
1841	13·9	1·3	15·2	*	250	*	*	*	*	—
1842	25·5	0·3	25·8	*	271	*	*	*	*	—
1843	3·0	0·6	3·6	*	480	*	*	*	*	—
1844	0·0	1·5	1·5	*	413	*	*	*	*	—
1845	5·0	6·4	11·4	*	475	*	*	*	*	—
1846	34·0	7·5	41·5	7·3	580	*	119	257	*	—
1847	61·0	7·6	68·6	11·9	540	604	144	227	233	—
1848	164·5	21·8	186·3	10·6	600	581	162	228	192	—
1849	52·5	5·3	57·8	11·9	692	596	153	222	95	—
1850	46·2	3·6	49·8	14·2	630	549	135	189	225	—
1851	5·5	3·7	9·2	26·1	775	700	193	260	247	—
1852	11·2	3·4	14·6	51·3	780	680	284	211	245	—
1853	7·8	4·8	12·6	56·5	720	950	318	317	315	—
1854	21·3	7·0	28·3	72·7	780	870	284	301	285	—
1855	25·7	8·2	33·9	87·4	820	840	244	298	298	—
1856	40·1	3·2	43·3	60·4	820	830	259	246	325	—
1857	20·0	8·3	28·3	59·2	900	832	294	234	304	—
1858	38·2	5·6	43·8	41·8	950	788	274	283	231	—
1859	37·1	7·2	44·3	36·8	980	920	254	315	351	—
1860	33·8	8·1	41·9	49·3	1000	890	255	318	317	—
1861	62·3	19·2	81·5	68·9	1040	940	267	328	345	—
1862	73·1	4·9	78·0	72·2	1080	980	270	300	410	—
1863	99·1	11·6	110·7	127·1	1150	1130	290	332	508	—
1864	65·7	16·6	82·3	189·8	1160	1120	324	352	444	—
1865	65·4	10·9	76·3	166·2	1164	1272	369	372	531	—
1866	51·7	14·8	66·5	124·2	994	1136	298	339	500	—
1867	54·4	8·8	63·2	111·9	1031	1068	338	309	420	72
1868	65·4	9·4	74·8	191·4	1068	973	324	261	388	154
1869	52·6	12·3	64·9	200·1	1150	1098	389	262	447	90
1870	90·7	20·1	110·8	195·7	1206	1161	389	266	506	110
1871	58·3	27·1	85·4	202·3	1160	1335	512	358	465	—
1872	74·6	28·4	103·0	231·0	1090	1386	617	299	470	—
1873	84·0	31·2	115·2	259·7	993	1067	399	295	373	125
1874	95·7	21·5	117·2	275·2	806	830	297	166?	317	200
1875	90·2	15·1	105·3	228·3	1050	976	(616)		360	220
1876	71·7	25·9	97·6	194·2	1103	910	(540)		370	285
1877	95·5	42·3	137·8	175·0	982	840	(505)		335	353
1878	117·7	17·1	134·8	229·3	902	728	(434)		294	325
1879	85·1	14·2	99·3	177·5	932	866	(564)		302	315
1880	93·1	24·5	117·6	237·1	1049	1055	(671)		384	335
1881	79·0	27·7	106·7	338·7	1176	975	(578)		397	420
1882	73·0	20·8	93·8	387·9	1126	1230	(645)		585	345
1883	73·9	27·0	100·9	413·4	1129	1130	(647)		483	432
1884	71·9	20·7	92·6	286·1	988	1002	(534)		468	369
1885	61·7	24·7	86·2	186·1	1004	774	(445)		396	465
1886	77·3	22·4	99·7	160·2	936	804	(381)		423	409
1887	72·4	21·9	94·3	170·2	932	887	(412)		476	434
1888	77·5	34·7	112·2	248·4	1028	1014	240	182	589	427
1889	54·6	35·4	90·0	296·4	978	1186	246	199	762	394

APPENDIX 4 (*continued*)

Year	(1)	(2)	(3)	(4)	(5)	(6)	(7)	(8)	(9)	(10)
1890	68·8	10·8	80·1	321·3	737	1160	237	216	766	*
1891	47·3	38·4	85·7	288·8	674	707	(314)		395	*
1892	58·8	37·2	96·0	298·5	972	1108	(395)		771	*
1893	78·8	25·7	104·5	248·5	793	*	*		*	*
1894	120·6	26·7	147·3	302·4	642	*	*		*	*
1895	97·3	30·7	128·0	319·1	1049	*	*		*	*
1896	118·7	44·9	163·6	373·4	1114	*	*		*	*
1897	124·7	27·2	151·9	301·6	1137	*	*		*	*
1898	108·1	39·6	147·7	414·2	1063	*	*		*	*
1899	91·8	47·7	139·5	435·8	1171	*	*		*	*
1900	88·2	36·2	124·4	431·6	1157	*	*		*	*

Notes and Sources:

All figures measure '000 tons. * Signifies not available.

(1) Railway demand for permanent-way iron expressed as pig-iron equivalent.

(2) Railway demand for rolling-stock iron expressed as pig-iron equivalent.

(3) Total railway demand for iron expressed as pig-iron equivalent.

(4) Demand for iron by the Clyde shipyards expressed in terms of pig-iron equivalent. Calculated from information in the annual trade reviews of the *Glasgow Herald*; W. S. Cormack, 'An Economic History of Shipbuilding and Marine Engineering' (Glasgow Univ PhD thesis, 1930), Appendixes B and D; I. F. Gibson, 'The Establishment of the Scottish Steel Industry', *ScJPE*, Vol 5, 1958, and I. L. Bell, *The Iron Trade of the United Kingdom* (1886), p 36.

(5) Scottish pig-iron production.

(6) Sales of Scottish pig iron.

(7) (8) Shipments of Scottish pig iron—(7) foreign, (8) coastwise—where the records fail to distinguish these, total shipments are shown in brackets. Coastwise shipments include those sent by rail.

(9) Scottish consumption of domestically produced pig iron. Computed by deducting (7) and (8) from (6) allowing for stocks held by the makers and in public stores.

(10) Imports of English pig iron into Scotland.

The source of columns (5), (6), (7), (8), (9) & (10) is the monthly circulars of William Connal, pig-iron storekeepers of Glasgow. A collection of these circulars is to be found in the Mitchell Library, Glasgow. Production statistics before 1850 were obtained from R. H. Campbell, 'Statistics of the Scottish Pig-Iron Trade 1830–65', *JWScI & S Inst*, 1856–7.

APPENDIX 5

SCOTTISH RAILWAYS: SCRAP IRON

	(1)		(2)		(3)
Year		*E*	*C*	*W*	
1840	—	—	—	—	—
1841	—	—	—	—	—
1842	—	—	—	—	—
1843	—	—	—	—	—
1844	—	—	—	—	—
1845	—	—	—	—	—
1846	0·1	—	—	—	—
1847	5·9	—	—	—	—
1848	7·0	—	—	—	—
1849	2·8	—	—	—	—
1850	2·9	—	—	—	—
1851	3·2	—	34	99	0·4
1852	4·8	—	7	23	0·1
1853	4·9	3	27	116	0·4
1854	6·7	2	9	103	0·3
1855	7·5	4	39	224	0·9
1856	9·0	3	NK	NK	0·1
1857	10·1	3	85	667	2·0
1858	12·5	8	71	805	2·5
1859	15·4	11	50	813	2·6
1860	17·2	13	59	578	2·7
1861	18·0	16	47	696	3·0
1862	24·3	8	50	293	1·2
1863	26·1	6	40	226	1·0
1864	29·8	7	49	436	1·5
1865	32·6	10	30	211	0·9
1866	35·6	4	17	228	0·8
1867	34·2	29	14	594	2·5
1868	30·7	41	41	1158	4·3
1869	25·3	41	102	1062	5·2
1870	35·3	68	11	1305	6·6
1871	41·2	41	82	1549	6·8
1872	48·3	81	37	1711	8·7
1873	55·1	55	60	1700	7·8
1874	60·5	63	37	1690	7·9
1875	69·6	42	22	1678	7·3
1876	64·8	55	41	1883	8·4
1877	75·8	53	69	3339	12·7
1878	80·7	50	134	1567	7·5
1879	73·5	49	145	2358	7·8
1880	71·4	58	135	3101	9·9
1881	67·5	70	164	3494	12·9
1882	63·6	41	123	2211	13·8
1883	59·3	52	172	3966	16·1
1884	54·3	80	192	3977	17·6

APPENDIX 5 (*continued*)

	(1)	(2)			(3)
Year		*E*	*C*	*W*	
1885	47·4	76	122	4448	18·6
1886	37·9	74	204	4199	17·9
1887	33·6	59	115	3913	15·8
1888	29·1	68	162	3974	16·3
1889	28·9	58	157	3222	13·9
1890	31·0	64	203	3218	13·6
1891	38·5	65	169	2932	13·1
1892	48·3	66	212	3174	14·3
1893	53·8	59	66	2646	11·6
1894	60·7	59	99	2887	13·0
1895	69·0	70	90	3278	14·3
1896	74·4	70	213	3535	15·8
1897	80·1	73	89	3275	14·6
1898	78·1	80	83	3523	15·9
1899	73·5	65	99	3301	14·8
1900	67·5	66	105	3241	14·2

Notes and Sources:

(1) Amount of rails taken from main lines and branches expressed in '000 tons of pig-iron equivalent. Estimated by multiplying renewals mileage by the average weight of rails laid *x* years before where *x* is the typical age of rails taken up.

(2) Number of engines, carriages and wagons scrapped each year. To 1869 these are totals of renewals, but thereafter are totals of vehicles actually scrapped. For method of calculation see text.

(3) Rolling-stock scrap expressed in '000 tons of pig-iron equivalent. For method of calculation see text, but note that the number of tenders scrapped is taken to be equal to the number of renewals throughout.

Pricing Policy of Railways in England and Wales Before 1881

By G. R. Hawke

Throughout the nineteenth century, much criticism was directed at the pricing policy of the railways. It was alleged to be detrimental to the trade of the country and to create unfair differences between groups of traders. The railway companies not unnaturally retorted that their policy was formulated with the precise purpose of promoting the trade of the country, and that there were no elements of inequity involved. It is here proposed to establish what the pricing policy of the railways was, what were the criticisms levelled against it, to what extent these were justified, and to explore the implications of the policy for overall economic growth. After 1881, railway prices became subject to more direct legislative interference, and 1881 is therefore taken as a convenient terminal date.

I

It is a commonplace that the original railway Acts assumed that charges for railway services would follow the pattern established by canals and turnpike roads, that is, the tolls received by the companies for the use of the line would be distinguished from charges for the actual conveyance of goods whether by the company or by other carriers. It is not surprising that it was proposed to follow a precedent of doubtful applicability; it is surprising that for a considerable time many people continued to regard the precedent as binding. As late as 1840 a parliamentary Select Committee commented; 'The Railway Directors have not usually kept their accounts in such a form as to enable them readily to distinguish the profits which they derive as carriers from the profits which they receive as toll proprietors.'[1] Throughout the nineteenth century, the railway accounts remained in the same condition. Except for the early Acts, Parliament usually provided

I am grateful for the permission of the archivist to the British Railways Board to use and quote the documents in his care. Such references follow the citation recommendations of the archivist and are indicated by BTHR: for the London collection, and BTHR (Y): for the collection at York. I am also grateful to Professor H. J. Habakkuk, Dr R. M. Hartwell, Dr P. S. Bagwell, Mr D. L. Munby, and Mr P. Cain for reading and commenting on earlier drafts of this paper.

[1] *Select Committee on Railway Communication, Report*, PP 1840, xiii, p 12.

different maxima for tolls and for rates, the latter including the services of a carrier.[1] But the distinction has no analogue in the accounts or other records of the companies.

The major legal issue arising from the railway Acts concerned the 'terminal charges' or 'terminals'. Many Acts which envisaged the railway companies acting as carriers distinguished the maximum charge that the company could make for its services as a carrier, from the charge that could be made for services rendered at stations. The legal provision for the latter was usually that a 'reasonable' charge could be made, and opinions differed as to the extent of the services referred to. It was widely agreed that terminal charges were intended to cover the cost of loading and unloading, collection and delivery where this was performed, and the provision of warehouse space, but companies could claim that the concept was much wider including such items as invoicing costs, the cost of station labour, and all other costs not explicitly and directly connected with the provision of locomotive power.[2] That is, it was generally agreed that in addition to the statutory maxima on carriage rates, railways could make an undefined, but reasonable, charge for terminal expenses, and differences of opinion occurred on what costs could be adduced to reach a judgment on the reasonable or unreasonable nature of a specific charge. This position created a fertile field for litigation.

There were some attempts to define the position more closely. In the early 1860s, the railway companies suggested that the following clause should be inserted into railway bills:

> It shall also be lawful for the company, acting as carriers, to make a reasonable terminal for the accommodation afforded, and services rendered by them in respect of any goods or minerals, other than the actual conveyance thereof along the railway; provided always that such charge shall in no case exceed the rate of 2s per ton for goods, and 9d per ton for minerals, at each terminal station of such traffic. . . .

but this attempt to bargain legal recognition of the companies' position for a statutory maximum foundered on the opposition of colliery owners.[3] A bill introduced by the president of the Board of Trade in 1865 and 1866 authorised a reasonable charge for:

> loading, covering, and unloading of goods at any station on the railway, being a terminal station in respect of such goods, and for delivery and collection and any other services incidental to the duty or business of a carrier.

[1] W. M. Acworth, *Elements of Railway Economics* (Oxford, 2nd ed 1932), pp 109–16, prints examples of early tables of maxima illustrating this point.

[2] The manager of the Great Western Railway suggested that even shunting expenses should be included, *Select Committee on Railways* (*Rates & Fares*), *Minutes of Evidence*, PP 1881, XIII, (Grierson) Q 12465.

[3] *Royal Commission on Railways, Report*, PP 1867, XXXVIII, Pt 1, p 22.

but this attempt to establish a narrow definition of terminals did not reach the statute book.[1] The legal position remained confused and cases continued to be heard by the Railway Commissioners and by the courts. In the opinion of W. M. Acworth, who as a counsel for railway companies in the later nineteenth century had an intimate knowledge of the legal issues involved, the law courts tended to favour the interpretation of the railway companies rather than the more narrow traders' view,[2] and the inclusion of the provision of stations as a terminal cost was accepted in *Hall v London, Brighton & South Coast Railway*.[3] But before the courts reached a binding decision, direct parliamentary intervention had begun.[4]

The other main legal issue in railway pricing was over 'undue preference'. After the 1854 Traffic Act, railways were prohibited from making charges such that one individual was given an 'undue preference' over another. The interpretation of this phrase was a major influence on the pricing policy of railway companies.

Before 1881 then, the legal position was in general that maximum charges for locomotive power were specified, undue preference between individuals was prohibited, and terminal charges were required to be reasonable. Remnants of the older toll/carriage charge distinction were inoperative, but as the law was formed mostly by Acts relating to individual railway companies, often amended by Acts enpowering extensions or amalgamations, the legal structure was confused and anomalies such as sections of track not covered by any statutory maximum were not uncommon.

II

Railway managers were not unwilling to describe their practice in price formation, but their descriptions were not always complete or consistent. The main public forum for managers' speeches on this subject was the Royal Commission on Railways of the 1860s, but Select Committees, especially that of 1881, also heard evidence on pricing policies. The managers examined by these bodies were not usually those involved in day to day rate setting, but their descriptions reveal what senior managers understood to be the policies of their companies.

[1] *Royal Commission on Railways, Report*, p 22.

[2] W. M. Acworth, *Railway Economics*, pp 140–2.

[3] 15 Queen's Bench Decisions. Described in W. M. Acworth, *The Railways and the Traders* (1891), pp 307–11. The judgments are printed in BTHR: RCH 4/17, pp 539–47.

[4] Henry Parris, *Government and the Railways in Nineteenth-Century Britain* (1965), p 224, suggests that *Hall v LBSCR* decided the issue in favour of the railways. But as Acworth's description cited in the preceding note makes clear, the traders were unable for technical reasons to take *Hall v LBSCR* to the House of Lords, and there was at the same time an analogous case that could have been taken to the higher court. The Queen's Bench decision cannot be taken as the final legal position.

The public pronouncements of managers confirm Acworth's description of the process as setting rates so as to maximise the company's revenue, subject to the constraints that no rate should be so high as to prevent freight from being offered to the railway, and no rate should be so low that the resulting freight became unprofitable.[1] But managers were prepared to go further in describing how a rate was settled in the indeterminate range between zero profit and zero output so prescribed. The availability of other railway routes or the availability of alternative transport methods were obvious limitations, but others were mentioned. Managers were seldom willing to accept that company profits were their sole concern; the needs of the customer and sometimes the general development of the area served by a particular company were frequently mentioned.

Few managers were indiscreet enough to declare that they were interested in maximum profits without regard to anything else.[2] A collective body, the Railway Companies Association, made the minimum of reservations in the 1850s when in the course of five resolutions aimed at increasing the profitability of the railways by diminishing competition between them, it resolved: 'That the rates and fares on the several railways of the kingdom should be so fixed as to realise the largest amount of net profits, due regard being had to the interests of the public.'[3]

No indication was given as to how this amalgam was to be made internally consistent, and in practice companies acted on the principle that profits were desirable but not the sole object of attention. Even in a report to a shareholders' committee of consultation, intended to persuade its members that the company was as profitable as it could be, the manager of the Great Western Railway did not claim that profit was his sole criterion in setting rates.[4]

Some idea of the other influences considered is given by notes appended

[1] W. M. Acworth, *Railway Economics*, p 78.

[2] W. M. Acworth, *Railway Economics*, p 83 quotes a French manager to this effect, without accepting his statement as an accurate observation.

[3] *Railway Record*, 11 (Sept 1858), quoted in P. S. Bagwell, 'The Railway Interest: its Organization and Influence, 1837–1914', *Journ Transport Hist*, VII (1965), 67. The ambiguity of the resolution annoyed the railway press; the *Railway Record*, for example, commented editorially, 'Nothing, we venture to say, so unmeaning has been enunciated at any time by any body of delegates . . . for it has been long ago admitted that the interests of the public and the interests of the Railways are identical,' and quoted the *Railway Gazette* as saying, 'We are told that one company actually dissented from so palpable a commercial truism; but we are not informed of the name of this eccentric corporation, which should be recorded in letters of brass. Nothing more absurd has been committed for some time'—*Railway Record*, 1858, 588, 611. That is, the railway press considered that the last clause of the resolution was redundant. But this is no more than special pleading. On some assumptions, the public interest might be considered best served by railways run at a loss and with zero rates. Given any monopoly element in the organisation of railways, and the overall purpose of the resolutions was to reduce competition between railways, it is not certain even on marginalist assumptions that the public interest would be best served by a policy of profit maximisation.

[4] BTHR: GW 18/4.

by two companies to the lists of their rates supplied to the Royal Commission. That of the London & North Western Railway read:

> In fixing the rates and charges regard is had to the local circumstances, the nature and value of the article to be carried, the existence and extent of competition by sea or by inland navigation or otherwise, between the same or neighbouring places, and also in the rates and charges for other producing districts to the same market.[1]

and that of the North Eastern Railway:

> The charges are not regulated by a mileage charge, nor solely according to distance. Within the limits of the company's legal powers they are determined by the consideration, in the special circumstances of each case, of what will fairly remunerate the company for their current and capital expenditure, and of what the traffic is able to bear.[2]

The oral evidence followed the same pattern, with no admission that maximum profit was the sole aim. An alleged quotation of the chairman of the Midland Railway to the effect that rates were always set high if it were possible to increase the dividend to the shareholders[3] was denied by the manager of the railway concerned.[4]

On the other hand, no manager could convincingly maintain that he disregarded profit. Usually, after apparent declarations of philanthropic behaviour, managers conceded that profit, at least in the long run, was important to particular rates as well as being an overall objective. Thus the manager of the Lancashire & Yorkshire Railway claimed that his company carried unprofitable freight to Manchester for the bleachers of Bolton because it liked to have all the freight of a district, but then conceded that he was also protecting the profitable freight carried in the reverse direction.[5] And his claim to offer unprofitable rates from the east coast to Lancashire to provide a wider market at the expense of the company was eroded when he admitted that he hoped that the rates would eventually be profitable, and in any case discouraged potential competitors.[6] Further, railway companies were not unobservant when opportunities of profit were presented; the chairman of the London & North Western Railway readily agreed in the boom of the early 1870s that the high coal prices should be exploited by raising railway rates on coal.[7]

The nature and value of the article to be carried was obviously one of the

[1] *Royal Commission on Railways, Appendices to Minutes of Evidence*, PP 1867, XXXVIII, Pt II, p 583.

[2] Ibid, p 648.

[3] *Roy Com on Railways, Min of Evid*, (Wright), Q 678.

[4] Ibid, (Allport) Q 12409.

[5] Ibid, (Smithells) QQ 13016–27.

[6] Ibid, (Smithells) QQ 12961–5.

[7] BTHR: RAC 1/234, p 225. It was claimed by a coal-owner in Yorkshire and South Wales, who did, however, have strong interests in railways, that the railways did not take maximum advantage of the high coal prices in the early 1870s, railway rates being advanced 'not at all proportionately'. *1881 Sel Com on Railways, Min of Evid*, (Baxter) QQ 9254–5.

criteria to be considered in fixing rates, and it was given approval in the maxima specified by Parliament. Charges could not be adjusted to the value of each particular commodity carried, but the Clearing House devised a classification mainly by value so that rate formation was facilitated. Coal and minerals were in the first class on which the lowest rates were charged and the classes ranged upwards to commodities of high value relative to weight such as hats and haberdashery. Adjustments were common and frequent but with the help of this classification companies were able to approximately relate charges to value as one of the elements in their pricing policy. The justice of this arrangement was seldom challenged. Complaints were occasionally made that the cheapest classes were carried at a loss[1] but the problem of distributing costs over different railway freights made it impossible to unequivocally prove this, and the issue of cross-subsidisation was not explicitly raised.

It is, of course, consistent with many pricing policies, including that appropriate to a situation of perfect competition, that lower rates per mile carried are set when another company has a shorter line between the relevant two points. The manager of the Great Western Railway told his shareholders' committee of consultation in 1867 that rates were always fixed by the shortest available line, and that after 1852 their company had not attempted to compete with a superior line by rate-cutting.[2]

Managers also admitted that rates were sometimes dependent on water competition[3] and that this resulted in differential rates according to whether a particular town had access to the alternative source of transport. This was frequently discussed with particular reference to the rates on agricultural produce because of the widespread feeling that English farmers were discriminated against. An assistant commissioner told the 1881 Royal Commission on Agriculture of the unanimous resolution of a meeting in Yorkshire that railway rates were unfair to the English farmer,[4]

[1] This charge was frequently made of coal rates during the 1860s and 1870s, eg BTHR: RAC 1/233, Feb 1862; BTHR: RAC 1/234, Aug 1863; *Edinburgh Review*, CXLIII (April 1876), 352–87. The claim was opposed by the railway press, eg *Herepath*, XXVII (1865), 480; *Railway News*, IV (1865), 513; and the article in the *Edinburgh Review* was criticised in *The Economist*, XXXIV (Jan–June 1876), 480–1. The difficulty of allocating expenses between freight classes precludes any definite conclusion to this debate, but it is true that some companies acted on the belief that coal rates were less profitable than they could be. The Great Northern Railway attempted to persuade the Midland Railway that this was true of coal supplied from Derbyshire and Nottinghamshire to London but failed to do so. BTHR: RAC 1/156, June 1869, Dec 1870, June 1871. Cf also the preceding footnote, and B. R. Mitchell, 'The Economic Development of the Inland Coalfields' (PhD Thesis, Cambridge, 1955), pp 41, 73–4.

[2] BTHR: GW 18/4, pp 22, 44.

[3] Land competition other than by another railway was uncommon but the first suggestion for fares on the London & Birmingham Railway was rejected because it was feared that coaches would survive 'prejudicially to the Passengers' receipts'. BTHR: LBM 1/54, July 1837.

[4] *Royal Commission on Agriculture, Reports of Assistant Commissioners*, PP 1881, XVI, (Coleman), p 176.

and railway rates were reported to be one of the chief subjects of complaint in Kent.[1] Farmers who gave evidence to the Royal Commission endorsed the complaint.[2]

The reply of the railways was convincing. Lower rates were charged on imported grain because the railways expected to receive a return traffic when flour was carried from the country millers to London.[3] On meat imports from America, lower rates were charged because the freight was available in full car-loads,[4] and because lower rates were essential if the freight were to be attracted away from direct sea transit to London.[5] The commission was forced to make the ambiguous recommendation that the law be changed to enforce equality of treatment as was envisaged by the existing law, but that this should not be interpreted as prohibiting lower through rates on goods imported from abroad.[6] It is difficult to see what changes the commission expected to be promoted by this recommendation. In the case of hops, the import rate was eventually abolished without any benefit to the English grower. The South Eastern Railway had a rate on hops imported through Folkestone and carried to London via Ashford only half of that charged on English hops carried from Ashford. When the import rate was abolished, the English grower had still to pay the same railway rate and compete with French hops carried direct to London by subsidised French steamers.[7]

This was not a new issue in the 1870s and 1880s. The 1865 Royal Commission on Railways was presented with exactly analagous arguments when the general manager of the London & North Western Railway defended the lower rates charged on Australian wool consigned to the London wool sales and imported through Liverpool.[8] But the issue probably intensified during the 1870s as declining sea-freight rates forced railway charges on imports to be reduced in order to prevent redirection of traffic to the competing transport medium, while the decline in price of agricultural products as imports increased reduced the capacity of English farmers to bear transport costs. But this element of the pricing policy of the railways was simply the reaction of a business interest that had some

[1] *Royal Commission on Agriculture, Reports of Assistant Commissioners*, PP 1881, XVI, (Little), p 406.

[2] *Royal Commission on Agriculture, Minutes of Evidence, Vol 1*, PP 1881, XVI, (Beadle) QQ 4856–64; (Roberts) QQ 7947–69; *Roy Com on Ag Min of Evid, Vol II*, PP 1881, XVII, (Jones) QQ 33742–5; (Barclay) Q 43198; (Booth) QQ 44850–7; (Frankish) QQ 49298–9; (Gardiner) QQ 53572–4; *Roy Com on Ag Min of Evid, Vol III*, PP 1882, XIV, (Swan) QQ 63006–34.

[3] *Roy Com on Ag Min of Evid, Vol I*, (Twelvetrees) Q 8253.

[4] *Roy Com on Ag, Min of Evid, Vol I*, (Twelvetrees) QQ 8280–2. Swan's evidence cited in note 2 above shows that this alone was not a complete explanation but it was not intended to be.

[5] Ibid, (Twelvetrees) Q 8286.

[6] *Roy Com on Ag, Final Report, PP* 1882, XIV, pp 18–19, 32.

[7] J. Grierson, *Railway Rates: English and Foreign* (1886), p 28, n 1. W. M. Acworth, *Railways and the Traders*, pp 71–3.

[8] *Roy Com on Railways, Min of Evid*, (Cawkwell) Q 11491.

control over prices; no conspiratorial discrimination was involved and no parliamentary inquiry could satisfy the English farmer.

The most controversial part of the railways' pricing policy was that involved with the differential promotion of the trade and industry of different regions. The companies felt that they were well advised to assist the trade of the region with which they were concerned, and to bring different areas of supply into competition at a given market. Their argument was frequently stated in the form of opposition to its converse; that is, in opposition to the theory that the railway rate for a given article per mile carried should always be the same.[1]

Thus the manager of the North Staffordshire Railway declared that his company would always seek to develop the trade of its region and to supply it with the necessary raw materials even though short-distance traffic was not remunerative;[2] the manager of the Great Western Railway thought that as labour costs and coal prices were relatively high in South Staffordshire, both his company and the London & North Western Railway should help the ironmasters of the region to compete in the London market;[3] and the manager of the Midland Railway declared: 'I think it is the duty of managers of railways to develop the resources of their districts to the utmost possible extent.'[4]

There is, however, nothing in this part of the policy immediately inconsistent with profit maximisation. The managers did not claim that profit was unimportant: 'If I saw an opportunity for developing a trade at Gloucester, so long as the rates left a profit, I should most undoubtedly endeavour to do it, without reference to the rates from Liverpool or London, or elsewhere; the only question would be whether the rates would leave a profit.'[5]

As the railway companies were approximately divided into geographical regions, a policy of regional development was easily made compatible with pursuing the company's interests. The manager of the Great Western Railway characterised his concern for South Staffordshire not as philanthropy, but as the result of considering the benefit of both company and district.[6] An ex-manager, agreeing that a railway company might become the arbiter of the trade of the district, thought that there could be no better candidate for the post, as the company and district had identical interests.[7]

[1] There is at least one exception to this general position. The 'Valley Clause' of the Taff Vale Railway's Act of 1836 prescribed equal ton-mileage rates, and this was applied also to the Rhymney Railway, and later to the Barry Railway. E. Brooks, 'Regional Functions of the Mineral Transport System in the South Wales Coalfield, 1830–1951' (PhD thesis, Cambridge, 1958), pp 20, 152, 173–4 and Appendix 2.

[2] *Roy Com on Railways, Min of Evid,* (Morris) QQ 14227–31.

[3] Ibid, (Grierson) QQ 11817–8.

[4] *Roy Com on Railways, Min of Evid,* (Allport) Q 12377.

[5] Ibid, (Allport) Q 12377.

[6] Ibid, (Grierson) QQ 11821–4.

[7] Ibid, (Sherriff) QQ 16286–94.

And a later manager expanded the same sentiment in declaring that the interests of a company and its district were necessarily the same since both would want to promote the traffic.[1]

But while profit maximisation and concern for the company's district could be reconciled, the policy went further than this. It was a policy of bringing different supply areas into competition at a given market, and conversely, a given trade was spread between different ports. Allport thought it would be disastrous for the whole trade of the country to be concentrated at one port,[2] although, under hostile questions, he conceded that this was the opinion of a private individual rather than of a railway manager, and that in the latter capacity his concern was with 'commercial questions' and not with holding the balance between regions.[3] It may be doubted whether Allport carefully maintained the distinction in practice, and in a later appearance before the commission, he declared that the policy of his company was so to fix prices that all collieries were able to compete with one another.[4]

The traffic manager of the Lancashire & Yorkshire Railway declared that it was the policy of his company to bring imports through Hull into competition at the Liverpool market with goods imported directly to that port,[5] but while this was presented as a case of promoting competition between areas, it would follow immediately from the need to meet sea competition. In the markets of the inland towns between Liverpool and Hull, however, the Lancashire & Yorkshire Railway was able to balance the rates from the two ports. In a similar situation, the manager of the Great Western Railway stated that the rates of his company were so set that Gloucester should not monopolise the import trade to Birmingham and South Staffordshire but that Liverpool and London should be able to compete for the traffic.[6] And while the evidence of the manager of the London & North Western Railway was not a model of lucidity, he did emphasise that his company was interested in promoting competition between areas, stating his company's policy

> enables the public to buy in a great many markets, whereas the other principle [enforced equal rates per mile carried for each commodity] would confine them to one particular market, that is to say, the producing district would have a certain circuit round it which would be a sort of protected ground, and have to be supplied from one particular market, and others would be shut out.[7]

[1] *Roy Com on Ag, Min of Evid, Vol I,* (Findlay) QQ 8662–4.

[2] *Roy Com on Railways, Min of Evid,* (Allport) Q 12377.

[3] Ibid, (Allport) Q 12378. The hostile questioner was the politician, Lord Stanley, who apparently believed in a firm distinction between 'Commercial' and 'Public' issues.

[4] Ibid, (Allport) QQ 13674; 13745–8; 13755.

[5] Ibid, (Smithells) QQ 12974–5.

[6] Ibid, (Grierson) Q 11959.

[7] *Roy Com on Railways, Min of Evid,* (Cawkwell) Q 11408. The question asked was actually about lower rates because of competition from water transport or other rail-

He agreed that his policy was not to create inequalities between areas, but rather to 'lower the natural inequalities existing between one place and another'.[1]

Further examples of how this policy worked in practice are not profuse but the manager of the Great Western Railway provided some in his book published in 1886. For coal exported through Birkenhead, the Great Western Railway assisted the coal of South Wales to be competitive with that of North Wales, charging the former only 0·45d per ton mile while the latter was charged 0·89d per ton mile.[2] Tin plates from South Wales carried to Liverpool were charged the same from wherever they originated between Carmarthen in the west and Monmouth in the east although the distance for which they were carried varied from 160 to 206 miles.[3] Grierson also quoted the example of a Wiltshire ironworks,

> About 30 years ago, when the ironworks at Westbury in Wiltshire were constructed, it was anticipated that fuel would be obtained from the Radstock district about 14 miles distant. But, after sinking collieries, it was found that the coke was not suitable, so it has now to be obtained from South Wales, a distance of about 130 miles. The pig iron is sent to South Wales in the return coke waggons, and also to South Staffordshire, a distance of 140 miles. The coke and pig iron are carried at special low rates below those in force for traffic to intermediate stations. Without such special rates, or if mileage rates were charged, the works would have to be closed.[4]

This is an extreme example, but a provision differing only in degree was made for South Staffordshire when the local raw materials became inadequate. Even while complaining that railway rates were strangling South Staffordshire, the spokesman of the regional iron industry conceded that low rates were being charged for the carriage of Northamptonshire ore to South Staffordshire.[5]

Examples can also be found in the coal trade. From the late 1850s the Great Western Railway had rates assisting coal from Ruabon to compete in the London market with that of the Forest of Dean.[6] In Yorkshire, Northumberland, and Durham, the North Eastern Railway was concerned to balance the advantages of the different coal-bearing areas and in 1862, the Traffic Committee resolved:

ways, but Cawkwell confused the two issues, lower rates where there was a competitive transport system and differential rates between the supply areas of a particular market.

[1] Ibid, (Cawkwell) Q 11409.

[2] J. Grierson, *Railway Rates*, p 164, n 1.

[3] Ibid, p 39.

[4] J. Grierson, *Railway Rates*, p 17, n 2.

[5] *1881 Sel Com on Railways, Min of Evid*, (Hickman) QQ 4493–8. The general complaint was really nothing more than the assertion that for an industry facing higher costs than its rivals, free railway transit would be an assistance. Ibid, (Hickman) *passim*.

[6] BTHR: RCH 4/17, pp 68–71.

> Laid before the Committee list of the rates on coals to stations on the Nidd Valley Branch.
>
> As it appeared that the rates charged to collieries in the North were somewhat higher in proportion than those charged to the West Riding Collieries, and on coal coming from beyond Leeds, the following reduction was ordered to be made. . . .[1]

The adjustment was not to equalise ton-mile rates—the committee did not worry about differences between areas other than the north—but to increase the number of collieries able to compete in towns along the Nidd Valley branch of the railway. When the Stockton & Darlington Railway reduced the discount it allowed on materials used in iron production, the North Eastern Railway responded by resolving:

> That on and after the above date [that of the change of the Stockton & Darlington Railway] the allowance made by this company on such dues be also reduced to 5 per cent, and that in order to place traders on the Newcastle & Carlisle line on the same footing as those on the other parts of the line, a discount of 5 per cent on such materials be allowed to them from 1st instant.[2]

That the company was concerned with the situation in the product market is shown by a resolution in 1863.

> Mr Anthony Bannister having asked the company to reduce the rates on Silkestone and Haigh Moor Coal to Withernsea in order to enable him to compete with water borne coal, Resolved, That a reduction of 1/– per ton be made, on condition that Mr Bannister makes a proportionate reduction in the selling price of the coal.[3]

The last clause was clearly designed to ensure that the application was justified and that the company was not being asked to make a transfer from its receipts to the collieries' profits. The company was acting to increase the supply area of a particular town although in this case the committee may have hoped that the elasticity of demand was such that its own receipts would rise, any loss falling on the competing transport medium.

The practice of making more even the transport costs of different suppliers has different implications for a railway company that serves all the suppliers involved than for a company which serves only one of a number of suppliers. The first case may involve a sharing of traffic between suppliers with no reduction in the railway's profits while in the second case the railway serving the most advantageously-placed supplier would presumably benefit from offering rates designed to exclude the more distant suppliers served by other railways. Most of the examples cited above are cases where

[1] BTHR (Y): NER 1/64, 24 Oct 1862, Resolution 5132.
[2] BTHR (Y): NER 1/64, 10 Oct 1862, Resolution 5091.
[3] BTHR (Y): NER 1/24, 23 Oct 1863, Resolution 5510.

a single company maintained the balance between a number of suppliers, but there were also cases where several railways were involved through agreements negotiated at inter-company meetings held at the Clearing House. Collieries in Derbyshire were grouped (that is, charged equal rates) for coal carried to eastern ports and this must have implied that some railways were making greater concessions than others as there was considerable variation in the distance of the collieries from the coast.[1] The agreement was made although a particular railway might have benefited from confining the trade to the collieries nearest the coast.

But although railway companies were arranged approximately regionally, the larger companies had lines extending far beyond their main region and companies involved in balancing the interests of different suppliers were usually concerned with the traffic of all the suppliers of a particular market. This limits any philanthropic element in the pricing policy of railways but it does not imply that such an element was entirely absent. 'If "grouping" were prohibited and the nearest collieries or works could supply all the coals or goods which were required, railway companies might, in some cases, earn as much net profit on the traffic carried as if grouping were adopted.'[2]

Whether or not one railway serves all of the potential suppliers makes only a difference of degree, and even where only one company is involved a policy of promoting competition between suppliers will not always be consistent with profit maximisation. The assertion of the managers was that when invited to assist a new supplier they did so if the variable costs involved in the new trade were covered, and did not seek to make greater profit by adjusting the rate on the former trade. There is no reason to doubt the assertions by the managers as to their intentions, and as complaints were made of the lower rates offered to competitors rather than of an increase in the rate charged to the complaining supplier, it seems that the intentions were carried into practice.

The pricing policy of the railways was not adopted by a conscious decision, but grew with the development of the railway system. The policy described above emerged from gradual adjustments of rates to the circumstances of the railways. The earliest rates of the Stockton & Darlington Railway distinguished between commodities but basically set rates per ton mile for each type of traffic.[3] Modifications were soon made, the first being to distinguish coal for export from coal for local consumption and to charge lower rates on the former.[4] Attention to the longer-run development of the traffic was soon apparent and the committee reported to the shareholders in 1827,

[1] J. Grierson, *Railway Rates*, pp 40–1.
[2] Ibid, pp 39–40.
[3] BTHR (Y): SAD 1/6, 5 Aug 1825, p 48.
[4] BTHR (Y): SAD 1/6, 9 Sept 1825, pp 57–8.

> Your committee hesitates to express a decided opinion as to the propriety of advancing the charges on Coal for the Export Trade. Whilst the conviction awaits them that the income rising from this source is nearly if not wholly absorbed by the attendant expenses, the fear of injuring a Branch of the Trade which may possibly ere long become of incalculable advantage alone prevents them from urging such an addition to the rates as might put them in possession of a just and equitable share of any profits arising from this Traffick. . . .[1]

In 1831, considerations of equalising the burden on different suppliers appear.

> The nett Gain upon the Bussiness [*sic*] of the Year are confessedly Small, but it must be remembered that with the View of Stimulating the Exertion of the Coal Owners, the Tolls have been low—
>
> Your Committee have nevertheless endeavoured anxiously to ascertain how far it might be consistant [*sic*] with the present and future Interests of the Concern to increase the Amount of Tolls. A Discount of 20 per Cent, has been allowed on the Export Tolls during the past year agreeably to the Order of the last Annual General Meeting the Policy pursued in this respect hitherto your Committee had Reason to approve—this abatement the Committee suggest ought to be reduced one Half—but on the other Hand, with the View of equalizing the Tolls throughout the Line some alterations in the Toll List are sugested [*sic*].;[2]

The need to preserve the trade against competitors was recognised when reductions were allowed on coal sent to the Stockton and Yarm depots, 'which was made to overcome all competition'.[3] Once rates were established changes were made in order to improve the income or to meet a new situation such as the appearance of a new potential supplier to a given market and the pricing policy described above. An example from the end of the period is the origin of cheap rates on imported wheat; inland millers needed the imported wheat to mix with the domestic product but were unable to compete with mills established at the ports until railways conceded new low rates on wheat travelling in the inland direction. The concession was made so that the railways would keep their wheat and flour traffic, and to promote competition between millers in different places, but the new rates became targets for critics of subsidisation of the foreigner.[4]

But much earlier than this, the pricing policy described above was recognisable. With the foundation of the Railway Clearing House in the 1840s, and especially after the extension of its mechanism to goods traffic at the end of the decade, inter-company co-operation in rate setting was facilitated, and a list of the 'factors influencing railway charges' made by

[1] BTHR (Y): SAD 1/6, 10 July 1827, pp 66–7.

[2] BTHR (Y): SAD 1/6, 30 July 1831, p 110. This quotation reproduces the syntax of the original.

[3] BTHR (Y): SAD 1/6, 12 Aug 1835, p 154.

[4] J. Grierson, *Railway Rates*, pp 25–6.

the Railway Commissioners in 1851 is virtually a summary of the policy outlined above.[1] With the development of inter-company co-operation fostered by meetings held at the Clearing House, and because the circumstances in which the companies were placed were similar, the behaviour described above can be regarded as *the* pricing policy of railways in England and Wales before 1881. There were some exceptions, such as the railways of South Wales that were subject to unusual statutory requirements, but most companies behaved similarly in the formation of their prices.

The policy of the railways was that of profit maximising discriminating monopoly with some modification. Regional policies went beyond those appropriate to this theoretical model, and pursuance of maximum profit was not energetic. As the alterations to rates for particular reasons became more numerous, energetic profit maximisation became impossible simply because the number of rates became immense, In the 1860s, there were said to be 3–4 million local rates on the North Eastern Railway,[2] 2 million freight and 1 million passenger rates on the Lancashire & Yorkshire Railway,[3] and ½ million rates with 20,000 alterations each year on the North Staffordshire Railway.[4] These figures should be treated with reserve as they were intended to show that publication of rates was impracticable, but in a system organised without basic prices per ton mile as reference points,[5] the number of rates becomes very large. Continual review and pursuit of maximum profit becomes difficult and it is easy for conventions to become established.

The second modification to the the theoretical model is that managers intended to promote competition between different sources of supply. In many cases, railways served their own interests, but the balancing of the interests of different suppliers was intended to foster a competitive 'framework of economic activity'.[6] Railways were willing to accept a new trade without considering whether more profit might be made by increasing the rate on the old trade and pricing the new out of the market.[7]

[1] *Report of the Commissioners of Railways for 1850*, PP 1851, XXX, pp 21–2.

[2] *Roy Com on Railways, Min of Evid*, (O'Brien) Q 12301.

[3] Ibid, (Smithells) QQ 13115; 13130.

[4] Ibid, (Morris) QQ 12236–46.

[5] In such a system the term 'special rate', used loosely in the debate on railway charges in the 1880s and 1890s, and again used after the regrouping in the 1920s to mean charges different from the standard ton mile rates then adopted, has little meaning. In a sense, all rates before 1881 were 'special rates'. The usual use of the term before 1881 was for a rate allowed to one individual but not to another in an analagous position, ie a rate prohibited by the Railway & Canal Traffic Act, 1854. But the term was also used, usually imprecisely, in other meanings.

[6] This phrase deliberately echoes the analysis of classical economic theory in L. Robbins, *The Theory of Economic Policy in English Classical Political Economy* (1952), pp 11–12, 34–67.

[7] The possibility that a higher rate might be borne by the older trade implies that the railway was not making maximum profits before the new trade appeared. That is, the operation of this second qualification depends on the first, that railways allowed rates to become conventional.

III

Criticism of the pricing policy of the railways in the mid nineteenth century was usually based on claims of inequity either between individuals, or between railways and traders, or between areas. There were more sophisticated arguments advanced by independent critics such as Galt, and by the Post Office.

There was a widespread belief among traders that railway companies discriminated between them, favouring one individual over another. Merchants from Liverpool told the Royal Commission of the 1860s that a railway's schedule of charges was illusory because of special rates,[1] and, more generally, that there was discrimination between parties.[2] They could present no evidence supporting these charges, and in one case where specific charges were made, the manager of the railway concerned was able to refute them.[3] And the managers were insistent in their rejection of the claim. The greatest concession was that there were two or three 'special rates' for individuals on the whole London & North Western Railway.[4] In most cases, companies gave lower rates if large quantities were guaranteed either as a total per year or as a minimum size for each consignment, but these rates were open to all individuals.[5] The manager of the Midland Railway went further than other managers and declared that his company not only allowed no 'special rates' to individuals,[6] but that all contract rates were being removed:

> That was the principle [ie lower rates for guaranteed large quantities] adopted years ago by many of the large companies, but when I took the management of the Midland Company I abolished the system that was in operation there. I did not consider it fair to a man of small capital, because it was as much as he could do to contend with the large capitalists even at the same rates, and gradually all those differential charges were abolished with reference to persons in the same trade in the same district.[7]

In view of the inability of the critics to produce any evidence, and in the absence of any evidence found subsequently, there is no reason to disbelieve the managers.

The other common complaint was that the charges of the railway companies varied between different producing districts, the argument usually

[1] *Roy Com on Railways, Min of Evid,* (Clark) Q 192.
[2] Ibid, (Patterson) QQ 240–55.
[3] *Roy Com on Railways, Min of Evid,* (Cosgrove) QQ 15680 ff; (Allport) QQ 16877 ff.
[4] Ibid, (Cawkwell) QQ 11596–602.
[5] Ibid, (S. Clarke) QQ 12631, 12716–20; (O'Brien) Q 11995; (Smithells) QQ 13121–9; (Grierson) QQ 11849–52.
[6] Ibid, (Allport) Q 12362.
[7] Ibid, (Allport) Q 12363.

being stated as the proposition that, in equity to all concerned, railway charges on a given commodity should always be so arranged as to imply a constant charge per mile carried. This is, of course, the converse of the companies' policy described in Section II, and the argument was therefore not over whether rates per mile were unequal, but over whether this was unfair to some traders. One railway manager listed nine previous occasions on which the question had been debated before a parliamentary body without the traders' case being accepted,[1] and the Royal Commission to which this was presented became the tenth. The argument in equity was never strongly made; although merchants of a particular town complained when the rate per mile on their freight was higher than that ruling for another town, in no case was there a complaint from merchants experiencing lower rates. Attempts to erect an economic argument from the base that charges should be related to costs and so be equal for any ton-mile of service provided by the railways foundered on the variation in costs of working between different railway lines. Arguments were sometimes based on the prohibition of 'undue preference' in the Railway & Canal Traffic Act of 1854 but the courts did not interpret this as requiring equal ton-miles rates. The judgment in the case brought by collieries in the Forest of Dean because the rates of the Great Western Railway assisted Ruabon collieries to compete in the London market read as follows:

> If we could say clearly that a scale of rates with respect to distance had been framed with a view of having the effect of favouring the Ruabon coal traffic and prejudicing the Forest of Dean coal traffic, we should hold that to be an undue preference within the act, in accordance with the decision of Ransome v. the Eastern Counties Railway Company, reported in the *Jurist* of the 16th April, -581. But we have no sufficient evidence to lead us to such a conclusion; and, although the complainants may suffer by this scale of rates, in consequence of their local position, that is a matter which the Court cannot interpose to remedy.[2]

The court held that proportionately lower rates on longer distance traffic did not constitute an 'undue preference' and this implies that the pricing policy of the railways was legal.

A few complaints were made formally, and no doubt many informally, of the absolute level of railway rates, especially of rates on Irish railways. These were usually based on notions of equity; an Irish grain merchant thought that Irish rates were based purely on the maximum obtainable, and not on 'what is a fair and regular rate',[3] and a Liverpool merchant thought that the Liverpool & Manchester Railway, begun to defeat a monopoly, had itself become one and had not lowered its rates in propor-

[1] *Roy Com on Railways, Min of Evid,* (O'Brien) Q 11969.
[2] BTHR: RCH 4/17, p 71.
[3] *Roy Com on Railways, Min of Evid,* (Perry) Q 6855.

tion to the reduction in its costs.[1] But the strongest argument against the level of rates was developed by the independent critic Galt, in a book[2] and in his evidence to the Royal Commission. His argument was not based entirely on equity; on the contrary, he considered that railway companies maximised their profits by experiments with rates in the early days and through the local knowledge of traffic managers in the 1860s,[3] and that to do so the directors were not abusing their power but simply fulfilling their responsibilities to the shareholders.[4] But he argued that the economy would gain from government purchase of the railways and the leasing of them to a number of companies on specific conditions including the reduction of rates to one third of the level prevailing.[5]

When questioned by the commission, Galt agreed that the 'English people' were 'generally very much opposed to Government interference in mercantile affairs and what is called centralisation generally', that the 'English people' considered that 'the system pursued by the continental governments in such matters is entirely opposed to the spirit of our constitution and the habits of our people' and declared that he agreed with such opinions.[6] But he argued that all this was irrelevant to railway management which was 'virtually a monopoly',[7] and he argued that even if the English preferred to pay high rates to avoid government interference, his scheme should be applied to Irish railways and he was confident that the result of such an experiment would be its eventual acceptance in England.[8]

Although the commission spent a large amount of time discussing such points as the relative advantages of competition generally, competition among railway companies, monopoly, and government management, only Galt formulated a coherent argument. While some of his figures were attacked,[9] and while the scheme drew some support from two commissioners,[10] the argument was unconsidered rather than refuted presumably because it was felt to be politically inappropriate. Galt's scheme was not accepted in England although the reorganisation of the 1920s included

[1] Ibid, (Patterson) QQ 317–18.

[2] W. Galt, *Railway Reform: Its Importance and Practicability* (1865). Galt published a pamphlet of the same main title during the debate that led to the Act of 1844 giving notice that the state might after 21 years compulsorily purchase railways sanctioned after 1844.

[3] *Roy Com on Railways, Min of Evid,* (Galt) QQ 7359–60.

[4] Ibid., Q 7425.

[5] *Roy Com on Railways, Min of Evid,* (Galt) QQ 7340 ff.

[6] Ibid, (Galt) QQ 7421–3. The words quoted are those used by the commissioner, Roebuck, to which Galt gave unqualified approval.

[7] Ibid, (Galt) Q 7424.

[8] Ibid, (Galt) Q 8510.

[9] eg Ibid, (Allport) QQ 13834–57; 16938–9.

[10] *Roy Com on Railways, Report of the Rt Hon W. Monsell* and *Report of Sir Rowland Hill,* PP 1867, XXXVIII, Pt 1, pp 93–105, 107–26. Monsell's support was limited to the case of Irish railways, and neither accepted all elements of Galt's plan.

some of the elements and it had earlier partial successes in other countries.[1] Whether his prescription would have been beneficial to the economy rather than merely transferring income from the railways to their users, depends on the price elasticity of the demand for railway services, and while this cannot now be conclusively determined a figure as large as Galt assumed would be surprising. The demand concerned, at least for goods services, was a derived demand and it is not likely that so many industries were sensitive to freight costs that a reduction of their level to one-third of that prevailing would have resulted in such an increase of traffic that railway receipts would not have declined.

Furthermore, if Galt's reorganisation scheme was to be compatible with his belief that railways were maximising profits and were to cover their costs after reorganisation, the low level of railway profits in the 1860s implies that the reorganisation was to be accompanied by considerable economies in costs and Galt was unable to specify where these would occur. He was almost certainly right in thinking that the cost of loans would be less for railways given a government guarantee, but this raises the question of how widely in the economy such guarantees should be spread, and the working costs of railways would not have been greatly affected. The value of Galt's scheme is highly dubious, and it was in any case irrelevant to the course of railway rates.

One particularly interesting critic of the railways' pricing policy was the Post Office. When the postal services were shifted on to railways in the 1840s, the Post Office was given power to requisition special coaches or trains but if it could not agree with the railway company concerned on the appropriate charge, the dispute was to be submitted to arbitration with an independent umpire. The Post Office claimed that it should pay for the accommodation with which it was provided, and interpreted this to mean the *additional* expense to which the company was put including a fair profit margin. The companies claimed that the charge should be the cost of the service provided including a share of the companies' fixed expenses, and this was the view generally favoured in arbitration.[2] The additional cost for a mail train was thought to be about 1s–1s 2d per mile whereas the actual rates settled in arbitration ranged up to 3s[3] and while the argument was usually stated in terms of mail trains, Sir Robert Hill carried it to its logical conclusion, requesting from Gooch an estimate of the additional cost involved in adding one carriage to a train of five or six.[4] The Post Office formulated its view during the 1840s when Robert Stephenson was

[1] See the remarks of an Australian High Commissioner and a New Zealand premier quoted in K. H. Johnstone, *British Railways and Economic Recovery* (1949), pp 104 and 321.

[2] *Roy Com on Railways, Min of Evid,* (Page) QQ 14946–7; see also the evidence of F. Hill at p 473.

[3] Ibid, (Page) QQ 15033–41.

[4] Ibid, (Gooch) QQ 17439–50.

requested to make an estimate of incremental cost,[1] but it was unable to secure its acceptance by the railway companies or in arbitration, and neither was it endorsed by the Royal Commission.

This is interesting as an early argument about marginal cost pricing, and the Post Office seems to have been the only advocate of marginal cost pricing in the mid nineteenth century. Its argument was not, of course, based on the premises used in modern welfare economics, but was merely the interpretation given by the Post Office to the concept of a 'fair price'. Not even the Post Office seems to have investigated the implications of its argument for the pricing of other freight.

IV

Further confusions about the pricing policy of railways arose over 'terminal charges' which, as noted in Section I, were usually allowed by railway Acts in addition to the maximum carriage charges. In practice, the concept of 'terminal charges' was used for two purposes, the first being the rebuttal of allegations that parliamentary maxima were exceeded, and the second being a mechanism internal to the railways for the allocation of through rates.

'Terminals' were an obvious weapon in a quarrel over the legality of a particular rate. To win a legal case, a trader had to prove not only that the rate charged exceeded the maximum carriage charge specified by the relevant Act, but also that the excess was greater than a 'reasonable' charge for the services rendered at each end of the journey. The task of showing that a rate was so high as to be illegal was greatly complicated, and the railways made full use of this weapon.

The Clearing House mechanism was concerned with the allocation of 'through rates', this term being used in England to denote rates between two stations such that the freight was required to pass over lines of two or more railway companies. The Royal Commission described the mechanism as,

> The railway company which accepts the traffic which is to pass over more than one line of railway specifies to the consignor the gross sum to be paid for it. From this gross sum a deduction at a fixed rate for terminal expenses at each end, of 4s per ton for the country and 8s 6d for London, is credited to the companies who receive and deliver the traffic, and the remainder is apportioned between the several companies, as a rule according to the relative lengths of those portions of their lines over which the traffic passed. . . .[2]

Questions then arose as to the nature of the deductions of 4s or 8s 6d. Railway managers argued that these were a device internal to the railways, approximately balancing out between companies, and having little or no

[1] *1846 Select Committee on Railways, Min of Evid,* PP 1846, XIV, (R. Stephenson) QQ 2846–7.

[2] *Roy Com on Railways, Report,* p 68.

relation to actual costs. Huish, formerly general manager of the London & North Western Railway, declared that they were merely an internal device and were not fixed 'with reference to the public' at all,[1] although he weakly conceded that as they had been unchanged for as long as he could remember they might be a reasonable approximation to the costs involved.[2] He could have argued with at least equal force that their constancy reflected their conventional nature, and this was to be preserved for another 50 years. W. M. Acworth thought that the same figures reflected actual costs, when their permanence at a particular level should have warned him of the dangers of this assumption.[3]

The particular figures of the Clearing House scheme were adopted in 1847 as the activities of the Clearing House were extended to goods traffic.[4] The principle of allocating through rates by a terminal allowance and division of the remainder by mileage was accepted in January of that year and endorsed in October.[5] Between these dates the country terminal allowance was fixed, and the higher figure for Camden station in London accepted,[6] this figure being later applied to other London stations.[7] Initially, the inter-company negotiations threatened to greatly complicate the work of clerks at the Railway Clearing House by creating variations in the terminal allowances to be made. In addition to the case of London, a lower figure was agreed to for heavy traffic despite the protests of the Midland Railway,[8] and railways involved in longer than average cartage requested higher allowance,[9] but the danger was eventually recognised and requests for local variation treated with greater caution.[10]

Attempts were made to reduce the level of the terminal allowances. A discussion of goods managers in 1848 ended in the resolution, 'That it is not expedient to reduce the allowances now made in London and in the Country for the Terminal expenses of the Goods traffic.'[11]

At the end of 1849, the Chester & Birkenhead and Scottish Central Railways reopened the question, initially proposing to reduce the allowance where the terminal station was in a small town. It was agreed, for unrecorded reasons, that no distinction should be made by the size of town,

[1] *Roy Com on Railways, Min of Evid,* (Huish) Q 16004.
[2] Ibid, (Huish) QQ 16005–7.
[3] W. M. Acworth, *Railway Economics*, p 128, n 1.
[4] The Clearing House did not make terminal allowances on through rates for passengers. The early through rates were simply the addition of the rates of the railways concerned, BTHR: RCH 1/13, 28 May 1845; and later rates were arranged by negotiation but still divided without terminal allowances. An attempt to introduce these in the 1850s was unsuccessful, BTHR: RCH 1/14, 11 Mar 1857, Resolution 452.
[5] BTHR: RCH 1/162, 19 Jan 1847, p 2; BTHR: RCH 1/162, 8 Oct 1847, p 34.
[6] BTHR: RCH 1/162, 17 Aug 1847, p 20.
[7] BTHR: RCH 1/162, 23 Jan 1851, p 193; BTHR: RCH 1/163, 19 Mar 1852, p 26.
[8] BTHR: RCH 1/162, 22 Feb 1849, p 108; 22 Mar 1849, p 111; 18 Oct 1849, p 137.
[9] BTHR: RCH 1/162, 22 Mar 1849, p 113.
[10] BTHR: RCH 1/162, 23 Jan 1851, p 194; 20 Mar 1851, p 197; 22 May 1851, p 201.
[11] BTHR: RCH 1/162, 21 July 1848, p 75.

but the same two railways then pressed for a one-third reduction of all the allowances, arguing that fairness to all companies required the allowances to be equal to the expenditure involved. Huish of the London & North Western Railway and Laws of the Lancashire & Yorkshire Railway argued that the figures adopted satisfied this criterion, and that a reduction of the allowances would lead to an inexpedient reduction of rates. The dissatisfied railways denied that there was any direct link between the Clearing House allowances and overall rates but could win no support for their proposal.[1] Either Huish and Laws were themselves confused about the Clearing House mechanism, since the allowances could have been set at any figure without necessarily affecting rates charged to the public at all, or they used a tactical argument to good effect.

There were no other significant attempts to change the Clearing House figures during the nineteenth century,[2] but this does not imply that the figures remained close to the costs involved. For if a company was not satisfied with its share of a particular rate, it could negotiate a variation of the usual procedure, or it could use the flexibility allowed in the setting of the gross rate. For example, when an allowance of 2s 3d instead of the usual 1s 6d was requested for non-carted goods at Fleetwood because of harbour and quay charges, the decision was eventually that the gross rate should be increased by 9d with no adjustment to the usual rules for dividing this between the companies involved. This did not have exactly the same effect as acceptance of the original request would have had; depending on its proportion of the total mileage, the company running into Fleetwood gained more or less than it would have had its own scheme been accepted, and the other companies involved gained at the expense of the public. But the decision satisfied the railways involved without complicating the work of Clearing House clerks.[3] Adjustment of the gross rate was a simpler method of modifying the effect on a particular company of the Clearing House rules than an attempt to relate the allowances to actual costs would have been. The conventional nature of the Clearing House figures was quickly accepted, and a rule approved by a meeting of general managers in 1854 read:

> Goods are invoiced through at two Rates only, Station to Station Rates, and Rates including Cartage. In the first case, neither company is entitled to any allowance for carriage; in the second case, both companies receive the allowance, whether the work of carting be performed by them or not 'except in those cases specially provided for'.[4]

Thus after some early confusion, the terminal allowances of the Clearing House became conventional figures used in the allocation of through rates.

[1] BTHR: RCH 1/162, 24 Aug 1849, p 130; 27 Sept 1849, p 134; 22 Nov 1849, pp 140–2.

[2] I am indebted to Dr P. S. Bagwell for this information, as well as for drawing my attention to the meetings of 17 August 1847 and 22 November 1849.

[3] BTHR: RCH 1/162, 23 Jan 1851, p 194; 20 Mar 1851, p 197; 22 May 1851, p 201.

[4] BTHR: RCH 1/70, 10 Aug 1854, p 129.

They had little relation to the costs of the services provided at the beginning and end of through transit, nor to the concept of terminals used by railways to disprove allegations that they set rates exceeding the parliamentary maxima, nor yet to the charges made to the public for railway services as a whole.

Managers were not very successful in conveying the nature of the Clearing House allowances to the public although they did try to do so. Attempts were made to describe the distinction between the function of the Clearing House itself and the functions of the various bodies that met at the physical site of the Clearing House. The manager of the London & North Western Railway told a Royal Commission in the 1880s:

> The Clearing House has nothing to do with the arrangement of rates, that is a neutral institution for dividing the proceeds of the traffic between the different companies. As a matter of fact the railway companies are associated together and we fix the rates by meeting and communicating with each other, and all the rates are arranged so that we may take it that everyone who is interested in the concern is consulted.[1]

and,

> . . . Although we meet at the Clearing House, the Clearing House has a distinct object and has nothing to do with the fixing of the rates.[2]

Rates were fixed at the periphery of the Clearing House; the terminal allowances belonged to its function of allocating through rates, and there was no relation between these.

That the charges made by railways to the public did not consist of two parts, a charge for terminal services and a haulage charge, is indicated by the railway managers' descriptions of their policy quoted in Section II. Managers did not say that they fixed rates in two parts. More direct statements were also made, such as, 'The question of mileage never enters into the calculation [of rates],'[3] and:

> The Midland Railway Company at the time I was one of their managers had, I think, four good managers, their line being divided for that purpose and the rates we fixed for goods and minerals were fixed at meetings in conference with each other. I am quite sure we never troubled ourselves about Acts of Parliament or our legal powers at all. We simply considered how much we thought the traffic would bear, and what the public would pay for it without making a disturbance.[4]

Allport also described a 2s 6d terminal allowed in an inter-company agreement on rates on Burton ales as a 'matter of account between companies' and not of concern to the brewers.[5]

The setting of rates by separate consideration of terminals and haulage

[1] *Roy Com on Ag, Min of Evid, Vol I,* (Findlay) Q 8618.
[2] Ibid, (Findlay) Q 8661.
[3] *Roy Com on Railways, Min of Evid,* (Allport) Q 13745.
[4] Ibid, (Wragge) Q 15533.
[5] *Roy Com on Railways, Min of Evid,* (Allport) QQ 16877 ff.

charges would be inconsistent with the general policy outlined in Section II, in the sense that such consideration would be superfluous. If a railway company adjusted its rates so that supply areas were brought into competition at a given market, or to meet competition from sea carriage, it would have been foolish to calculate terminal charges separately. Consider a market, C, served by a supply area, A, with a gross railway charge on freight from A to C of x shillings. Another supply area, B, suggests to the railway company that given a rate of y shillings, it could compete at C. The railway gains nothing by dividing the suggested rate into 4s terminals and $(y - 4)$ shillings for haulage. Provided y gives a profit over the incremental cost incurred by carrying freight from B to C, the railway is likely, according to the evidence presented in Section II, to accept the proposition. If more than one railway is involved, then each has to be satisfied that its incremental cost is covered, but there is still no point in considering terminals separately.

Further, the nature of terminals is indicated by the records of rates set. One element of the pricing policy described in Section II, is that rates would generally fall with distance as different supply areas were assisted to compete in a common market. If terminal charges had been made separately, the constant charge would affect the relationship between gross rates and distance, and a statistical measurement should reveal a closer relationship between rates net of terminal charges and distance, than between gross rates and distance.[1] In general, this is not the case; to present only the example illustrated in Figures 1 and 2, for a group of rates on timber and deals collected by the Royal Commission of the 1860s,[2] the coefficient of correlation between the gross rate and distance is 0·65, that between rates net of terminals and distance is only 0·43.[3]

Terminals were not in general a separate element in the prices charged by railways to the public, but a qualification should be made to this. In the coal trade, railways sometimes provided depots for merchants, and the charge made for this service was sometimes known as a terminal.[4] But in general, the rates set were required in total to give aggregate receipts that provided a margin of profit, and any individual rate was not decomposable into terminal and carriage elements. It was the gross rate that managers

[1] The relationship will not be exact because distance was not the only consideration in setting rates. For the same reason, the exercise does not furnish irrefutable proof, but read in the context of the rest of this section, it gives support to the argument advanced.

[2] *Roy Com on Railways, Appendices to Min of Evid,* pp 349–50.

[3] Only one example is presented here, but the same exercise has been performed for groups of rates relating to chemicals, sugar and sundries, corn and grain, bar iron, pig iron, hardware, encaustic tiles, and ale, with the same result in each case. The regressions were made on the Oxford University KDF9 computer, and I am grateful to Mr K. MacDonald for programming assistance and for arranging computer time.

[4] *Roy Com on Railways, Min of Evid,* (Allport) QQ 5323–4; (Bidder) QQ 4440–1; *1881 Sel Com on Railways, Min of Evid,* (Findlay) QQ 14128–9.

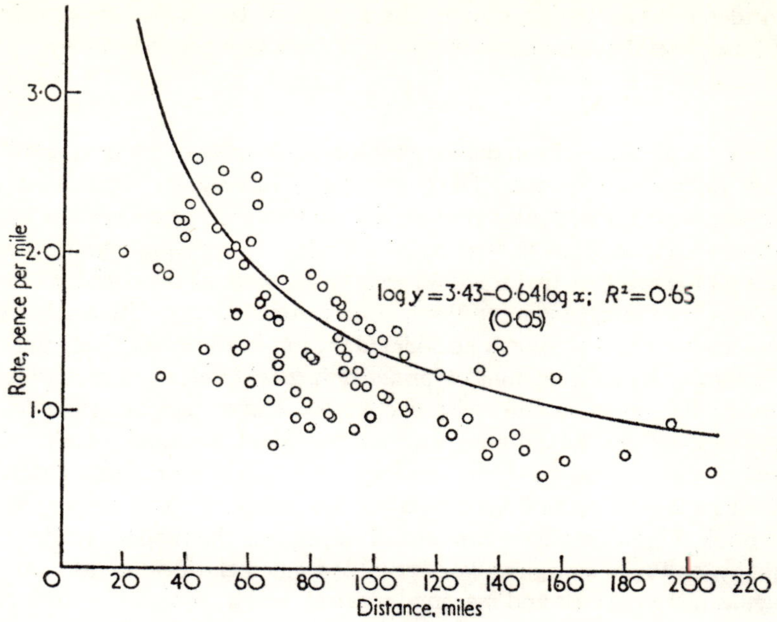

FIGURE 1. Railway rates (including terminals) and distance-rates on timber and deals, 1865.

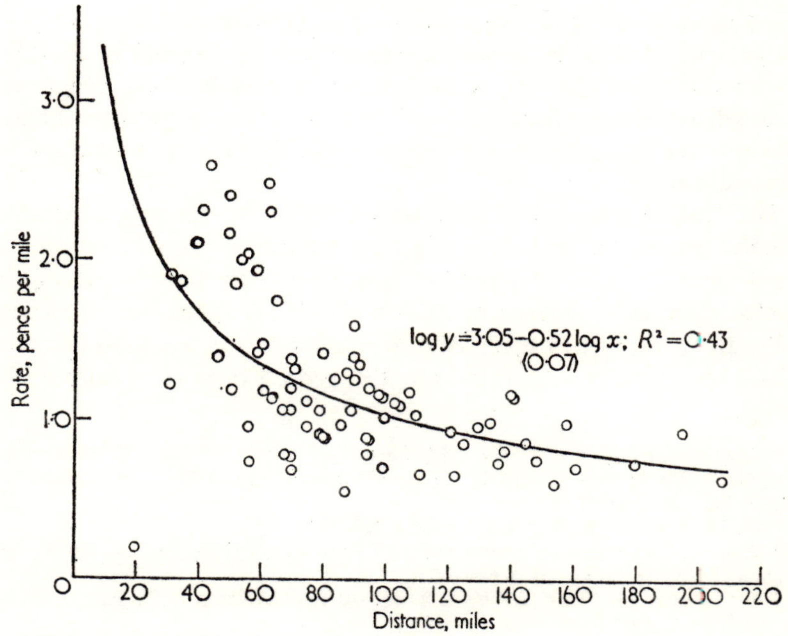

FIGURE 2. Railway rates (excluding terminals) and distance-rates on timber and deals, 1865.

considered when setting prices. The notion of terminals served several purposes, but the actual determination of rates was not one of these.

V

Few attempts have been made to explore the impact of the pricing policy of the railways on the overall level of national income. By implication, the contemporary railway managers considered that their pricing policy raised national income since they rejected the idea of applying equal mileage rates on the grounds that it would restrict the trade of the country.[1] Later analysts have largely ignored the question. Acworth explicitly excluded it from his book and obviously considered the implications of pricing policies to belong to legal discussions of 'undue influence'.[2] Sherrington considered price formation as an administrative matter, and while he considered the legal implications, he did not concern himself with economic results.[3] The most thorough analysis is that of Pigou,[4] in which he considers railway rates as a special case of discriminating monopoly. As with other parts of his book, Pigou's analysis cannot fail to impress the modern reader, but equally, as Pigou's original work preceded much clarification of concepts such as marginal cost and marginal revenue, and as some of his own concepts did not find a permanent place in the literature,[5] the analysis appears dated. Because of this, only a severely modified form of the argument is considered here.

Pigou was concerned with discrimination between the different types of freight carried. That is, he was concerned with the practice of classifying commodities and charging a different rate for each of the classes constructed. He was not concerned with discrimination between areas and so was able to assume that the terminal points of the railway under consideration were given.

His method was that of comparative statics, comparing competition, simple monopoly, and discriminating monopoly. Perfect competition would lead to equal rates per ton mile for all commodities, since 'when competition really prevails, seller A must always endeavour to undersell seller B by offering to serve seller B's better-paying customers at a rate slightly less than B is charging, and this process must eventually level all rates'.[6]

[1] *Roy Com on Railways, Min of Evid,* (Sherriff) Q 16258; (O'Brien) Q 11970; (Grierson) QQ 13255 ff; (S. Clarke) QQ 12796–807; (Smithells) QQ 13036–69; (Morris) QQ 14197–246; (Stewart) Q 14893.

[2] W. M. Acworth, *Railway Economics,* p 138, n 1.

[3] C. E. R. Sherrington, *Economics of Rail Transport in Great Britain,* Vol II, 1928, second edition 1937), Chapters 6 and 7.

[4] A. C. Pigou, *The Economics of Welfare* (1920, fourth edition 1932), Part II, Chapter XVIII, 'The Special Problem of Railway Rates'.

[5] Eg 'Ideal Output', which survives in a modified form in modern welfare economics, but is no longer given the same prominence as 'national income'.

[6] A. C. Pigou, op cit, p 291, n 2.

This conclusion is subjected to several modifications or reservations; the absolute level of the rate per ton-mile so established depends on the circumstances of the particular railway under consideration;[1] charges would vary if the services required by different commodities varied because of such considerations as packaging arrangements; rates may vary with time and season, or between continuous and intermittent demands. But Pigou argues strongly and convincingly against Taussig[2] that railway costs would not, in general, diverge from equality because of the incidence of joint costs. Conceding that the existence of joint costs can be made into a purely semantic question, Pigou correctly indicates that the most relevant sense of the term is to denote a situation in which costs are so related that perfect competition would evolve divergent prices for the products, and for this the appropriate condition is that investment *necessarily* involves output of more than one product. Investment in sheep produces wool and mutton and the costs of those products are joint. Railway investment could be used for several types of product, in the sense that it could carry freight of different kinds, but in general it is not such that it must do so. Railway investment could usually be confined to one particular freight if this was wanted, and the costs of railways are not usually joint in the relevant sense. The main exception to this conclusion arises from reverse freight; investment to carry goods from A to B necessarily involves investment to carry goods from B to A, and hence perfect competition may evolve rates dependent on the direction of traffic. But 'joint costs' is not sufficient reason for expecting charges for the same journey by rail to vary between types of freight.

Pigou considered the pricing policy of railways to be that appropriate to discriminating monopoly and he compares the implications of this with those of a competitive policy. The argument is a variant on the now familiar monopoly-competition comparison, and Pigou proceeds by comparing each of discriminating monopoly and competition with simple monopoly.

The first part of the argument is the proposition that competitive output must exceed monopolistic output because of the divergence between the average and marginal revenue curves facing the individual seller in the latter market situation. A second proposition results from the comparison of simple and discriminating monopoly, and may be stated as: if discri-

[1] Such as variations in construction costs, or in the population of the district served, etc.

[2] F. W. Taussig, 'A Contribution to the Theory of Railway Rates', in W. Z. Ripley (Ed), *Railway Problems* (Boston, USA, 1907), pp 123–44. Taussig's position was accepted uncritically in W. M. Acworth, *Railways and the Traders*, p 85. The controversy between Pigou and Taussig carried on in the *Quarterly Journal of Economics* in 1913, and in the other publications cited here, was the immediate inspiration of Chamberlin's theory of monopolistic competition, see E. H. Chamberlin, 'The Origin and Early Development of Monopolistic Competition Theory', *Quart Journ Econ*, LXXV (1961), 515–43.

mination is applied only to demands not satisfied by simple monopoly, output will in general be greater under discriminating monopoly than under simple monopoly. Pigou's argument is complicated by his concern with social returns and ideal output but the essential notions for our purposes can be seen in Figure 3.

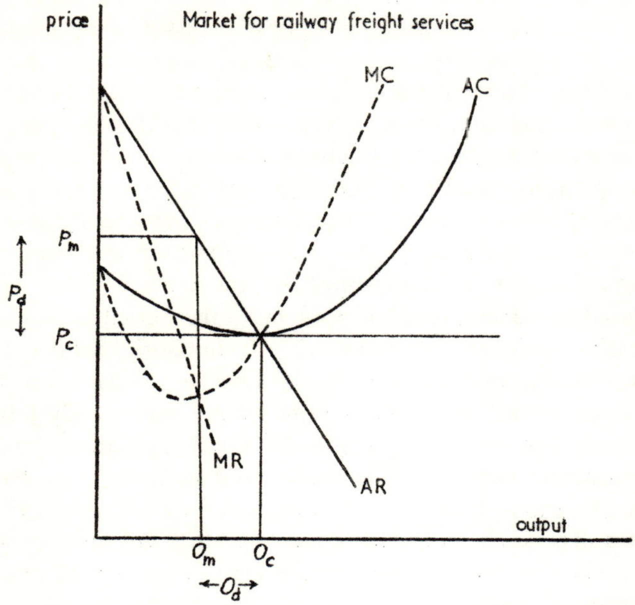

FIGURE 3. *Comparison of Competition, Simple Monopoly, and Discriminating Monopoly; the Conventional Case.*

Discriminating monopoly of the first degree leads to output equal to that of competition. Discrimination of lesser degrees leads to an output between that appropriate to competition and that appropriate to simple monopoly, assuming in each case that discrimination is applied only to demands not satisfied by simple monopoly.

The diagram refers to the market for railway services and it is the usual price-output diagram with average and marginal curves for revenue and costs. Perfect competition, including in that concept freedom of entry to the market, establishes output O_c and price P_c, while the subscript 'm' refers to the corresponding position established by simple monopoly. With perfect discrimination,[1] the average revenue curve becomes the appropriate marginal revenue curve since the maximum demand price is extracted from each customer. If discrimination is practised only on those demands not satisfied by a simple monopolist's policy, output would range from O_m to O_c, and price from P_m to P_c, tending towards the competitive position as discrimination becomes more refined. This argument, with the apparent implicit ranking by output of competition, discriminating mono-

[1] More precisely, Pigou's 'discrimination of the first degree'.

poly, simple monopoly, depends on the form of the various functions involved.

Given that railways through discrimination reduced prices to meet some demand prices not accepted by simple monopoly, and did not introduce discrimination to those demand prices accepted by simple monopoly,

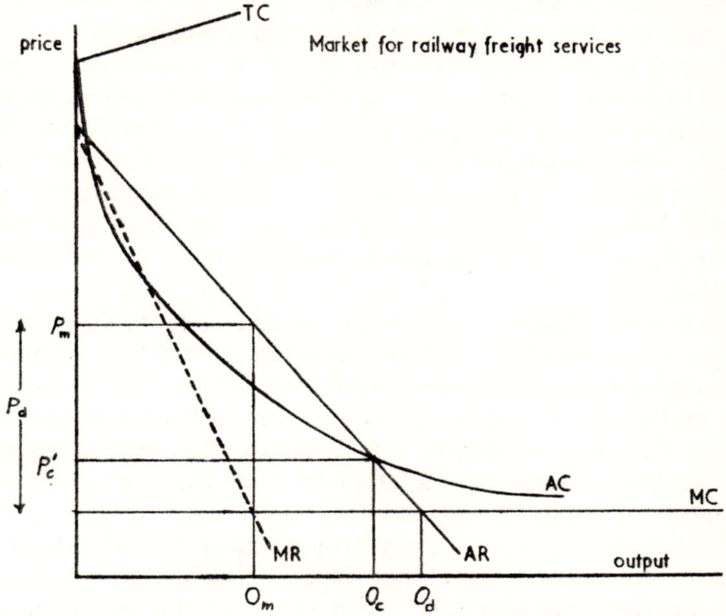

FIGURE 4. *Comparison of Competition, Simple Monopoly, and Discriminating Monopoly: A Special Case.*

Under certain assumptions, those often thought to apply to public utilities, competitive output is not finite, but if non-negative profits are required, the output of discriminating monopoly may exceed that appropriate to competition.

then their output would be increased by discrimination. The question of competition, however, is more complicated. Pigou explicitly assumed that the same cost curve was appropriate to competition as to monopoly,[1] being concerned with the imposition of a competitive position on a railway rather than with the likelihood of a spontaneous realisation of a competitive position. But the analysis also assumes that output under perfect competition is determinate; that is, it presupposes the existence of a unique minimum to the average cost curve. It is not difficult to construct a case in which this condition is not satisfied. Indeed, under the usual assumptions about public utilities, namely, a large capital investment and low, approximately constant variable costs, and assuming that the plant is not used to physical capacity, the minimum of the average cost curve is not finite, and

[1] Thus avoiding the usual criticism of demonstrations from diagrams such as Fig 3 that competitive output exceeds that of simple monopoly.

competitive output is indeterminate unless a constraint such as the requirement of non-negative profits is imposed.[1] As shown in Figure 4, this case can lead to a larger output resulting from discriminating monopoly than from competition. Any attempt to enforce a uniform rate per ton-mile is more likely to have induced the railways to operate a simple monopolistic pricing policy than a competitive policy, but even had attempts been made to prescribe a fixed price at the level appropriate to constrained competition (that is, competition with the added requirement that profits be not negative), output may have been reduced. However, given the difficulties involved in attempting to prescribe a competitive price, that is the difficulties of determining the shape and position of the relevant curves, and given also the attitude to such proposals by such political bodies as the Royal Commission, the relevant question about the effect of discrimination on output refers to the comparison of simple and discriminating monopoly.

Two points of Pigou's own argument should be reintroduced here. In considering the possibility that discriminating monopoly might produce some output where competition would produce none,[2] a possibility that Pigou thought to be empirically unlikely, the basis of the argument is changed. Pigou concerns himself with the possibility of some output under discrimination and no output at all under competition (or under simple monopoly). The point at issue, however, is a situation of no output in a particular sub-market under competition or monopoly, and some output in that market under discriminating monopoly. Considering the complaints made of the lowest rates in the 1860s, those on coal, it is quite conceivable that a simple monopoly rate over all commodities might have led to the cessation of the coal trade on certain railways, and it is conceivable that a competitive rate would have had the same effect. Pigou's assessment of the empirical situation does not relate to the relevant question.

The second point made by Pigou[3] is theoretically valid but substantially irrelevant. This is the suggestion that state bounties might replace monopoly charges if a railway needed assistance to extend its services to commodities that could afford less than the prescribed uniform charge per ton-mile. This is obviously theoretically valid, and even on some ethical assumptions preferable, but as was shown by the reception of Galt's plan of little relevance to the nineteenth-century situation.

The conclusion of this Pigou-inspired[4] analysis is then that in so far as

[1] In the case of one enterprise required to adopt a competitive price, this leads to a one-sided unstable equilibrium. This construction is a variant of the standard proposition that competitive equilibrium requires increasing marginal costs.

[2] A. C. Pigou, op cit, pp 309–12, and Appendix 3, article 26. The argument of this appendix article can be restated as a comparison of simple and discriminating monopoly.

[3] A. C. Pigou, op cit, pp 313–5.

[4] It should perhaps be made explicit that Pigou's own conclusion was that the competitive solution, with bounties etc, was to be favoured. It should also be made clear that Pigou was concerned with the situation at the time he wrote, with the early twentieth

discrimination enabled commodities to be carried that would not have been carried at a simple monopoly rate, without restricting the freight obtainable at the monopoly price, the policy tended to promote railways' output and the national income.[1] But the precise theoretical result cannot be applied immediately to the empirical situation. Historically, railways did not begin with a monopoly rate and subsequently introduce discrimination to the demands for railways services not initially accepted. As discrimination was applied, through the classification scheme, over all commodities, those commodities in the higher classes were probably paying more than the simple monopolist's rate. But if we divide all commodities into two classes, those that would travel at the simple monopolist's rate, and those that would not travel at this rate, then if discrimination induced a greater increase in the output of the latter than it restricted the output of the former, the theoretical conclusion can be applied. And this is the likely empirical situation. The commodities discriminated against by being placed in the higher classes were mostly articles of large value relative to their weight such as hats and haberdasheries, and only in unusual situations of the product markets would the railway rate have greatly restricted their output.[2] On the other hand, the lower rates on goods in the lower classifications may have considerably increased the output of these commodities since their weight/value ratio implied that high rates could stop the trade completely. Further, the commodities favoured by discrimination such as coal and minerals had greater linkages in the input-output pattern of the economy than did such consumer goods as hats and so the conclusion that national income was more increased by the lower discriminatory rates than it was diminished by the higher discriminatory rates is strengthened. It seems highly likely that the pricing policy of railways before 1881 tended to promote the increase of national income, in so far as it discriminated between freights of different kinds.

It is possible that various schemes of government regulation would have promoted the national income even further,[3] but this is not certain, and the political situation before 1881 excluded the possibility of the necessary adjustments.

century, and not with the nineteenth. But he did not consider the legislative adjustments after 1881 that made railway rates much less flexible, and in particular made reduction of particular rates more difficult.

[1] We assume, realistically, that railways were not employed to physical capacity, and that resources invested in railways were not readily transferable to other uses.

[2] ie the market would have to be in such a position that a very small increase in price leads to large reductions of output. This is not impossible, but is unlikely to be widely prevalent for expensive consumer goods.

[3] As well as distributing transport costs in a way, which on some ethical assumptions, would have been fairer to the users of railways for different freights.

VI

Pigou dealt with the less unusual aspect of discrimination in the railways' pricing policy. The most interesting question is not whether the discrimination between freights of different commodities was beneficial to economic growth, but whether the discrimination between different supply areas was so beneficial. To this problem, even less theoretical attention has been devoted.

In a very brief consideration of the effects of rates in the USA, in some respects similar to those in England and Wales, P. W. MacAvoy comments:

> To be sure, less discrimination between local and through transport would have been desirable in a world of perfect competition in all other markets,* but raising through transport rates, and lowering some local rates, may or may not have increased economic welfare in the framework of these transport markets . . . [which included producers' cartels etc].
>
> * Since this is no more than a requirement for Pareto optimum conditions of production and exchange. . . .[1]

As MacAvoy is concerned with welfare, the absence of perfect competition throughout the economy allows him to dismiss this consideration. But it is of interest here because the particular Pareto condition referred to is also a condition of maximum production and is not confined to welfare. This condition is: 'The ratio of marginal products of any two "factors of production" must be the same for every "good" in the production of which they both co-operate.'[2]

The usual simple proof of this proposition is in terms of a box diagram of isoproduct curves requiring the absence of external economies and diseconomies and it implies that producers must be faced with the same relative prices.[3]

This argument might seem to imply that taking railway services as a 'factor of production', dissimilar railway rates charged to different producers would imply that production is not maximised. But to treat the problem in this simple way is to ignore some problems of location—to accept assumptions related to the 'Anglo-Saxon bias' discerned by Isard[4]—assumptions more than usually implausible when dealing with problems of railway rates. In theoretical terms it is to ignore the significance of the condition that the factors must co-operate in the production of more than one good, and to ignore the impact of transport costs.

If it is not assumed that resources are geographically mobile and can

[1] Paul W. MacAvoy, *The Economic Effects of Regulation* (Cambridge, Mass USA, 1965), pp 201–4 and 201, n 9.

[2] I. M. D. Little, *A Critique of Welfare Economics* (1950, 2nd ed 1957, paperback 1960), p 136.

[3] Ibid, pp 136–40.

[4] W. Isard, *Location and Space-Economy* (Cambridge, Mass USA, 1956), pp 24–7.

produce more than one good, the Pareto condition stated above is not a condition of maximum output. In Figure 5, a variant on the box diagram referred to assuming that railway services and other resources are not substitutable,[1] we have two producers A and B, B requiring more transport to take his product to a given market. The total factor supply other than railway services at each location is A_f, B_f respectively, and given the initial

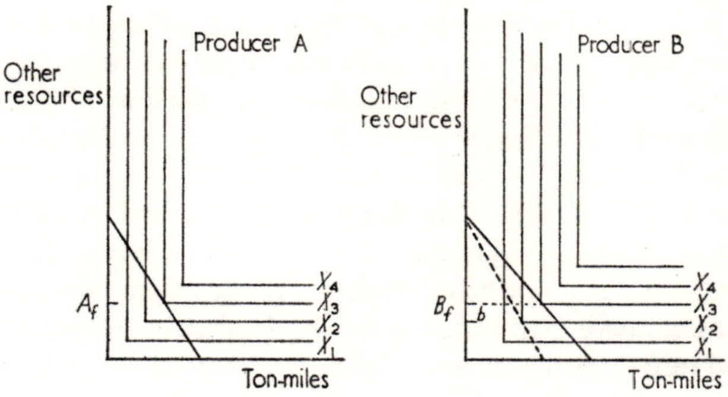

FIGURE 5. *Maximum Production with Immobile Resources.*
In initial conditions, with discriminating rail prices, each producer has output X_3. If producer B is required to face freight rate per ton-mile of producer A his output falls to X_2 and b of other resources becomes unemployed. Producer A is unable to expand his output as resources are immobile. Output of the good concerned, and railway freight fall.

discriminating railway rates shown by the non-parallel price lines each producer has an output of X_3. If the railways were required to establish a uniform price per ton-mile and did this by adjusting the lower rate charged to B to that charged to A, the output of B would fall to X_2 and b of resources at B would become unemployed. If A could obtain these resources, he could expand to X_4 but the resources are assumed to be geographically immobile, and specific to a particular use. Therefore total output falls, as does railway freight receipts. If the adjustment to equal rates is made by altering only A's rate, output of the good remains constant, but in all intermediate adjustments, that is, changes in both rates, output falls because some resources become unemployed at B without becoming available to A.

If it is not assumed that the resources other than railway services are specific to one use, but it is still assumed that resources are geographically immobile, then some of the resources made unemployed at B as far as the original good is concerned may be used in the production of another good. But only if the proportion of transport required per unit of other resources is less for the alternative good than it is for the original product will output

[1] As seems reasonable in discussing railway services. This assumption is not needed for the case in which rates are equalised at the level charged to A, but is needed for the other cases in which rates are equalised.

be increased. Otherwise, output remains at best constant. Thus discriminating railway rates, in the situation described by Figure 5, will increase output unless the rates established maintain a transport intensive industry the resources of which could be efficiently used in a less transport intensive use.

This is not an unrealistic construction. Two coal mines, or two blast furnaces, at unequal distances from a market could fulfil all the conditions of Figure 5. The railway managers attempting to describe such a situation used the extreme case where one producer could not enter the market at all unless a rate lower than that on existing suppliers was offered. But the principle remains the same; in effect, the railways brought more resources into a given 'economy' by tending to equalise the natural barriers of distance. This conclusion fails if the barriers are equalised by raising the rate on the more favourably located producer, but the railways claimed not to do this, and there is no evidence to disprove the claim. Nor are there any obvious cases where a transport-intensive inefficient industry was maintained, and rare occurrences would be outweighed by other discriminatory rates.

Some relevant empirical material can be obtained from the exceptional case of the South Wales railways required to charge equal ton mileage rates. The Taff Vale Railway lost some trade because it could not reduce its charges to compete with other railways for the trade of some areas because this would have required reduced charges on the more important freight from the Rhondda valleys. In this case the services required were provided by other railways but in the early twentieth century a planned extension of the Barry Railway was frustrated because rates would have had to be lowered to attract traffic to the branch and so all rates would have had to be reduced. The branch was not built, although it would have been useful to the area it was proposed to serve.[1] In South Wales, the prohibition of discriminatory rates restricted the railway services provided.

Not all the discrimination practised by the railways is of the type analysed with the aid of Figure 5. Where railways were concerned only with redirection of a trade so that not all fell into the same hands, output was affected only if external economies or diseconomies were involved. In the particular case of imported freight in which the alternative to lower rates by rail was sea freight, domestic income was affected only if the sea freight was in the hands of factors resident in other countries, that is, if non-English ships were used. But only if external economies were frustrated by actions of the railways could national income have been reduced.

There is something slightly ironic in the railways acting so as to dis-

[1] E. Brooks, 'Regional Functions of the Mineral Transport System in the South Wales Coalfield, 1830–1951' (PhD thesis, Cambridge, 1958), pp 20, 152, 173–4, and Appendix 2.

courage monopoly in other trades. But railway managers, at least in the 20 years before 1881, thought that they had responsibilities to the public, and in their behaviour towards the regional allocation of trade and in some other respects 'they acted for the most part as if they were public utilities'.[1] It is likely that the railways' policy of discriminating between supply areas promoted rather than restricted national income.

VII

Problems of the nature considered above do not arise to the same extent from the passenger traffic. This was divided into classes, but the fares were related to, even if not precisely proportional to, the service provided. The comfort, convenience of timing, and often the speed of a journey increased with the class fare. Between districts little discrimination was practised, and the rates were close to a mileage rate modified in the few cases where there was an alternative source of transport, and where there were competing railways that with the longer line had to accept a lower fare per mile carried. Some managers felt that the charges for different services should be more differentiated; the manager of the Great Western Railway would have liked to charge higher fares for faster trains more frequently than was done, but other railways did not consider it worth while and their competition prevented a unilateral change.[2]

The main factor preventing discrimination between classes from giving rise to the same criticism as it did in the case of goods traffic is that the units to be carried could readily transfer from one class to another.[3] Railway managers sometimes showed irritation over this ease of movement. The manager of the Lancashire & Yorkshire Railway thought that if third-class carriages were attached to all trains, 'people who have risen' would travel in that class when it was 'natural to expect them' to use the first or second.[4] More often irritation was shown at some uses of the excursion trains, which by the 1860s were simply trains, especially common at holi-

[1] D. E. C. Eversley, 'The Great Western Railway and the Swindon Works in the Great Depression', *University of Birmingham Historical Journal*, V–VI (1955–8), p 190, referring to the investment and employment policies of the Great Western Railway.

[2] BTHR: GW 18/4, p 19. The trend was eventually in the other direction, with express fares nearly disappearing by the end of the nineteenth century. In the early 1870s the Midland Railway abolished the second class and this was gradually copied by other railways. But in 1865 the manager of the Midland reported an experiment indicating that the abolition of the second class would lead to reduced railway income, and did not look on the move with favour. *Roy Com on Railways, Min of Evid,* (Allport) QQ 5357–69.

[3] There were isolated cases of 'cheating', of disguising freight so that it was treated as belonging to a class on which lower rates were charged. The feeling of the railways that carriers were doing this with 'smalls' was one of the bases of the legal battle of *Pickfords et al v Grand Junction Railway*. See W. T. Jackman, *The Development of Transportation in Modern England* (1912, 1965), Appendix 14.

[4] *Roy Com on Railways, Min of Evid,* (Smithells) QQ 12996–7.

day times, offering rates lower than the standard charge.[1] Managers felt that these should not be treated as convenient low-cost transport, and the manager of the Great Western Railway recounted with indignation the story of the six county families of Lancashire using an excursion train provided for the London Exhibition of 1862 to transfer their households including the servants to London for the season.[2] But the railways could do little to preserve the class differences; apparently it was only in Ireland that managers felt that the company to be found in the third class would keep people in the appropriate compartments![3] Elsewhere they were helpless.

Railways did not discriminate between passenger traffic in different areas. The managers asserted this to be the case,[4] and the record of rates set confirms the assertion.[5] Presumably this was because the railways felt that passenger traffic was largely a pleasure trade, or at least that personal travelling expenses were not a significant business cost, and that there was therefore no reason to assist certain areas. From the point of view of their own profits, managers did not think that the passenger traffic in country districts could be greatly stimulated.[6] The attitude is consistent with that adopted towards freight rates, that is, to offer lower rates if there is potential new traffic but not to energetically pursue profit if this involved restrictions on the existing traffic.

VIII

The pricing policy of railways in England and Wales before 1881 was basically that of discriminating monopoly with company profit as the major aim. But a policy of maximising profit on existing traffic was not energetically pursued, and the railways recognised a special responsibility for developing the trade of particular regions. Critics of the railways did not develop strong arguments against their pricing practice, and much discussion of it, especially of terminal charges, was misdirected. Despite the frequency with which the railways' policy was criticised, it is unlikely that it restricted the growth of the national income.

[1] Excursion trains began with organisations such as branches of the temperance movement hiring a train for a special purpose, and developed with the 1851 London Exhibition.

[2] *Roy Com on Railways, Min of Evid,* (Grierson) Q 13298. See also (Gooch) Q 17488; (S. Clarke) QQ 12848–60. Not all managers agreed, see ibid, (Smithells) QQ 13000–2.

[3] Ibid, (Barrington) QQ 7110–3; (Murland) QQ 4911–3.

[4] Eg ibid, (Cawkwell) Q 11636.

[5] Eg *Roy Com on Railways, Report,* p 53; and *Appendices to Minutes of Evidence,* Inquiry 5.

[6] *Roy Com on Railways, Min of Evid,* (S. Clarke) Q 12881; (Grierson) QQ 13290–1; (Morris) Q 14371.

The Great Western Railway and the Swindon Works in the Great Depression

By D. E. C. Eversley

For the historian interested in the fluctuations of the British economy in the nineteenth century, there is now a formidable array of books and articles, mostly of a statistical nature, which provide a great deal of information on global movements. Already, 20 years ago, H. L. Beales pointed out that the period known as the 'Great Depression', which figures so largely in textbooks of economic history, was not so much a time of widespread misery as an era of falling prices and loss of confidence.[1] Since then, the books of W. W. Rostow, W. G. Hoffmann and J. Tinbergen, to name only a few, have amplified this general judgment.[2] Professor A. K. Cairncross, in his book on investment, has provided a detailed study of building in Glasgow from 1856 to 1914 as well as convenient summaries of the levels of investment in other fields.[3] In Chapter 6 of this work a section is devoted to the investment programme of the main British railway companies of the period 1870–1914. Unfortunately, for reasons which the author himself appreciated, his statistics were least reliable for the years before 1893. Although there is a table of 'Factors influencing fluctuations in railway investment', only a few of the variables which may have influenced investment decisions are printed here, and of course no particular instances of the process of decision-making are recorded. Lastly, the figures given in the main table of railway investment are given in uncorrected money values at a period of very rapidly falling price levels, especially for

This article was first published in the *University of Birmingham Historical Journal*, (1955–6), 167–90, and is based on a paper read to the Economic History Society in the University of Birmingham in 1953. The documents used here were investigated in connection with the preparation of a chapter on engineering industries and the railway works, which will form part of the forthcoming Vol IV of the *Victoria County History of Wiltshire*. For their help with the preparation of the statistical material I am indebted to Miss Edna Davies and Miss Janet Blackman. Thanks are also due to the British Transport Commission's Archivist for permission to consult material and to quote from it.

[1] H. L. Beales, 'The "Great Depression" in Industry and Trade' in *Economic History Review*, V, No 1 (1934).

[2] W. W. Rostow, *British Economy of the Nineteenth Century* (1952): J. Tinbergen, *Business Cycles in the United Kingdom, 1870–1914* (1951): W. G. Hoffman, *British Industry*, 1700–1950 (1955).

[3] A. K. Cairncross, *Home and Foreign Investment 1870–1913* (1953).

this type of commodity, so that no true picture of the level of activity is obtained.

Yet a more detailed study of railway activity during this period is long overdue. There are good reasons for choosing the railways as a case-history: after the end of the stage-coach era, and before the advent of the motor-car, practically all long distance movement of people and goods took place by rail. The canals, by 1870, had to a large extent been taken over by the railways and no longer seriously competed with them. Though there may have been some substitution of canal for rail transport of bulk goods in bad times, this could not seriously affect the issue.

Given this function, we may assume that even slight changes in production and consumption would be reflected in the sensitive barometer of railway activity. This is true both of capital or investment goods (iron and steel, bricks, plate-glass, machinery), of consumer goods (imported and home-produced foodstuffs, textiles, pottery and other articles usually described as 'General Merchandise'), and of the consumption of 'services'—this item appearing in the guise of journeys to work and on business, holidays and excursions, as well as the carriage of mail and parcels. The correct use of this indicator of economic activity is a specialised operation for an economic statistician, and no attempt will be made in this article to make such an investigation.[1] The intention is, rather, to see how the management of the Great Western Railway responded to the difficulties of the period, and what effect their decisions had on the welfare of the railway town of Swindon.

The study of the years 1866–1900 in the microcosm of the works at Swindon, and the town which grew up around them, is designed to supplement the available general statistics and to illuminate both the causes of fluctuation in the level of activity and, more especially, the agencies of stabilisation. It is not possible, from such a study, to set up valid generalisations, but it can help us towards an understanding of the causes of human behaviour in industrial and commercial fields. This type of inquiry is what Schumpeter has called economic sociology, and as such a branch of economics. But the relationships which emerge from such an inquiry also tell us a good deal about class structure, occupations and urban growth—that is, they are part of our social history.

To formulate our starting question more clearly, how did it come about that in the period 1873–96, when there was widespread gloom in the business world, and a consequent failure of the level of investment to remain where it was, let alone continue to rise, Swindon, a town dependent on the production of investment goods and the maintenance of a service closely tied to the level of business activity, did not fall into the grip of a serious depression, and in fact, by most tests, continued to flourish? From the

[1] For such an investigation in American history see A. F. Burns and W. C. Mitchell, *Measuring Business Cycles* (1946), pp 414–16.

answer to this question, we may derive also a contribution to the history of modern economic policies. It is the aim of every government to eliminate as far as possible the wasteful recurrent crises which result in unemployment and idle machines. They therefore try to organise the economy so as to maintain a high level of investment. These policies have, in part, been worked out from historical studies showing that it is the cessation of investment which leads to the initial fall in demand and thus begins the vicious circle which is known as the 'downswing' period of the trade cycle. Eventually, in any case, the downward trend is reversed by forces which appear to occur spontaneously. The aim of economic policy is to make such forces appear earlier. What we observe in action in the nineteenth century are instances of these factors operating in a contra-cyclical manner.

The material available for the study of the course of events at Swindon is fuller than that used by Professor Cairncross. In addition to the national statistics such as those collected by the Board of Trade, and the printed half-yearly reports of the Great Western Railway, there are the minute books of the various committees set up by the directors to control expenditure and to make recommendations on policy. For Swindon itself, the sources are summarised in a volume issued in connection with the fiftieth anniversary of the incorporation of the borough, and drawing on material then being prepared for the forthcoming volumes of the *Victoria County History of Wiltshire*.[1] From this it is possible to derive some indication of building activity in the town during our period.

As far as the railway statistics are concerned, they are not above suspicion as a source of historical evidence. The definitions of what they measured changed quite frequently in the early days. 'Engine miles' might include non-operational runs in one year, and not in the next. Perhaps the Trevannock & St Mullion Joint Mineral Line was counted as a leased line in 1889 and not at all in 1890. More seriously, changes in fares and goods charges could affect receipts just as much as changes in the volume of traffic. Improvements in locomotive design made it possible for goods trains to be heavier, and thus reduced running mileage while traffic increased. Most of these factors are known, and adjustments could be made. But for the purposes of a survey of investment decisions, these small matters are less important. We know that the figures which appeared in the various returns were also those laid before the engineers and directors and shareholders—and they formed the basis of their deliberations. Nevertheless, it is important at all times to bear in mind running mileages, money receipts and traffic-volume figures, since together they provide a true picture of activity and profitability.

Other errors can arise from a loose definition of what is meant by 'investment'. Professor Cairncross' series were derived from contemporary

[1] L. V. Grinsell and others, *Studies in the History of Swindon* (1950); esp H. B. Wells, 'Swindon in the 19th and 20th Centuries', pp 93 ff.

newspaper sources,[1] and it may therefore be claimed that a summary from the minute books, which describe the actual orders or purchases behind the money values, are more reliable. Nevertheless, even these primary sources present difficulties. As will be shown, not all true investment was necessarily defrayed from special capital allocations. Sometimes, also, current maintenance costs may have been charged as part of a large item of capital expenditure. Accountancy was still in its infancy. Business men may have had a notion of the importance of setting aside funds out of profits to cover depreciation and thus create a source from which replacement of capital might be financed. Practice, however, was often confused. In bad years, reserves created from profits might be raided for dividends, and in the next good year capital might be raised to pay for postponed renewals. Since the control of expenditure was strict rather than logical, we find in the minute books authorisations for the construction or purchase of items ranging from a one-horse-bus costing £75 to carriages and wagons worth a quarter of a million pounds at the time of the gauge conversion. Nevertheless, an analysis of all these various items, thanks to the full description, is possible and the statistics in Table 3 should represent a fairly reliable guide to the volume of investment.

I THE RISE OF SWINDON

The new town of Swindon had been created by the decision of the board of the company, in 1840, to site there its principal locomotive depot. In that year, the line from Paddington had reached a point a little to the north of the declining market town of Swindon, a place of less than 2,000 inhabitants and in danger of total decay. The suggestion to site the works there had come from Daniel Gooch, then aged 24 and already superintendent of locomotives to the company.[2] The considerations in his mind were purely technical. Gradients on the line determined the site of the junction with the Cheltenham Railway, and the configuration of the ground also led to a meeting at this spot with a canal affording direct connection with the Somerset coalfield. Here, too, engines had to be changed, since one type of locomotive pulled the trains along the easy gradients from London, and another continued the journey across the hills to Bath and Bristol. Nearby was the Wootton Bassett incline which was thought to demand a ready stock of banking engines to assist the ascent.[3]

[1] A. K. Cairncross, op cit, p 135.

[2] The office of the chief technical officer of the company was variously described as 'superintendent' or chief superintendent of locomotives, etc, or chief engineer, and later chief mechanical and electrical engineer. The person referred to in this article as the chief engineer was the holder of the office filled in our period by Daniel Gooch, Joseph Armstrong, William Dean and George Churchward.

[3] Letter from Daniel Gooch to I. K. Brunel dated 13 September 1840, quoted in E. T. MacDermot, *History of the Great Western Railway* (1927), I, 120.

At first, in addition to a station with its refreshment rooms, there were only some primitive locomotive-repair shops and cottages for the men employed there. The place was ready for use in January 1843, but even then employed over 400 men, of whom 72 were highly skilled engineers. After 1845, locomotives were also constructed at Swindon, and from then on steady expansion took place. The driving force behind this movement came from the technical men—Isambard Kingdom Brunel, Daniel Gooch and Archibald Sturrock, the first works manager.

In these early days, there was continuous friction between these technicians and their masters, the directors in London. After each period of expansion, the slightest sign of a trade recession led to economy measures. Already in 1843, a 'sub-committee of economy' was appointed, which put Brunel on a part-time basis, ordered wage cuts and a change from piece-work to day-work. But, significantly, the numbers of those employed were not reduced below the figures recommended by Brunel as being consistent with efficiency and safety.[1] A second feature of this period was a propensity on the part of the directors to favour the supply of equipment and parts by outside manufacturers, whereas the technicians were always in favour of having the job done, more economically and more thoroughly, under their own control. Economy was to the directors' liking, but on the other hand those who, like the Baldwins, had their own interests in that sphere, did not like to see business diverted from those already engaged in it.

The history of the expansion of the works, however, shows that the technocrats usually won in the long run. Moreover, the time lag between recommendation and execution tended to grow shorter. From 1840 to 1865, when Gooch himself became chairman of the company, the directors at Paddington made a constant nuisance of themselves to their resident representative at Swindon. They wanted to know trifling details and queried most estimates. But even then, they always gave way in the end. The board could see no reason, one of the directors remarked, why they should pay their engineer a large salary, as being the best man in his trade, and then disregard his advice. Thus the company made its own engines in increasing numbers after 1846, and from 1861 it made rails in its own mill at Swindon. The ironmasters fought Gooch tooth and nail over this last innovation, and shamelessly harassed him over his cost accounts,[2] until he resigned from his position—only to reappear a year later as chairman of the company, and as the victor in the battle between technology and finance.

Yet it was understandable that the directors should be cautious about expansion at that time. The mid-forties were the period of George Hudson, the 'Railway King', a fraud remarkable even in that age. In 1847, the

[1] Great Western Railway Board Minutes, 13 February 1843 (BTHR, GW 1/3).

[2] GWR Board Minutes, 12 February 1852: GWR Correspondence, BTHR, HL 1/1/2, 3 (BTHR, GW 1/6).

empire he had built started to collapse, and every respectable company felt the draught. Railways were in bad odour and caution was natural. Moreover, a blow had befallen the Great Western Railway in 1846 which was to have consequences of importance to investment policy for 45 years. Parliament had decided that the standard gauge was to be the narrow one (4 ft 8½ in), and thus Brunel's broad gauge was doomed to extinction. The company could keep its broad lines for the time being, but competition forced it to conform gradually, first by 'mixing' the gauge and finally changing over completely to the narrow pattern. In view of these uncertainties, a contraction seemed to be called for, and a shareholders' committee was appointed under the chairmanship of T. S. Gladstone[1] to which Gooch made a report showing how the works had grown by that time. This report[2] shows, on the technical side, how much had been achieved. By 1848, 1,800 men had been employed. The place repaired and made engines, undertook general repairs of stock in connection with the locomotive department, and even built bridges which Brunel needed for South Wales. Now the directors wanted to reduce the scale of operations. But Gooch did not think that this would save money:

> Swindon has been designed and built to employ 1,800–2,000 men, and all the arrangements of tools and shops have been made to employ that number of men to the best advantage, and are therefore not so well adapted for our present diminished numbers, the fixed charges or shop expenses are in consequence heavier than they would be in a plan better proportioned to the work to be done. Any work that can be obtained will therefore assist to reduce these expenses; in fact we have the means at Swindon if we had the work, of earning at manufacturers' prices at least £20,000 p.a.

The directors, however, proved adamant for a time. Employment dropped to 600, of whom only 100 were retained on new engine construction.[3] The directors wished to exercise closer control over their expanionist engineer and a permanent expenditure and stores committee was formed.[4] It is easy to see why this was done. Gooch, for instance, took it upon himself to make goods for other companies without permission, without

[1] GWR *Half-Yearly Reports and Accounts*, 20 September 1849 (BTHR, RAC 1/165).

[2] GWR Secretary's Special Reports (BTHR, GW 18/339).

[3] The loss of the Bristol & Exeter line just before this date helped to reduce demands on Swindon. In the early days, activity was often affected by fortuitous parliamentary upheavals in shares and speculation. This element of instability gradually disappeared.

[4] Great Western Railway, Copies of the Minutes of the Directors on Locomotive matters, Swindon, contain the decisions of this and subsequent committees. They begin in September 1849. (Referred to as Loco Minutes.) The decision to establish the committee is in the GWR Board Minutes of 15 September 1849.

Editor's note. These 'Loco Minutes' do not appear to have been transferred from Swindon to the British Transport Historical Records Office. However, the main series of Great Western board minutes for this period (BTHR, GW 1/3–45) contains many of the references cited.

worrying too much about payment. This was to be stopped.[1] Fortunately for Swindon, this period of extreme caution did not last long. The dishonesty of some of the outside contractors, whom the directors insisted on employing, helped to convince them that there was something to be said for the engineer's attitude, and in the early fifties, expansion once more took place, with facilities for wagon and carriage repairs and the installation of powerful new machinery.[2] As the township around the works grew, the company began to provide certain local amenities, in part through the New Swindon Improvement Society founded in 1853 with a capital of £3,000.[3] In the sixties, in addition to the rolling mill, the company added its central carriage workshops to replace those which had previously been in existence elsewhere, but found to be uneconomical. This new venture was decided upon in 1866, precisely when the business world was shaken by a financial crisis of the first magnitude. Since the initial outlay required was £26,000, the directors were understandably reluctant to embark on the project. But by this time, Gooch was firmly in the saddle, and he knew how to sway them.[4] The new chief engineer (Joseph Armstrong) was right in claiming that carriages could be produced more economically in a place specially designed for them, and if economy could only be achieved by fresh expenditure, then expenditure there must be. Although this development was obviously unfavourable to the places where carriages had been made previously, it greatly benefited the one-industry town where the economies of scale were so manifest.

II THE GREAT DEPRESSION

Although there were recurrent trade crises, the major part of the history of the Swindon works consists of a record of continuous expansion in a booming economy between 1850 and 1873. Parliament forced the railways to keep uniform records of their traffic, and thus we know that the rise in activity was almost uninterrupted. With extensions of the system, and widespread changes in social habits, the total of miles run went up practically every year, and the intensity of traffic also increased. Receipts, too, increased almost proportionately. By 1873, the company was paying a dividend of 6¼ per cent, more than at any time for 25 years. (See Table 3.)

[1] Loco Minutes, 22 September 1849. The condition that two-thirds of such work must be paid for before it leaves Swindon works is an apt comment on some of their shaky customers. It was not a usual commercial practice.

[2] 'The advantage of making all the ironwork which can be made at Swindon for the use of the line was recognised and ordered to be the principle of arrangement with a view of getting rid of the extra Bills of contractors as much as possible.' (Loco Minutes, 22 September 1849). Some of the buildings and machinery added to the works for this new phase of expansion are in *Illustrated Exhibitor and Magazine of Art*, 3 January 1852 (BTHR).

[3] Loco Minutes, 1 September 1853.

[4] Loco Minutes, 13 May 1868.

All this might also have been said of a good many other British industries of that time. But in 1873 came a turning-point, and by most indexes of production, consumption, investment and employment, activity in Great Britain ceased to expand as fast as it had previously done. The dates at which the turning-point came vary according to the field investigated,[1] but the picture is the same almost everywhere. The internal and external causes of this change in the economic fortunes of the country are many, and not universally agreed.[2] Chief amongst the explanations are the monetary ones, relating the fall in prices, and therefore in confidence and enterprise, to the direct and indirect effects of falling gold production and rising demand. Other explanations were concerned with the costs of production, the fall in demand for shipping after the opening of the Suez canal, the emergence of Germany and the United States as serious competitors in the industrial field, and of the New World and Australasia in the production of agricultural commodities. All these eventually led to the same attitude: that expansion of capacity was a doubtful speculation, since total demand might fall, and in any case purchases should be postponed, since the same article could probably be purchased a year later at a much lower cost—an expectation which tends to bring about its own fulfilment.

As far as the railways were concerned, they were certainly not immune from the consequences of this fall in general investment on one hand and the particular consequences of certain labour-saving investments at earlier dates on the other. But the impact was both smaller and later than one might have expected. Continuous statistics are available only after 1866, but the picture they present shows clearly enough how and when the 'depression' made itself felt.[3] Investment programmes in new lines to be built which had been started before 1873 meant a steady increase in total mileage open to traffic until 1877 (Table 1), and consequent heavy orders for rolling stock down to that date. After 1877, however, only 400 miles were added to the network in 20 years. Passenger traffic receipts climbed steeply up to 1876 and then very slowly to 1888. Goods receipts, however, did not begin to stagnate until 1880. To some extent these receipts are influenced by charges, but the volume figures tell a similar story. The number of passengers carried was stagnant between 1876 and 1881, and then climbed after 1882. Since receipts did not also rise, one at once assumes the correct connection—that charges were lowered.[4] Goods traffic may be divided into

[1] Cairncross, op cit, p 69, Table 38. This shows a fall in the value of new construction in the building industry from 1877, shipbuilding from 1874, railways from 1875 and local authorities from 1878. But the four series together fell from 1874.

[2] Cf: Rostow, op cit, p 45 ff for a summary of the main explanations.

[3] All figures from Board of Trade *Railway Returns*, 1866–1900. (*Returns of the Capital, Traffic, Receipts, and Working Expenditure of the Railway Companies of the UK.*)

[4] Cheap Trains Act of 1883, abolishing duties on fares and inaugurating workmen's fares. Cf: C. E. R. Sherrington, *Economics of Rail Transport in Great Britain* (1928), p 239.

mineral traffic (particularly important for the GWR because of South Wales coal production) and general merchandise carrying. Mineral traffic failed to increase between 1882 and 1888, general merchandise between 1888 and 1895. Once again changes in charges mean that receipts and volume do not move together. But the fact which immediately strikes one in looking at these figures is that the periods of stagnation do not coincide so much as one might expect. The result is that total receipts rise over most of the period, with an intermittent drop only from 1883–6. But it has to be remembered here that all this took place at a time of rapidly falling general price levels, so that the drop in revenue is apparent rather than real. If one revalued the receipts at constant prices, the rise in real income would be continuous. It was precisely this relationship between prices and incomes which lay at the base of the continued increase in activity, albeit at a slower rate. The index of real income per head of the population constructed by Mr Prest[1] also shows a continuous rise during our period except for the years 1874–80, and 1890–3. (See Table 3.) In terms of individual families, this meant that their standard of living went up. In part, of course, this was due to cheaper imported foods.[2] If this development did not benefit the British farmer, it certainly benefited the consumer and the railwayman—before the days of lorries, the imported produce was carried to the urban markets by rail. In 1874, Acklom's refrigerator van was introduced on the Great Western Railway.[3]

The increasing real income also probably meant more passenger journeys for pleasure. The introduction of a shorter Saturday working day[4] in the seventies meant more excursions, as did relaxations in the strictness of the Victorian sabbath. As towns grew, so more people moved to the suburbs, and the seventies and eighties were the heyday of the steam train carrying folks to work from the salubrious villas of Acton and Edgbaston. The word 'suburban' first appeared in the timetables of the Great Western Railway in 1869.[5] The seaside holiday was becoming possible for ever-increasing numbers of people. These features also introduced a measure of competition into an industry where, owing to amalgamations, local monopolies were gradually emerging.

[1] A. R. Prest, 'National Income of the United Kingdom, 1870–1946', in *Economic Journal*, Vol 58 (1948), 58–9.

[2] Cf: the index of imported food prices in P. Rousseaux, *Les mouvements de fond de l'économie anglaise, 1800–1913* (1938), pp 264–5. This index fell from 145 in 1874 to 77 in 1896—almost half.

[3] Loco Minutes, 22 July 1874.

[4] The GWR reduced its working week in conformity with the practice of other companies to 57½ hours in 1871 (Loco Minutes, 4 October 1874), and then to 54 (Board Reports and Memoranda, 15 November 1871) (Swindon).

[5] T. B. Peacock, *Great Western Suburban Services* (1948), p 3.

III INVESTMENT POLICY IN THE GREAT DEPRESSION

Within the Great Western Railway policy was made, as we have seen, by the board of directors on the advice of their engineers. To some extent, both these sets of people must have been affected by the prevailing pessimism of the time. Gooch, though by training also a technical man, and first and foremost a devoted servant of the company, was not by any means insensitive to financial considerations. Following the peculiar customs of his time, he engaged in private business even while he was the salaried employee of the company. When the directors once refused to ensure a good permanent coal supply, he himself went into business, setting up the Ruabon Coal Company which sold fuel to his own employers.[1] When he left their service and returned as a director, he had numerous other irons in the fire, and was, by 1873, a wealthy business man. When he took over the direction of the company at a critical moment, he said that 'economy was the watchword', but always subject to efficiency being maintained.[2] As for his fellow directors, they were much less likely to sanction large capital expenditure in difficult times for purely technical reasons.

On the other hand, a particularly close relationship existed between the engineers and the chairman who had once been their colleague, and this probably helped to preserve the balance. One of the first factors in keeping investment going was the manifest absurdity of abandoning at the half-way stage projects which had been conceived before 1873, for which parliamentary sanction had been obtained and which shareholders had already approved. The impetus of this movement may be said to have carried the business through at any rate to 1876–7, when orders for new engines effectively ceased for a while. The fact was that the new mileage did not come up to expectation in expanding the company's business. A careful scrutiny of the accounts showed the directors an alarming state of affairs. From 1876–7 the track mileage of the company expanded by about one-sixth, yet passengers and goods carried, and consequently receipts, failed to expand at all. In other words, the lines were less intensively used than formerly and the need for renewal of equipment, much of it brand new, was much smaller than before. This phase—when inventories are full of recently completed stocks—is well known to students of trade cycles, and this, added to a bad trade outlook, meant a momentary cessation of investment. The year 1880 marked the smallest annual investment in our table of corrected moving average figures. (See Table 3.) But it also marks, in most of the series of statistics relating to the period, the beginning of a notice-

[1] *Diaries of Sir D. Gooch* (ed Sir T. Martin, 1892), p 68.

[2] Op cit, p xix. There is no suggestion that Gooch had ever wasted money. An inspection committee under Frederick Ponsonby in 1857 (Appendix to GWR Board Minutes, 25 June 1857, BTHR, GW 1/11) suggests that Gooch achieved economy by manipulating piece work rates whenever the men appeared to earn too much.

able, though short-lived, revival of buoyancy, reaching its peak in 1883. Prices, production and foreign trade all rose in 1880 compared with 1879, and railway traffic went up *pari passu*.

Yet the response in investment was slow. In part this must have been because, as already mentioned, so much equipment was still relatively new. Between 1871 and 1878, the number of locomotives went up from 959 to 1,530, of which at least 240 were new ones. Between 1878 and 1888, only 70 engines were built at Swindon—a fraction of the former rate. A similar story emerges from statistics for coaches and goods wagons. (See Table 2.) But this does not mean that all activity at Swindon came to a standstill. Admittedly, not so much new stock was required. But old stock had to be brought up to date. The lines were not fully used—hence the drop in profitability. To use them more fully meant attracting new business—excursions, holidays, a predilection for suburban houses on that line. This meant investment in safety and comfort.

In the period 1875–6, a large number of accidents gave rise to urgent discussion about brake systems.[1] The government was pressing for research to be done so that an effective system could be made the subject of legislation. Continuous brakes, as developed by the firm later known as Westinghouse, had been experimentally introduced before that time, and most new carriages built seem to have been fitted with one or other type of continuous brake. From 1878 the pressure mounted to such an extent that the directors were obliged to vote a sum each year, usually amounting to about £20,000, to convert existing stock.[2] This went on until the fitting of such brakes finally became law, and public opinion asserted itself more strongly than through the price mechanism. Competition also forced the company to adopt upholstery for third-class carriages from 1865 onwards. Gas lighting to replace the smoky oil lamps came in, only to give way later to electric lighting.[3]

There were other factors which, by 1880, secured Swindon against the full rigours of depression. The vast increase in stock and activity in the seventies meant an expansion of the minimum maintenance work which had to be done to keep the system going. Engines, carriages, signals, lamps, water tanks, pumps—all came back to Swindon to be repaired. Moreover, as the directors' reluctance to commission fresh equipment increased, so much more repair work had to be done. Engines, in particular, underwent a process of refurbishing which must have meant little less demand on capital and manpower than a new order. One year the boiler was renewed,

[1] Cf: letter from general manager of Metropolitan Railway, 22 January 1878 (Board Reports and Memoranda). He claimed that if continuous brakes had been fitted, a bad accident could have been avoided.

[2] Saunders and Bolitho's system was used in the main. Loco Minutes, 6 November 1878.

[3] After 1900. Locomotive Carriage and Stores Committee Minutes, 25 February 1900. (These will be referred to as LC & S Minutes) (BTHR, GW 1/265).

the driving wheels the next, and the cab and main body the next, until nothing remained except the nameplate and number, like the famous pipe which the old gentleman kept going 60 years, nothing being renewed except, alternately, the stem and the bowl.

From the minutes one has an impression that the work did not suffer as serious an interruption as mere annual summaries make one suppose. For one thing, there was a time lag. If we speak of orders ceasing in 1879 this does not mean total cessation of work even in one department. The orders of 1879 were not completed until 1881, and so on. Moreover, the money values attached to the orders are not good guides. For reasons of their own, the engineers put in estimates for new locomotives year after year at £2,000 each (or £1,500 in the case of a smaller type), quite regardless of the fact that engines were all the time becoming more elaborate and costly in real terms (though falling prices in the depression period may to some extent have countered this tendency). Ten engines were asked for at £20,000 in 1867, 20 at £30,000 in 1873, 30 at £45,000 in 1876, 20 again at £35,000 or £36,000 in 1882, 1887, 1891 and 1897—hardly a good index of technical or price changes.

One is inclined to attribute this curious state of affairs partly to the primitive state of the science of cost accounting, so that with the best will in the world the engineer at Swindon could not accurately say what the 'real' cost of each completed engine should be, allowing for all overheads. But one suspects that even if he knew the answer, he was reluctant to alter the traditional figure. It is easy to see why. Firstly, if the directors inquired from outside contractors (as they still did occasionally until Gooch became chairman), the price quoted would be, inevitably, much higher than their own engineer's. This would ensure a continued pressure on the directors to give all possible orders to the establishment. Secondly, the main difficulty between the financial and technical direction lay in the separation of capital from running expenditure. It was hard to persuade the shareholders, through the directors, that the time was opportune for fresh capital outlay. The need to maintain existing stock in good order was not questioned, subject to general economy. If, therefore, a good deal of the work done on new stock could be put down to ordinary repairs and maintenance and if, in particular, none of the overheads such as engineers' salaries, were charged to the capital account, a great deal more work could be done at Swindon than one would guess from the capital investment figures.

Apart from the engineer's natural anxiety to keep his equipment up to date, he would have another strong reason for doing all he could to keep work flowing. The labour force at Swindon was highly skilled. Exact statistics are not available. But in the earliest days about one-sixth of the total force consisted of qualified engineering workers. This proportion is not likely to have dropped over the years. In 1875, 4,000 people were employed in the works, and thus it is not unreasonable to assume a concentration of something like 1,000 specialised workmen. The future expansion of the undertaking, which was confidently expected, would depend on these workmen being available. As we know from social surveys of this period, men with such high qualifications were not dependent on a single employer. There were plenty of openings for them in the United States and elsewhere, where the period of railway expansion had not yet come to an end. The census reports[1] show how Swindon had, in the sixties, acquired many people from South Wales—many of them skilled ironworkers at the time of the opening of the rail rolling mills. Such men would go where the work was, and the chief engineer, looking forward to the great task of conversion to the narrow gauge, as well as the inevitable trade revival, would do his best to keep his force intact.

Different questions of policy are raised when one examines the type of machinery installed during the years of depression. One of the explanations often advanced for the falling prices of the seventies concerns the re-equipment of industry with labour-saving devices as the result of high wage costs in the boom years. One possible corollary to that view is that the cheapening of real labour costs in the depression would lead to a reduction in investment in specifically labour-saving devices. But such a change would be the result of an examination of the position by a cost accountant or financial director, and even then it would presuppose that costs of labour had fallen faster than costs of capital equipment, or that the marginal productivity of labour had risen faster than that of capital equipment. For such a view there is no evidence. In fact prices of investment goods fell much more drastically:

Index numbers (1907 = 100)

	1873	*1880*	*1885*	*1892*
Wage rates	85	81	82	89
Prices of investment goods	125	77	75	84

Source: Tinbergen, op cit, Table 1A.

Thus we find that expensive items were purchased or constructed during some of the time here described which are definitely to be classed as 'labour-saving', such as portable riveting machines (January 1882) or a wagon lifting shop costing £8,500 in January 1887, and so on.[2]

[1] *Studies in the History of Swindon*, table, p 144, showing that in 1871 those born in Wales formed the largest group of residents apart from those born in Wiltshire. (These will be referred to as *Studies*.)

[2] Loco Minutes, 18 January 1882; 6 June 1881 (sandblaster); 14 March 1883 (welding machine). One of the difficulties here is that one cannot be sure that the full extent of the adoption of labour-saving tools is measured by authorisations of capital expenditure. (See p 178 above.) In the Loco Minutes for 20 February 1861 Gooch was shown as asking for £5,000 worth of tools. After much discussion, it was decided that these were to be charged to capital, in the same way as engines, apparently after someone had worked out that the construction of 20 locomotives at Swindon would show a 'profit' of

IV THE FALL OF 1884–6 AND THE RECOVERY

However great the desire of the engineers to keep the works going at full stretch, the second trough in the depression was bound to have far-reaching consequences. The short-lived boom of 1883–4 collapsed, and with it the railway's traffic. Throughout the history of the company, total traffic increased with only minor lapses. If we take the number of miles run by passenger and goods trains, rather than receipts or volume of traffic, as our index figure, we have the even more astonishing fact that these mileages actually increased every year (comparing the half-yearly figures—the first half of the year always showed lower returns than the second half, owing to obvious seasonal influences). Only a few exceptions occur to this—passenger mileages dropped in 1879 and between the first half of 1884 and the first half of 1885, and goods mileages in 1874, 1878, 1881 and continuously from 1883 to 1886. (See Table 1.) The significance of this drop in passenger mileage should be appreciated. By 1885, railways were an institution and a public service to a sufficient extent to make their passenger schedules almost sacrosanct. Trains might be more or less full—but they would run, since the public expected it. Trains might be added as traffic demanded it—but to withdraw them, as the managers did in 1885, meant a really serious loss of confidence. This alone would indicate widespread unemployment, since the principal trains affected were workmen's trains and excursions. This supposition is fully confirmed by evidence relating directly to employment figures.[1] With these facts before them, the directors naturally reduced authorisations for fresh capital expenditure to a new low record of only about £2,000 for new machinery in 1885. But even at this rather grim period, we can see that the depression must be temporary. The conversion of the Cornwall Railway to narrow gauge running was urgent, partly so as to provide the convenience of through trains—an operation which would cost £128,000.[2] But although the directors approved of this operation in principle, in April 1885, they could not yet authorise the work to begin. In March 1886 it again came up for discussion, and was again turned down. Finally, in February 1887 came the only recorded instance when a direct application by the engineer for fresh authorisations of rolling stock for ordinary operating purposes was turned down.

Now one would expect that this black period would be reflected in employment figures at Swindon. But once again the works weathered the

£6,000—more than the cost of tools. The profit is to be seen as the difference between the potential contractors' prices and Gooch's. These tools may well have been machine tools, at least in part, but the practice may not have been followed at all times.

[1] W. W. Rostow, op cit, p 49: 'The years 1884–7 were probably the worst continuous sequence from the point of view of unemployment, of any throughout this era'. The tables in Tinbergen (op cit) suggest that 1879 was worse, but the trough not so prolonged.

[2] MacDermot, op cit, II, 374.

storm. In October 1884, William Dean, the chief engineer, reporting on the economies he had made as a result of the reduction in train mileages, announced that he had arranged for a general laying off of hands—except at Swindon.[1] In other words, depression meant concentration for the sake of efficiency. The large unit triumphed at the expense of the smaller ones.

1887 saw a general revival of trade similar to that of 1880. Once again the statistics of the railways provide an extraordinarily sensitive barometer to general conditions. The half-yearly returns for the first six months of 1887, laid before the directors in August of that year, at once showed that the downward trend of traffic had been reversed, and the first order for locomotives since 1884 was put in.[2] This was followed in February 1888 by a large order for rolling stock, all goods wagons.[3] By 1889, orders for passenger stock were also resumed, together with a large number of specialised wagons for purposes clearly indicating the changing demands of the economy—fish, meat and poultry vans, and trucks for carrying agricultural machinery.[4]

With 1889, we enter on the last big phase of investment at Swindon, and with it the final triumph of technical necessity over mere financial considerations. The minor boom which was noticeable in the economy as a whole from 1888 to 1891, indeed, coincided with the beginning of a large programme of construction on the railway. But in this case, the technical impetus carried forward the high level of employment and production at Swindon until 1894. 1895 was a year of comparatively few fresh orders, but the upward trend was resumed in 1896. After that date, there were, admittedly, a few more years when the level of orders temporarily dropped, for one reason or another (1898, 1900, 1905, 1909) but on the whole the advance continues unchecked. By 1905, employment at Swindon had reached the record total of 14,000—nearly three times as many as there had been in 1875. In 1873, the stock and buildings ordered on capital account were valued at £371,000, in 1891 the figure was £681,000, and £1,183,000 in 1913.

How did this come about? First of all, the completion of gauge conversion, which had been suspended in 1886, could now no longer be delayed, and once it was decided to reduce the number of lines still running on the broad gauge, the matter gained momentum of its own account—the fewer of the old lines there were, the more unprofitable it became to maintain them, their engines and rolling stock. In February 1891 it was finally resolved to complete the conversion operation by May 1892.[5] This meant an ambitious programme of some hundreds of locomotives and thousands of wagons, whose construction had, of necessity, to be spread over a few years.

[1] Loco Minutes, 29 October 1884.
[2] Loco Minutes, 3 August 1887.
[3] Loco Minutes, 1 February 1888.
[4] Loco Minutes, 5 February 1889.
[5] MacDermot, op cit, II, 375.

The second influence was that of public safety and convenience. In 1890 came a Board of Trade order making the block telegraph system of working trains compulsory, and also ordering interlocking points and continuous brakes. The engineer estimated that this would take a four years' programme of making and installing equipment and of course there was no question of refusing this order.[1] Coming on top of the gauge conversion, it meant a considerable enlargement of premises, machinery and employment at Swindon. Although exact figures are not available, it may be assumed that employment in 1892 exceeded 10,000. At any rate the reduction of hands ordered early in 1893[2] is to be seen only as a removal of some temporary staff engaged to cope with the exceptional rush, and not as an interruption of the upward trend of employment figures. In addition to technical change and measures for safety, passenger comfort became increasingly important. In 1863 a carriage had cost about £250 at the most. By 1883, the eight-wheeled, upholstered and gas-lit carriages cost £720. By 1892 the price was over £1,000.[3] We may be certain that these improvements did not proceed from the aesthetic predilections of the engineer or the directors. The family's choice of Newquay as a holiday resort, rather than the nearer Brighton or Eastbourne, would depend on the discomfort one might experience on the longer journey. The fare from London to Birmingham was the same on the Great Western as on the LNWR.

Soon, these heavier carriages presented the company with a fresh problem. A train composed of 10 or 12 of them could no longer be hauled at the advertised speed by most of the existing engines. For some time, the matter was solved by having only a few of the better carriages on each train, for first-class passengers. This soon became unworkable. The design of locomotives, which had not varied significantly from the days of Gooch's reign at Swindon through that of Armstrong and Dean, underwent a revolution at the hands of G. J. Churchward, who had become assistant chief superintendent at Swindon in 1897 and was in charge from 1902. The monsters he built cost over £4,000 even by the extraordinary method of estimation used at Swindon. They could no longer be built by the orthodox methods, and a constant stream of new sheds, presses, lifting tackle, traversing bays, heavy presses, and such like, was ordered and could not be refused, since each new development followed logically from the last. In the reign of Churchward, as the awed reader of his memoranda is inclined to call it, the process of expansion had finally become an autonomous force. That this was not so, events after 1920 demonstrated only too clearly, but the appearances are certainly impressive. The shareholders had no reason to complain, since after the beginning of Churchward's tenure, the dividend

[1] Loco Minutes, 27 March 1890.

[2] LC & S Minutes, 12 April 1893 (BTHR, GW 1/263).

[3] These prices are approximately comparable. Cf: Tinbergen, op cit, Table 1A, investment goods price index.

did not drop again below 5 per cent and reached 6 per cent in 1913. The statistics of receipts and volume of traffic are equally formidable. The number of passengers carried, which had been 50 million in 1885, reached 80 million by 1900 and 100 million by 1908.[1]

V WAGES

Only very little evidence is contained in the Swindon minutes and reports with regard to earnings in our period. In general it is known that wage rates and earnings fell much less sharply than prices, and the series in the work of Tinbergen and others suggest a very substantial rise in real wages. The boom of the early seventies had already brought a rise in money wages as well as a reduction in hours, that is, an increased hourly rate of pay. Even meal hours were extended.[2] In September 1872, the mechanics asked for a rise, and Armstrong was given a free hand by the directors to accede to this demand or not as he thought fit.[3] Detailed results of this application are not known, but certain concessions were announced early in 1873, including 2s 6d extra for London residents.[4] It may be assumed that some general improvements in earnings resulted from these changes. After this, we hear nothing until 1879, the year we have already characterised as one of the two periods of deepest depression. William Dean's report to the directors is not specific,[5] but he indicated that all grades would be reclassified 'in proportion to the nature of the work performed'. Undoubtedly this indicates the dismissal of some unskilled men and the downgrading of skilled ones. Lest one should be in doubt as to the effects of this regrading the minute goes on to say 'that in consideration of the saving to be effected under the new regulations it was agreed to increase the subscription to the Enginemen's and Firemen's Mutual Assurance Society from £800 to £1,200 pa'. The new system (which applied only to footplate staff—nothing is said about the engineers) seems to have been grossly unfair, and a number of protests are recorded[6] but upward readjustments were not made until December 1880, with more substantial concessions, following prolonged and bitter negotiations, in 1883.[7] No fresh reductions seem to have been made during the second deep depression period in 1885, and in 1889 a further restoration of the 1879 cuts was granted.[8] Since the annual cost of

[1] A superficial study of the statistics leads to errors here. After 1900, train mileage for passenger and especially for goods trains fell, or failed to rise. This seems to contradict the expansion of traffic noted elsewhere until one remembers that Churchward's engines pulled twice the load of their predecessors.

[2] Loco Minutes, 22 January, 1873.

[3] Ibid, 2 February 1872.

[4] Ibid, 22 January 1873.

[5] Ibid, 27 August 1879.

[6] Ibid, 22 October, 12 November, 17 December 1879, 7 April 1880.

[7] Ibid, 1 December 1880, 18 July 1883.

[8] Ibid, 4 December 1889. Cf: detailed accounts in Board Reports and Memoranda, July–November 1889.

this was to be £10,000, the extra contribution to the assurance fund of £400 appears cynical.

This information, it must be emphasised, relates only to a small part of those involved at Swindon, namely the footplatemen who were based on the town. There are no *a priori* grounds for assuming that the men (and women) in the workshops were treated differently. The engine drivers were highly skilled men, the firemen less so. The same distinctions would apply to people in the works, though the latter also included a proportion of totally unskilled workers. Perhaps nothing is heard about them because they were less well organised than the footplatemen. At any rate no strikes seem to have been threatened by either set of men, though deputations were frequent. No mention of trade unions occurs in any of the minutes until 1891,[1] though even in 1872 Armstrong had suspected the presence of 'agitators'.[2]

On this basis, it is clearly impossible to say what happened to real wages during our period. The most likely interpretation is that wages were steady in the seventies while activity still continued at a high level, and therefore real wages increased quite considerably. In 1879, a sharp reduction was made, which was not remedied until 1889, but since prices were also much lower, it is at least possible that real wages did not deteriorate. Hours were shorter, and, as we have seen, there was no general dismissal of hands until after the conversion boom of 1891.

VI SWINDON TOWN

In the absence of unemployment statistics and other relevant material, it is difficult to make any precise statement of the impact of the years here described on the life of Swindon. If what we have described is correct, there were two periods of hardship, culminating in 1879 and 1885. The census figures suggest that Swindon population expanded more rapidly in the seventies than in the eighties—but that applies to the country as a whole and may have as much to do, directly, with more successful birth-control propaganda than with economic circumstances—though it could no doubt be argued that depression made the adoption of birth control more necessary. A far better indication of what went on is provided by a tabulation of public building investment in the town.

There were, in the main, four sources of capital for such projects. First of all, there were the buildings put up by the company for the welfare of its employees. These would naturally be dependent on the same sort of considerations as other works investment. Secondly, there was municipal building, by which we mean the work of such agencies as the health board and the school board as well as the proper local authority which followed

[1] Loco Minutes, 8 January 1891.
[2] Board Reports and Memoranda, 12 December 1872.

it. The decision to borrow on the security of the rates would also be partly dependent on the state of prosperity—quite apart from the fact that the company's senior employees were also the most active members of the local boards and that the company, one way or another, was the principal ratepayer. Thirdly, there were the voluntary religious bodies, whose subscribing members were, once again, the employees of the railway or the tradesmen who supplied them. Lastly, there were buildings of a commercial nature, put up privately, but depending for their profitability on the expenditure of the local employees. In a word, everything that was done depended on the level of income of the Swindon citizens. The state was not responsible for subsidising any of this expenditure, and as a market town for the farmers of the surrounding countryside, Swindon was of little or no importance.[1]

If, therefore, the periods of depression listed, as well as the whole long period from 1873 to 1896, were of great significance to the town, this should be reflected in the rate of local building. But the record does not suggest any such effect. Admittedly, years like 1891 stand out in the burst of civic pride and expenditure they generate—a new school, the town hall and municipal buildings, and Regent Circus were all opened in that year. But in 1877–9, the newly established school board also built four schools, and the company built another in 1881. In 1887, the jubilee celebrations were fittingly marked by the start of the Victoria Hospital. Even commercial building did not come to a standstill during the black period, if Mr Betjeman's dating of the terraces of shops in Milton Road may be accepted.[2]

But the most formidable array of building in the depression period is ecclesiastical. Apart from a Particular Baptist chapel built in 1843, and the Old Town parish church erected in 1851, there were six 'pre-depression' nonconformist chapels all built in the sixties. The cost for the rebuilding of the Methodist chapel in 1862 (£1,200) is probably representative of all of them. The comparative lack of new buildings in the seventies should probably be put down to the fact that there were for the time being enough religious edifices. A Catholic church was built in 1875. But from 1877 to 1890, covering the two major periods of recession, a total of ten churches were built, and a rough comparison shows that on the whole these were larger and better edifices than the earlier ones. They include the Anglican churches of St Paul's (1881) and St Barnabas (1885) as well as the curious building of St Saviour's, opened in 1890, built by railway workers in their spare time. This may in itself be taken as an indication of rather more leisure than was wanted in the eighties—nevertheless, the costs must have been considerable. On the nonconformist side we have the impressive Baptist chapel in Regent Circus, opened in 1886 and reported to have cost £6,000 —a large sum to defray from voluntary contributions if a significant part of the population is unemployed or under-employed. Six other chapels

[1] *Studies*, p 136. [2] Op cit, p 176.

fall into the same period. The historian fond of dating his periods of prosperity in an area from its architecture would be misled by Swindon's appearance, unless he chose to take into account the poverty of the design.

The census figures of private dwelling houses, unfortunately, like the population as a whole, are available only in decennial periods. But at least they suggest that housebuilding kept pace with population, and that the degree of overcrowding did not become worse. The houses might be drab, but they were sound enough to survive to our own day. In the nineties, various municipal improvements such as electric lighting were begun, a technical school started and the hospital enlarged. Looking back over the growth of Swindon as a whole, it is impossible to detect any sure signs of a serious setback in development.

VII THE STABILISING FACTORS

We must now sum up by examining the factors operating in the industrial and social pattern of the place to prevent a collapse. Many people have pointed out that a 'one-industry town' is not a healthy place, and Swindon itself has made great efforts, now successful, in reducing its dependence on a remote board of directors at Paddington. Looking at the organisation superficially, it certainly appears that the board, with one stroke of the pen, could have deprived thousands of their livelihood and killed the town—a phenomenon not unknown in the nineteen thirties. Why did this not happen?

The first answer undoubtedly lies in the position of the chief engineer. Gooch was the prototype of a new man. His origins were not humble—he came from a family with industrial interests, and received a good education. When he was appointed as locomotive superintendent under Brunel in 1837, he was only 21, but his knowledge of the subject was great. He had worked under the Stephensons and other well-known engineers. Even then, his salary was therefore £300, or five to six times the income of a fairly skilled workman. It was a gentleman's salary for an engineer's job. He thought it was too little, and in less than ten years it went up to £1,000. From 1851 until his retirement it was £1,500. This, as we have seen, did not constitute his sole income. Apart from his private financial ventures, he served as adviser to other undertakings, his own employers occasionally paid him a handsome bonus (£500 in 1846), and like most professional men, he took pupils. After 1850, he probably never earned less than £2,000 a year. This income put him on a footing of equality with his directors. Technically, he was their master, financially their equal, by origin he was superior to some and equal to most of them. He established a position of great authority. His income and status should be compared to what he would have had in an industrial undertaking of the conventional sort, where the manager was the creature of the partners and had an income of perhaps £300 per annum. Much of this may have been due to Gooch's personality. But the main reason is to be sought in the organisation and legal position of a railway company. The directors were not proprietors. They were merely elected by the shareholders of a joint stock undertaking. The capital involved was so large that, except in the early stages, no family could hope to hold a controlling interest. There were few full-time directors and those who had another occupation served on more than one board. The chief officer was a secretary who was responsible for finances, knew little or nothing about technology, and was the servant of the board in law and of the engineer in fact. Moreover, as Parliament not only created each company, but by successive Acts (especially Gladstone's of 1844) controlled what the railways might and might not do, the companies were, increasingly, public utilities. In 1844, Gladstone had uttered the threat of nationalisation if they put profit before safety and efficiency. One department of state after another made orders or contracts—the Board of Trade, the War Office, and especially the Post Office. The Great Western Railway was the Royal Line ever since Queen Victoria chose to travel to Windsor by train, which she then did invariably, until she took her last journey.[1] The standards of conduct of railway servants were always a favourite topic for writers of letters to *The Times*. Each apparent dereliction of duty was the occasion for a demand for legislation. Accidents were matters for public inquiry and stern rebukes in official reports. Economy measures were thus handicapped from the start.

In the face of such pressure, the railway directors had to rely on their chief executives to judge what was right and necessary. That is why they gave them freedom, responsibility and a large salary. The office of the chief engineer or superintendent assumed increasing dignity with the years. Churchward, who controlled 14,000 workers at Swindon alone, as well as some 5,000 engine drivers and firemen, was probably the head of the largest single industrial establishment of his day in England, if not in Europe. He was also the foremost designer of locomotives, and built every other sort of equipment. He was, to a large extent, his own personnel director and conducted his own wage negotiations. He had many apprentices and pupils, who between them paid him £2,500 per annum in fees. The company paid him as much again. His income, allowing for price changes and taxations was probably on a level with that of the highest paid industrial executives of today. He took an active interest in the town of Swindon and was its charter mayor.

William Dean and Joseph Armstrong were less formidable figures than their predecessor Gooch or their successor Churchward, but their position was similar. All designed locomotives as well as retaining general charge of

[1] There are numerous references in the minutes to the construction and alteration of royal carriages. This work might also be deemed to have been independent of trade fluctuations.

the works. (There were, of course, managers in charge of the locomotive and carriage works respectively, but they played, apparently, a subordinate part.) Though all these men had their battles with the directors in their early days especially, it is easy to see why the board had to give way. The engineer had two aces up his sleeve: one was the threat of accidents due to faulty equipment,[1] and the other was the demonstration that in the long run a financial saving would result from the step recommended. This is why we seldom hear of prolonged friction, except for the episode about the rolling mill in the sixties.

We interpret these relationships as the beginnings of the rule of the technocrat, the 'managerial revolution' of the twentieth century. These engineers were men who held their posts through strength of their professional qualifications and their character. In the days of Stephenson and Brunel, technical knowledge was still something of legendary quality. By the end of the nineteenth century, there were recognised professional institutions for civil and mechanical engineers. These bodies, through their membership, conferred status on their members. Even without patrician birth or landed property, the new professional class could aspire to the magistracy, a seat in Parliament, and even a baronetcy.

It is not surprising, then, to find the new technocrat playing the role of a public servant. Despite their obviously intense loyalty to the company employing them, the engineers had a wider responsibility, in the same way that an officer owes his duty to the crown, however intense his attachment to his regiment. This type of man was to be found also in the Post Office, and in later ages the industrial civil servant became a common figure. One source of stability, then, was the emergence of the professional engineer-manager.

A second set of factors tending to work in the same direction must be sought in the pressures set up by the need to remain competitive within the framework of a public service—a contradiction in terms as it appears to us now, and an economic tightrope even in the 1880s. Mere caution might have led to safety, accompanied by economic ruin. In the days of George Hudson, anxiety to pay a dividend where there were no real profits, and need to advertise efficiency by boasting about speed led to hair-raising performances on a meagre budget. The regulations in force by the end of the century, which ran to volumes, prevented this sort of criminal behaviour. This then was the task of the engineer: to ensure the standards laid down by Parliament and jealously watched by the public without prejudicing, at least, the maintenance of the customary dividend. If rails had to be re-laid on the narrow gauge, and rolling stock renewed, the conversion had to be made to coincide as accurately as possible with the end of the useful life of the obsolete equipment, or else, if unavoidably something was left in serviceable condition, it had to be sold off to some other concern. If new

[1] Loco Minutes, 4 October 1882: 'New engines cannot be delayed any longer.'

carriages were constructed, it would be necessary to foresee the next public or parliamentary demand for comfort or safety, so as to save expensive rebuilding and the loss occasioned by having the stock out of service.

A third set of factors operated particularly in the case of Swindon. The place had been carefully chosen by men who knew their work. From 1840 onwards, the chief care of the men in charge was to promote the efficiency of the place. The successive heads of the workshops took an active part in Swindon's local life and felt a sense of personal responsibility, reflected in their requests to the directors for money for amenities which benefited both their workpeople and the town as a whole. Although there is no specific reference to this point in the Swindon papers, one feels that Dean, for instance, was aware that the town depended on the railway alone, and that a reduction of staffs elsewhere was not so disastrous as it would be to Swindon. But even without this philanthropic motive, the advantages of concentrating all work under the direct supervision of the chief engineer were patent. This was shown in the debate over the siting of the carriage works in 1866. There had been a strong argument in favour of Oxford. Daniel Gooch advocated Swindon. The University of Oxford objected to the proposal to use Port Meadow for the purpose. When Richard Potter (Beatrice's father) was still chairman, the matter was as yet undecided. As soon as Gooch took over the direction of affairs, Swindon got the works, and not from any sentimental regard for the Meadow.

It was possible to prove that concentration kept down costs. Today, the industrial economist might doubt whether the assembly of such a large mass of skilled workers was necessarily the most efficient way of organising the concern, on managerial grounds. In the days of Churchward no such qualms were felt. That the policy was not unsuccessful may be judged by the fact that, in time, other companies followed the example of the Great Western, when they grew to sufficient size, and concentrated their works either in a town practically created for the purpose (as at Crewe) or at any rate largely dependent on this one industry (Eastleigh, Wolverton).

The conclusions from this investigation seem to be fairly clear. The 'Great Depression' was essentially a crisis of confidence—a time of falling prices when the profitability of capital fell. New ways of investment had to be found, many of them advantageous to the community. But where profit was the sole criterion projects important to the social or economic future of the country would be neglected. The idea that the state should make it its business to ensure investment for minimum standards was not yet born. Successive housing Acts attempted to lead private individuals and local authorities to provide accommodation without helping them to do so. From the Fabian Society first came coherent suggestions that this type of investment might best be undertaken under circumstances where there was no need to ask, in each accounting period, whether the provision of a public service paid for itself. This view seemed outrageous to orthodox finance. Yet, on the railways, something very nearly akin to a public service not primarily concerned with profit was being slowly developed. As it happened, after the initial period of speculation the railway services in the British Isles were not again in danger of suspension through bankruptcy, without a public subsidy, until much later. But if railways were not made a state concern, as a whole or in part, as in most European countries, it was surely because they acted for the most part as if they were public utilities. It is suggested that this organisation proved itself to be useful in times of crisis in promoting contra-cyclical investment, and in saving Swindon from the worst effects of the 'Great Depression'.

TABLE 1 GREAT WESTERN RAILWAY: TRACK MILEAGE AND INTENSITY OF TRAFFIC, 1866–1900

	Miles of Line Open (*)	*Passenger Engine Miles Run* (000's)		*Intensity Passenger Traffic* (†)	*Goods Engine Miles Run* (000's)		*Intensity Goods Traffic* (†)
		Jan-June	*July-Dec*		*Jan-June*	*July-Dec*	
66	1254	3277	3643	5520	3114	3584	5340
67	1276	3467	3696	5610	3438	3586	5500
68	1306	3565	3746	5600	3524	3684	5520
69	1321	3748	3975	5850	3720	4017	5860
70	1321	3971	3996	6030	3879	4209	6120
71	1321	3986	4143	6150	4219	4675	6730
72	1325	4141	4313	6380	4862	5073	7500
73	1384	4355	4464	6370	5190	5418	7660
74	1500	4388	4578	5980	4932	5440	6910
75	1548	4556	4797	6040	4950	5832	6970
76	1777	6086	6090	6850	6521	6918	7560
77	2053	6028	6152	**5930**	6671	6920	6620
78	2092	6240	6431	6060	**6625**	**6916**	**6470**
79	2099	**6200**	**6384**	6000	6793	7163	6650
80	2100	6487	6715	6290	7258	7396	6980
81	2124	6638	6988	6420	**6218**	7913	6650
82	2170	6661	7123	6350	7744	8061	7280
83	2205	6881	7416	6480	7949	8098	7280
84	2235	7138	7482	6540	7937	7899	7090
85	2281	**6918**	7513	6330	7641	7777	6760
86	2328	7035	7597	**6290**	**7488**	**7687**	**6520**
87	2361	7219	7906	6410	7486	7858	6500
88	2382	7419	8115	6520	7829	8072	6680
89	2391	7698	8682	6850	8137	8528	6970
90	2401	8140	9160	7210	8441	8842	7200
91	2404	8537	9622	7550	8851	9157	7490
92	2405	8889	9693	7730	9040	9224	7590
93	2413	8973	9843	7800	8784	9137	7840
94	2421	9247	10054	7970	9405	9367	7750
95	2429	9338	10334	8100	9216	9657	8180
96	2453	9772	11082	8500	9807	10286	8190
97	2475	10256	11502	8790	10264	10629	8440
98	2493	10441	11870	8950	9951	10331	8140
99	2505	10890	12195	9220	11097	11464	9010
00	2515	11127	12151	9260	11632	11503	9200

urce: Half-yearly Reports.

(*) Average of figures of 31 December of previous year and 31 December of current year (from MacDermot, op cit).

(†) Intensity = Number of miles run in year divided by mean number of miles open to traffic.

ote: In all tables, the years in which the most marked drop in activity or the bottom of the trough occurred, are distinguished by bold figures. The two troughs of 1879 and 1885–6 are thus clearly indicated.

TABLE 2 GREAT WESTERN RAILWAY: RECEIPTS AND VOLUME OF TRAFFIC CARRIED, 1866–1900

	Receipts				*Number of Passengers carried*	*Goods Carried*		*Rolling Stock in Service*		
	Passenger (£000's)	*Goods* (£000's)	*Total* (£000's)	*Per Mile* (*)	(000's)	*Minerals* ('000 *tons*)	*Gen Merch'ise* ('000 *tons*)	*Loco-motives*	*Carriages*	*Goods Wagons*
1866	1947	1950	3897	3100	19504	6012	2379	814	1351	15897
1867	1940	1974	3914	3070	20925	6423	2267	842	1441	16169
1868	1958	2017	3975	3040	23304	6453	2302	867	1441	17226
1869	2005	2109	4114	3060	23103	—	—	903	1581	17693
1870	2031	2219	4250	3070	23779	—	—	929	1643	18462
1871	2143	2394	4537	3170	25390	7943	2771	959	1776	19583
1872	2244	2668	4912	3260	30040	8833	2944	1009	1867	21183
1873	2365	3004	5369	3880	32628	10434	3283	1082	2002	24516
1874	2462	2926	5388	3590	32662	10005	3373	1142	2091	25712
1875	2528	3140	5668	3670	36025	12351	4037	1225	2192	26446
1876	3182	3718	6900	3890	42280	14212	4672	1471	2746	30801
1877	3168	3772	6940	3430	42627	14698	4756	1514	2815	31381
1878	3156	**3713**	6869	3290	42980	**14578**	**4510**	1530	2815	31565
1879	**3089**	3762	**6851**	**3270**	**42791**	15148	4692	1550	**2812**	31589
1880	3199	3936	7135	3410	44418	16216	4831	1550	2853	32229
1881	3059	3822	6881	3240	42608	16525	4475	1553	2862	33190
1882	3400	4225	7625	3520	47784	18129	5154	1553	2882	33845
1883	3474	4344	7818	3540	49509	18904	5341	1557	2977	34794
1884	3554	4229	7783	3500	50917	18504	5323	1577	3050	36024
1885	**3504**	4079	7583	3340	**50003**	17959	**5286**	1582	3073	36324
1886	3507	**3976**	**7503**	**3220**	51130	**17340**	5501	1600	3079	36336
1887	3541	4076	7617	3230	51466	17785	6170	1600	3099	36336
1888	3573	4214	7787	3280	52327	18762	6255	1600	3165	37705
1889	3802	4473	8275	3520	55098	19654	6291	1620	3253	40267
1890	4006	4536	8542	3570	58105	19608	6395	1620	3398	41353
1891	4105	4652	8757	3650	60079	20150	6235	1660	3549	42856
1892	4159	4659	8818	3680	62575	20773	6004	1690	3623	43538
1893	4102	4504	8606	3570	61168	19883	5821	1700	3733	44043
1894	4143	4743	8886	3670	65703	22659	6149	1713	3786	44887
1895	4186	4726	8912	3680	66695	22567	6117	1750	3853	46129
1896	4386	4992	9378	3830	70338	24314	6551	1790	4015	47892
1897	4595	5167	9762	3950	74481	25520	6875	1837	4167	50118
1898	4724	4916	9640	3880	76468	22815	6417	1885	4264	51357
1899	4979	5578	10557	4300	80933	28345	7249	1933	4365	53271
1900	5165	5698	10863	4330	80944	30077	7424	1988	4450	55172

Source: Railway Returns (B of T Returns of the Capital, Traffic, Receipts, and Working Expenditure of the Railway Companies of the UK 1866–1900).

TABLE 5 INDICES OF GENERAL ECONOMIC ACTIVITY, INDICES OF GWR TRAFFIC, AND INVESTMENT AT SWINDON

	(1) *Total Value of Investment Goods (National) (Mln £s)* (at 1907	(2) *Value of Consumption of Consumers' Goods (Mln £s)* Prices)	(3) *Cost of Living Index* (1907=100)	(4) *Index of Income Per Head at* 1900 *Prices* (1900=100)	(5) *Total employment (£ millions* at 1907 *Prices)*	(6) *Price Index of investment Goods* (1907=100)	(7) *Engine Miles Run (Annual Totals, '000 miles)* *Passenger*	(8) *Goods*	(9) *Receipts Per Mile Open*	(10) *Dividend Paid* %	(11) *Investment at Swindon in £000's at* 1907 *Prices 5-yr moving Average*
1866	—	970	103	—	—	93	6920	6698	3100	$1\frac{1}{2}$	—
1867	—	960	109	—	—	84	7163	7024	3070	$1\frac{3}{8}$	—
1868	—	1030	108	—	—	82	7311	7208	3040	$1\frac{3}{8}$	89
1869	—	1000	104	—	—	82	7723	7737	3060	$2\frac{5}{8}$	143
1870	—	1040	104	57·72	511	82	7967	8088	3070	$3\frac{3}{8}$	204
1871	271	1090	105	59·10	526	84	8129	8894	3170	$4\frac{15}{16}$	254
1872	286	1100	111	58·10	528	103	8454	9935	3260	6	256
1873	282	1170	112	61·64	537	125	8819	10608	3880	$6\frac{1}{4}$	236
1874	278	1200	110	64·78	548	120	8966	10372	3590	$4\frac{1}{2}$	209
1875	285	1210	107	63·63	551	106	9353	10782	3670	$4\frac{1}{4}$	276
1876	285	1210	105	63·72	550	94	12176	13439	3890	4	215
1877	301	1200	107	63·35	554	86	12180	13591	3430	$3\frac{7}{8}$	183
1878	292	1210	106	64·96	553	82	12671	**13541**	3290	**$3\frac{3}{4}$**	202
1879	**279**	**1140**	**100**	**63·04**	**537**	**72**	**12584**	13956	**3270**	$4\frac{1}{8}$	185
1880	328	1270	104	63·21	570	77	13202	14654	3410	$5\frac{1}{8}$	**76**
1881	343	1260	102	65·97	577	75	13626	14131	3240	$5\frac{1}{2}$	133
1882	360	1280	103	68·48	588	76	13784	15805	3520	$6\frac{1}{4}$	162
1883	364	1320	100	69·51	597	78	14297	16047	3540	$6\frac{3}{8}$	131
1884	342	1340	99	69·96	596	80	14620	15836	3500	6	123
1885	321	**1290**	97	72·77	587	75	**14431**	15418	3340	$5\frac{1}{2}$	129
1886	**318**	1300	94	74·90	593	69	14632	**15175**	**3220**	**$5\frac{1}{4}$**	**116**
1887	324	1340	**91**	77·08	603	**67**	15125	15344	3230	$5\frac{1}{2}$	160
1888	354	1370	**91**	81·88	619	75	15534	15901	3280	$5\frac{7}{8}$	230
1889	403	1430	94	85·92	634	77	16380	16665	3520	$6\frac{3}{4}$	377
1890	398	1490	94	89·43	642	89	17300	17283	3570	$6\frac{1}{2}$	406
1891	368	1540	96	87·88	650	91	18159	18008	3650	$6\frac{1}{4}$	445
1892	368	1480	96	84·63	642	84	18582	18264	3680	$5\frac{7}{8}$	424
1893	360	1450	94	82·92	640	82	18816	18921	3570	$4\frac{3}{4}$	373
1894	369	1520	93	89·10	655	82	19301	18772	3670	$5\frac{1}{4}$	258
1895	385	1550	91	94·73	667	78	19672	19873	3680	$5\frac{1}{8}$	236
1896	424	1600	91	95·71	685	79	20854	20093	3830	6	176
1897	456	1610	93	95·71	685	78	21758	20893	3950	6	162
1898	457	1680	94	96·09	696	85	22311	20282	3880	$3\frac{7}{8}$	170
1899	487	1730	93	101·69	712	86	23085	22561	4300	$5\frac{1}{2}$	—
1900	486	1720	95	100·00	717	108	23278	23135	4330	$4\frac{5}{8}$	—

Sources: Cols: 1, 2, 3, 5 and 6; Tinbergen, op cit, Table 1A. Col: 4; A. R. Prest, op cit, App I, Table II. Cols 7, 8 and 9; as in Tables I and II. Col 10; MacDermot, op cit, Vol II, App III, 637. Col 11; Manuscript minute books.

Note: The value of investments at Swindon has been corrected by the price index for investment goods as in Col 6.

Aspects of Railway Accounting Before 1868

By Harold Pollins

The railway age in Britain, when about three-quarters of the country's route mileage were built, may conveniently be limited to the four decades between 1830 and 1870. Near the end of that period, in 1868, the Regulation of Railways Act was passed, and for the first time railway companies were given fairly detailed guidance as to the form and content of published accounts.[1] In particular they were required to adopt the 'double-account' system[2] for their published accounts, and uniformity as between one company and another was secured after many years of chaos. While the Act did not settle all the problems and difficulties of railway accounting,[3] the form of accounts which it prescribed remained unchanged until

This article first appeared in *Studies in the History of Accounting*, edited by A. C. Littleton and B. S. Yamey on behalf of The Association of University Teachers of Accounting and The American Accounting Association (London: Sweet & Maxwell; Homewood, Illinois: Richard D. Irwin; 1956), pp 332–53. A number of revisions have been incorporated.

I am particularly grateful to Professor B. S. Yamey for suggesting I work on this subject and for providing guidance and help. I have also benefited from the criticisms of Professor David Solomons and Dr S. A. Broadbridge.

Note on Sources:

The most obvious sources for the study of railway accounts are the published *Reports and Accounts* of the companies, copies of most of which are in the custody of the British Railways Board. A few are to be found in other places such as the British Library of Political and Economic Science. The volumes of *Reports and Accounts* often include reports of the shareholders' meetings (viz, the chairman's speech and shareholders' comments), extracts from which have been quoted in this article. Before the Act of 1911 railway accounts were made up twice yearly, normally for the six months ending June 30 and December 31, respectively. However, some companies published annual accounts and others balanced their books at dates other than in June and December. The company *Reports and Accounts* and reports of shareholders' meetings were also printed, in varying degrees of detail, in the railway periodicals, such as *Herapath's Railway Journal*, *Railway Times*, *Railway Record*, and *Railway News*.

[1] The Act was generally welcomed at the time: see, for example, the views of one accountant, H. Lloyd Morgan, *Accounts and Audits: Remarks on the new 'Regulation of Railways Act'* (1868). A short note on the origins of the Act is to be found in the Report of the Departmental Committee on Railway Accounts and Statistical Returns, PP 1910, LVI (Cd 5052), pp 405–6. See also C. C. Wang, *Legislative Regulation of Railway Finance in England* (Urbana, Illinois, 1918).

[2] So called because, under this system, the balance sheet is divided into two sections, one dealing with fixed capital and the other with circulating capital.

[3] See the Departmental Committee on Railway Accounts, PP 1909, LXXVI (Cd 4697) and 1910, LVI (Cd 5052).

the Railway Companies (Accounts and Returns) Act of 1911; in general the Act of 1868 marked a turning point in the history of railway accounting after a long period of uncertainty.

There are many topics of interest to students of history and accounting which it would be worth while examining in the formative period of railway history before 1868.[1] One might try to trace the origins and development of the double-account system. The history of railway auditing is also of importance.[2] Again, the development of the organisation and methods of the accounting departments of the railway companies would repay study. Many of the companies were large; some in the 1860s had a paid-up capital of as much as £30–£40 million. They needed highly elaborate systems of accounting and financial control to avoid misappropriation of resources. Not all of them had the necessary safeguards. Several published *Reports and Accounts* reveal that the secretary or treasurer had absconded with the funds, and registrars misappropriated dividends by forging stock. Leopold Redpath, the registrar of the Great Northern Railway in the 1850s, who after his conviction in 1857 was transported for life, was a notable example.[3] A study of the methods adopted by the companies to prevent financial irregularities would usefully add to our knowledge of the history of financial administration in business concerns.[4]

However, in this article it is not intended to do more than discuss certain accounting practices affecting the determination of profits, primarily those concerned with the distinction between capital and revenue receipts and expenditures, and with the depreciation of fixed assets. On the basis of this discussion it will be possible to exhibit differences in the accounting practices of different railway companies, and to trace the changes over a period of years.

Although it is possible to indicate some general lines of development, the

[1] It is not always very profitable to date periods in economic history, but it is interesting to observe that one eminent railway historian dates the virtual completion of the British railway network at 1868: L. M. Jouffroy, *L'Ere du rail* (Paris, 1953), p 78.

[2] S 30 of the Railway Companies Act of 1867 (30 & 31 Vict c 127) raised the status of auditors by providing that:

> No dividend shall be declared by a company until the auditors have certified that the half-yearly accounts proposed to be issued contain a full and true statement of the financial condition of the company, and that the dividend proposed to be declared on any shares is bona fide due thereon after charging the revenue of the half year with all expenses which ought to be paid thereout in the judgment of the auditors.

Any difference between the auditors and the directors over the deduction of expenses from revenue was to be decided by the shareholders; but 'if no such difference is stated, or if no decision is given on any such difference, the judgment of the auditors shall be final and binding'.

[3] See C. H. Grinling, *History of the Great Northern Railway* (1898), Chap 11; and D. Morier Evans, *Facts, Failures and Frauds* (1859), Chap 9: 'The Great Northern Railway Frauds and Forgeries by Leopold Redpath'. See also a letter to the *Railway Times*, 14 August 1869, 788.

[4] In this connection see a description of the financial methods of Thomas Brassey, the great railway contractor, in A. Helps, *Life and Labours of Mr. Brassey* (1872), Chap 9.

very multiplicity and variety of the accounting practices adopted by the several hundred companies before 1868, for which they were notorious, make a comprehensive treatment of these matters quite impossible. Walter Bailey, the accountant of the Midland Railway, wrote in 1914 that 'the accountants of those days [*sc* before 1868] must have been giants indeed if they were able to make useful comparisons with each other's accounts from the published material at their disposal. There is scarcely an account, abstract, or statement, in either of these early half-yearly reports which is paralleled by a corresponding account, abstract, or statement in the report of another company.'[1] In addition, it was said, railway accounts were 'so intricately framed that they are calculated either to conceal the truth, or to lead to erroneous conclusions'.[2] In 1850 *The Times* referred to the financial affairs of the Caledonian Railway in these terms: 'The Caledonian Railway Company, the work neither of lawyers, nor of old women, nor spendthrifts, but of shrewd middle-aged mercantile men, is just such a tangle as one might dream of after supping on lobster salad and champagne.'[3] This kind of comment was constantly made throughout the nineteenth century about railway finance and accounts.[4] Professional accountants too were criticised for their inconsistency.[5]

THE RAILWAY AGE

Railways had a long history before the introduction of the locomotive; the use of rails has been traced back to the sixteenth century. But railway history has little significance before the 1820s when important developments in the locomotive led to the success of George Stephenson's *Rocket* in 1829, at the Rainhill Trials,[6] organised by the Liverpool & Manchester Railway. In 1830 that line was opened and was immediately successful, paying good dividends at once.[7] The railway age had begun, although the locomotive required further development and improvement before it could completely supersede other forms of traction. By the middle of the 1830s Acts of Parliament had been passed to authorise the incorporation of many main line companies, and by the late 1830s and early 1840s their lines had

[1] W. Bailey, 'Railway Accounts—Old and New', in *Jubilee of the Railway News* (1914), p 78.

[2] H. Ayres, *The Financial Position of Railways* (1868), p xxv. See also a letter to the *Railway Times*, 23 September 1843, 1060: 'I fear that deceptive Reports and deceptive balance-sheets are a growing evil.'

[3] *The Times*, 30 September 1850, leading article.

[4] For some further references see my 'A Note on Railway Constructional Costs, 1825–1850', *Economica*, XIX (1952), 400–1.

[5] *Herapath*, 27 September 1851, 1051–2.

[6] On 6 October 1829, 'date marquant véritablement le début de l'histoire des chemins de fer proprement dits'. (J. Dessirier, 'Chemin de fer et progrès technique', *L'Année Ferroviaire* [Paris, 1952], p 25.) The trials lasted several days.

[7] H. Pollins, 'The Finances of the Liverpool and Manchester Railway', *Economic History Review*, second series, V (1952).

been built and opened (apart from one or two which, for financial reasons, had abandoned part of their route).

Railway promotion and construction came in bursts. There was a mania of railway company promotion in 1835 and 1836. Then between 1837 and 1842 hardly any promotion took place, but in the mid 1840s the famous 'railway mania' led to the promotion of about a thousand companies. Lines were promoted throughout the country; shares were at enormous premiums; high guaranteed dividends were promised by main line companies to small branch line companies with little regard to earning capacity. In 1847 financial conditions adversely affected the raising of capital and in subsequent years share prices fell as dividends fell, partly because construction was proceeding faster than the increase in traffic. Between 1847 and 1851 there were few promotions of new companies, and much authorised mileage was abandoned. However, the most significant feature of railway history in the 1840s was the extensive mileage that was built despite financial difficulty. The mania added about 5,000 miles of railway, but it also resulted in the downfall of one of the major characters involved, George Hudson, the 'Railway King'. In the late forties most railway companies appointed some sort of committee of inquiry to investigate alleged frauds, scandals and abuses or to prove that the particular company had been free from irregularities. Judging by the course of share prices, and the comments of such observers as Herbert Spencer,[1] railways were no longer the favourite child of investors or the public.

Nevertheless, some 8,000 miles were built between 1850 and 1870, part of this having been authorised in the mid forties. Improved trade in the early fifties led to a veritable boom in 1852 and 1853, and again in 1856 (the Crimean War intervening). After the financial crisis of 1857 the period of 1858–65 was full of railway excitement, particularly in 1863–5, and by 1870 some 15,000 miles were open in the United Kingdom.

Though an extensive mileage was built between 1850 and 1870, the period was one of financial difficulties for the railways. Dividends rose only slightly despite continuous increases in the traffic carried, and equity share prices hardly improved until the sixties. There was a shortage of equity capital and some companies had to resort to unusual methods of finance, for example, paying contractors in the company's shares, usually at a discount. The financial crisis of 1866 showed up not only the imperfections of the 'contractors' lines' but also the unsoundness of many apparently solid railway companies. In particular their habit of over-issuing short term debenture debt left them, in 1866, when rates of interest were high, unable to renew their debt on favourable terms, or indeed on any terms. One effect of the crisis and depression was the hasty conversion of short term mortgage debentures into long term debenture stock. Another was a series of

[1] H. Spencer, *Railway Morals and Railway Policy* (1855).

legislative enactments laying down more detailed rules for railway companies to follow.[1]

RAILWAY LEGISLATION

Railway companies were statutory companies, their powers being conferred directly by Parliament. Each company had to obtain an Act of Parliament to give it authority, amongst other things, to build the line and to raise capital. The clauses in these Acts came mainly from two sources: the standing orders of both Houses of Parliament, and various general railway Acts. Standing orders had little to say on accounts,[2] and it was not until 1844 and 1845 that general Acts were passed which affected railway accounts.[3] These were: the Railway Regulation Act (1844) (7 & 8 Vict, c 85); the Companies Clauses Consolidation Act (1845) (8 & 9 Vict, c 16); and the Railway Clauses Consolidation Act (1845) (8 & 9 Vict, c 20). Of these the most important for present purposes was the Companies Clauses Consolidation Act.

Before the general Acts were passed the accounting provisions in the various private Acts were not uniform. It was normal for them to require that accounts should be kept, but often they demanded little beyond that. There was seldom any reference to auditors. For example, the Act incorporating the Stockton & Darlington Railway in 1821[4] consisted of 104 sections, but the only reference to accounts was the requirement that the company should keep 'proper Books of Account' (s 56). The company was empowered to pay dividends:

> All Persons . . . who shall severally subscribe for One or more Share or Shares . . . shall be entitled to and receive . . . the entire and net Distribution of an equal proportional Part, according to the money so by them respectively paid, of the net Profits and Advantages that shall and may arise and accrue by the Rates and other Sums of Money to be

[1] For more details and discussion of the development of railways in the period under review, see H. G. Lewin, *Early British Railways* (1925), and *The Railway Mania and its aftermath* (1936); J. H. Clapham, *Economic History of Modern Britain* (3 vols, Cambridge, 1930–8); G. H. Evans, *British Corporation Finance 1775–1850* (Baltimore, 1936); L. H. Jenks, *The Migration of British Capital to 1875* (1938); R. C. O. Matthews, *A Study in Trade Cycle History 1833–1842* (Cambridge, 1954); J. R. T. Hughes, *Fluctuations in Trade, Industry and Finance: a Study in British Economic Development 1850–1860* (Oxford, 1960); G. Cohn, *Untersuchungen über die englische Eisenbahnpolitik* (3 vols, Leipzig, 1874–83); B. C. Hunt, *The Development of the business corporation in England 1800–1867* (Cambridge, Mass, 1936); and T. Tooke and W. Newmarch, *A History of Prices* (Vol 5, 1857).

[2] See O. C. Williams, *The Historical Development of Private Bill Procedure and Standing Orders in the House of Commons* (1948–9); F. Clifford, *History of Private Bill Legislation* (1885–7).

[3] See Wang, op cit; C. H. Newton, *Railway Accounts* (1930); A. M. Sakolski, 'Control of Railroad Accounts in Leading European Countries', *Quarterly Journal of Economics*, xxiv (1910).

[4] 1 & 2 Geo 4, local Act, c xliv.

raised, recovered, or received by the said Company, by the Authority of this Act. (s. 38).

There is no reference to a balance sheet or to the shareholders' right to examine the accounts. Indeed the shareholders did not automatically receive a copy of the accounts, as a letter of 1836 demonstrates:[1]

Cotham Mill,
Near Uxbridge.
10 of 3rd Mo. 1836

Resp. Frd.,

The proprietors of the Stockton and Darlington Railway residing in the neighbourhood of Uxbridge, feel themselves disappointed in not receiving an annual statement of the accounts of the above named concern.—I find upon conferring with Joseph Pease that it is not customary to transmit a statement without an application from the proprietors, these are therefore to request thou will send a copy of the last year's accounts as early as thou conveniently can, which is wished to be transmitted regularly every year in future addressed to 'Will Hull, Uxbridge'.

I remain respectfully,
Thy friend,
Thomas Smith.

To Sam Barnard.

Another company, the Liverpool & Manchester, obtained its Act in 1826. This time the Act was more specific as to dividends. In order to reduce the possibility of excessive profits the company's charges were to be related to its dividend. If the dividend exceeded 10 per cent, the rates charged by the company were to be reduced by 5 per cent for each 1 per cent of dividend above the 10 per cent.[2] But nothing was said as to the method of determining the net profit. A later, and larger company, the Great Western, though its Act contained 251 sections, had only a little more detail in it on accounting matters. Accounts were to be made up half-yearly and to be laid before the half-yearly general meeting of the company; if the shareholders at the meeting considered the accounts to be unsatisfactory, they could appoint a committee to examine them and make a report.[3] Dividends could be declared from the 'clear Profits' of the company, provided that 'no Dividends shall be made exceeding the net Amount of clear Profit at the Time being in the Hands of the said Company, nor whereby the Capital of the said Company shall in any degree be reduced or impaired' (s 146).

Gradually more detail was included in these private Acts so that as early as 1842 (three years before the general Acts were passed) a body of regula-

[1] BTHR (Y), SAD 8/145/8.

[2] See the discussion in H. Pollins, loc cit, 93–4. At least one other railway company had a similar limitation: Garnkirk & Glasgow Railway, 7 Geo 4, local Act, c ciii (1826), s 88.

[3] 5 & 6 Will 4, local Act, c cvii (1835), s 145.

tions had been built up which the general Acts took over. Thus the various sections, relating to accounts, in the Warwick & Leamington Union Railway Act of 1842[1] were similar to those, to be quoted below, of the Companies Clauses Consolidation Act of 1845. By 1844 the clauses in the new private Acts were virtually identical with those to be prescribed in 1845.[2]

There was little in the private Acts to guide railway companies on the keeping of accounts or the determination of profits. However, it should be mentioned that gross income was regulated in part, since each Act laid down maximum charges that could be made, and interest on loans was declared a prior charge. Sometimes part of the gross profit had to be reserved as a contingencies fund.[3]

The following changes were introduced by the general legislation of the 1840s. Under sections 115–19 of the Companies Clauses Consolidation Act of 1845 a book-keeper was to be appointed to 'enter the accounts . . . in books', and accounts were to be kept and books were to be balanced at the prescribed periods.

> On the books being so balanced an exact balance sheet shall be made up, which shall exhibit a true statement of the capital stock, credits, and property of every description belonging to the company, and the debts due by the company at the date of making such balance sheet, and a distinct view of the profit or loss which shall have arisen on the transactions of the company in the course of the preceding half-year.

The balance sheet was to be examined by at least three of the directors and signed by the chairman or deputy chairman. The directors were to produce the balance sheet at shareholders' meetings. The balanced books and the balance sheet were to be available to shareholders at the company's office 14 days before the shareholders' meeting, and for one month after it. Auditors, holding at least one share in the company but not holding any office in it, were to be appointed.[4] They were to receive the accounts from the directors fourteen days before the shareholders' meeting 'and to examine the same'. They could make a report or simply confirm the accounts (ss 101–8).[5] They did not have to sign them, though in fact auditors often did.

This was the sum and substance of the statutory provision governing railway accounts during the most important period of railway develop-

[1] 5 & 6 Vict, local Act, c lxxxi, ss 103–7, 111–13.

[2] See, for example, the North Wales Mineral Railway Act, 7 & 8 Vict, local Act c xcix (1844), ss 106–10, 114–15.

[3] An analysis of the Acts relating to 26 railway companies, contained in Appendix 31 to the Second Report, *Select Committee on Railways*, PP 1839, X, pp 449–541, shows that there were important variations in these enactments.

[4] Some of the major companies in fact also employed full-time professional accountants, as permitted by the Act.

[5] This Act applied to companies incorporated thenceforth. Many of the older companies did not appoint auditors until after the crises and scandals of the late 1840s.

ment. Clearly it did not amount to very much.[1] Although there was government supervision of railways in such matters as safety in operation, as far as accounts were concerned the companies had only to deliver copies of their balance sheets to the appropriate government department, together with other prescribed statistical information. The officially published annual railway returns invariably contained a pathetic statement to the effect that the statistics printed were those given by the companies, and the compilers of the returns had no responsibility for their accuracy or for their completeness; and there were always delinquent companies which did not bother to deliver any information at all.

A great deal of latitude was left to the companies in the calculation of profit, with little power of control by auditors or by the government. This was realised at the time. Thus Gladstone's Act of 1844,[2] which provided for the eventual purchase of new lines by the state at prices to be based on their annual divisible profits, was criticised at the time for not 'establishing a systematic control over the method by which profits were calculated'.[3]

Although throughout the early period of railway development there were few legislative and administrative changes affecting railway accounting, it is convenient to draw a dividing line at about 1850. Before that time there was little experience on which the companies could draw, and the majority were cavalier in their attitude to railway finance and accounts. After 1850 there were attempts to improve matters, at least on the part of some of the major companies. In the late forties, too, public concern about railway matters led, amongst other things, to the appointment of the Select Committee on the Audit of Railway Accounts.[4] Dionysius Lardner's book entitled *Railway Economy*, which was published in 1850, was perhaps the first attempt to lay down principles for railway administration and accounting.[5] Both the select committee and Lardner scrutinised past practices and tried to establish some principles that companies ought to follow.[6]

[1] Sometimes other Acts of Parliament affected railway accounts. Thus the Stage Carriages Act (2 & 3 Will 4, c 120 [1832], ss 50, 51) and the Railway Passenger Duty Act (5 & 6 Vict c 79 [1842], s 4) required railway companies to keep books giving details of passenger receipts. Copies had to be sent monthly to the Commissioners of Stamps and Taxes. This was for the purpose of assessing liability for passenger duty.

[2] 7 & 8 Vict c 85.

[3] E. Cleveland-Stevens, *English Railways, Their Development and their Relation to the State* (1915), p 111.

[4] Its report is in PP 1849, X (371) (421).

[5] For a note on Lardner's work, see M. Robbins, 'Dr Lardner's "Railway Economy" ', *Railway Magazine*, March 1950.

[6] Other writers on that period were Mark Huish, *On the Deterioration of Railway Plant and Road* (1849), and Samuel Laing, *Report on the Question of Depreciation and on the Policy of establishing a Reserve Fund* (1849).

THE DISTINCTION BETWEEN CAPITAL AND REVENUE

In the discussion of the determination of the amount of net profit available for distribution as dividend, the most important question was the allocation of items of expenditure between the revenue and capital accounts. Net profits could be increased, and the rate of dividend raised, by debiting capital with expenses which should have been debited to revenue, and vice versa. Until the Regulation of Railways Act of 1868 the law did not attempt to detail or specify the items of expenditure which belonged in each of the two accounts; and in practice there was no uniformity in the treatment of important expenditures before that date.[1]

It should be stressed that contemporary opinion realised the necessity of keeping separate the two accounts of capital and revenue. The separation was emphasised over and over again in the evidence submitted to the Select Committee on Audit of 1849. Throughout the nineteenth century one of the recurring themes of the pamphleteers was that railway companies had not properly kept the two accounts separate. One commentator wrote of the important Lancashire & Yorkshire Railway, in the late forties, when railways were in the doldrums: 'No one can examine the capital accounts with any degree of attention without being impressed and—were it not for the *declarations* of the Chairman to the contrary—being convinced that this Company paid all dividends out of capital.'[2] This was not an isolated case. The recent accounting habits of one company were summarised in 1867 in these terms: 'Dividends have only been paid by a wholesale system of charging to Capital not only interest on new lines, but repairs, renewals, law charges, and other accruing expenses on completed lines.' This was the London, Brighton & South Coast Railway, whose accounts had been specially audited in that year by Price, Holyland and Waterhouse.[3] The flexibility in the treatment of items of expenditure naturally lent itself to fraudulent management. The most notorious case was that of the Eastern Counties Railway which, between 1845 and 1848 (when George Hudson was chairman), paid out in dividends some £115,000 more than the 'accounts in their books stated they had earned', by the conscious transfer of items from revenue to capital account; 'traffic accounts were altered, and the expenses were squared to suit the dividend'. This was in addition to some £200,000 'improperly charged to capital'.[4] Some companies may

[1] There was room for discussion even after 1868; see, for example, the complaint of lack of uniformity in the treatment of expenditures in the *Railway and Tramway Express*, 4 April 1885, 216–17.

[2] Arthur Smith, *The Bubble of the Age* (1848), p 49.

[3] London, Brighton & South Coast Railway, *Reports and Accounts* for the period ending 30 June 1867 (BTHR, RAC 1/250).

[4] *Select Committee on Audit of Railway Accounts*, PP 1849, X, Appendix A, p 362. The Report of the Committee of Investigation is reprinted in *S.C. on the Eastern Counties*

even have paid dividends directly from moneys raised to defray capital expenditure; although it is difficult to find specific evidence of this,[1] some contemporary comments seem to imply it. 'So long as you have a capital account open, you have two sources of receipts, one a much larger source of receipt than the other; and I am afraid, that with the best intentions, even on the part of such a board as the London & North Western, they can hardly avoid occasionally a little tripping, in spite of themselves.'[2] Another factor making for imperfect accounts was the inefficiency of the clerks; details of this sometimes appear in the companies' minutes.

Most companies seem to have been aware of the difference between capital account and revenue account. The assistant accountant of the ill-fated Eastern Counties Railway, who was in charge of the construction ledger, explained that 'blue checks are issued for traffic, and red checks for construction expenditure'. It was true that 'some of the blue checks were afterwards charged to capital, and portions of others; whether properly or not, I cannot say'.[3] The point is that the company drew a distinction between revenue and capital expenditure, though sometimes it took little notice of that distinction.

Many companies opened part of their line for traffic while the rest was under construction, and did not have a separate revenue account until the whole was open. The income and expenditure on current working were entered in the capital account. When the line was fully opened, the accumulated revenue items were transferred to the revenue account.

During the period of construction interest was paid on long and short term loans, sometimes on all calls paid by shareholders (until this was prohibited in 1847), and on calls paid in advance; interest was meantime earned on temporary balances. The amount paid in interest was usually greater than that earned. These interest payments had to be made while the company was building, when there was no revenue; they had, therefore, to come out of capital. Most companies seem to have debited their current interest payments to revenue account once the line was opened, leaving the

Railway, PP 1849, X (366). The published reports of both these Select Committees include a full report on this railway by a firm of accountants, Quilter, Ball, Jay & Crosbie. The amount improperly charged to capital included interest on lines in operation.

[1] This appears to have been the burden of the complaint against the Liverpool & Manchester Railway in the 1830s (H. Pollins, loc cit). In the 1860s the Metropolitan Railway intended paying a dividend out of funds applicable to the construction of a branch line; directors' and auditors' fees and office expenses were also charged to capital. (See H. Godefroi & J. Shortt, *The Law of Railway Companies* [1869], p 112 for a discussion.) The Companies Clauses Act of 1845 (s 121) specifically prohibited the payment of any dividend by railway companies 'whereby their capital stock will be in any degree reduced'.

[2] *SC on Audit*, PP 1849, X, Q 1110 (Mihill Slaughter, of the Stock Exchange).

[3] Committee of Investigation, p 367.

amount previously paid as interest in the capital account.[1] Although one firm of accountants in 1849 thought that such accumulated interest should eventually be written off in the revenue account,[2] only one example has been found where a company subsequently transferred the interest paid out of capital to the debit of revenue.[3] At the other extreme the London, Chatham & Dover Railway was still debiting interest against capital account after the line was open, because, the company explained, there was insufficient revenue to cover it.[4]

Some companies drew a distinction between 'productive' and 'unproductive' capital; that is, between capital invested in lines earning revenue and that spent on branch lines still in course of construction. The interest on money borrowed to build the revenue earning lines came from revenue, while that on the uncompleted branch lines was charged to capital. In 1845, for example, the report of the South Eastern Railway stated: 'The Directors recognise the propriety of the principle . . . that the net[5] revenue on the Main Line should be divided among the Proprietors, and should not be charged with the interest on the capital employed in constructing Branches, and other ancillary works, while in progress'.[6] On the other hand, the London & South Western Railway in 1849 charged all interest to revenue, even though some of the capital was 'unproductive'.[7]

The costs of obtaining a company's Act of incorporation were invariably debited to capital, but the costs of unsuccessful applications to parliament as well as the costs of opposing the Bills of other companies were sometimes charged to capital and sometimes to revenue. The object of opposing other companies' Bills was to prevent possible competition. In 1853 the London & South Western Railway charged capital with all parliamentary costs; three years later the costs of opposition were debited to revenue.[8] In 1853 the auditors of the South Eastern Railway thought that the costs of

[1] For example, London & Birmingham Railway, *Reports and Accounts*, 31 December 1838 (BTHR: RAC 1/226. Line opened throughout on 17 September 1838; interest paid after that date debited to revenue.

[2] Quilter, Ball, Jay & Crosbie in Appendix to *SC on Audit*, PP 1849, X, p 389. One journal said it was illegal not to pay it back from revenue: *The Railroad Quarterly Journal* (London), January 1841, 117.

[3] Great Western Railway, *Reports and Accounts*, 31 December 1840 (BTHR, RAC 1/165). Transfer of net interest.

[4] London, Chatham & Dover Railway, *Reports and Accounts*, 30 June 1861 (BTHR, RAC 1/126) (statement of the secretary at shareholders' meeting). One of the reasons given for the fact that the nominal capital of this company was in excess of the amount actually received and spent on construction was the large amount charged to capital for interest and commission: LCDR, *Committee of Investigation* (1866), p 13.

[5] The report gives 'next'. This is probably a misprint for 'nett'. *Railway Times*, (22 March 1845, p 394) reprinted the report and gives this word as 'net'.

[6] South Eastern Railway, *Reports and Accounts*, 31 January 1845 (BTHR, RAC 1/377).

[7] London & South Western Railway, *Reports and Accounts*, 31 December 1849 (BTHR, RAC 1/245).

[8] London & South Western Railway, *Reports and Accounts*, 31 December 1853; 31 December 1856 (BTHR, RAC 1/245A).

parliamentary opposition should be debited to revenue.[1] Eventually the best railway practice was to charge expenditures on successful applications to capital and those on unsuccessful applications and on opposition to Bills to revenue.[2]

DEPRECIATION

Although the accounting treatment of the depreciation of fixed assets is frequently referred to in the reports and accounts of the various railway companies, as might be expected, little was said about it in the Acts of Parliament governing railways. Perhaps the nearest reference to it was contained in the Companies Clauses Consolidation Act of 1845 (s 122):

> Before apportioning the Profits to be divided among the Shareholders, the Directors may, if they think fit, set aside thereout such Sum as they may think proper to meet contingencies, or for enlarging, repairing, or improving the Works connected with the Undertaking, or any part thereof, and may divide the balance among the Shareholders.

But this gave no detailed guidance to railway directors and accountants, and in practice a variety of methods of accounting for depreciation were adopted.[3] It is true that the important case of *R* v *Grand Junction Ry*[4] upheld an order of quarter sessions that in assessing a railway company for a poor rate, the proper measure of the rateable value was the gross receipts less various items of expenditure (interest, working expenditure) including a percentage on the capital invested in the movable stock for the annual depreciation beyond the ordinary annual repairs. But the railway companies did not necessarily take note of the fact of depreciation, much less the sum proposed in this case (*viz*, 12½ per cent of the capital sum).

The variety of methods illustrated in this section followed not only from the lack of experience in matters such as the life of assets but also from the absence of any clear definition of what was meant by depreciation. Some meant a fall in the market value of the assets when they spoke of depreciation (thus when the price of locomotives rose some companies assumed that their assets had improved); others meant no more than current repairs and maintenance; others again were concerned with replacement.

In the discussions of depreciation, a difference of emphasis can be detected as between the years before the mania of the mid forties and the subsequent period. Before the mania the discussion chiefly concerned roll-

[1] South Eastern Railway, *Reports and Accounts*, 31 July 1853 (Auditors' Report). (BTHR, RAC 1/377).

[2] J. A. Fisher, *Railway Accounts and Finance* (1891), pp xii–xiii.

[3] Similarly American railway accounting at this time showed important variations in the treatment of depreciation; see the quotations and extracts collected by Perry Mason, 'Illustrations of the Early Treatment of Depreciation', *Accounting Review*, September 1933.

[4] (1844) 4 QB 18.

ing stock; afterwards the emphasis shifted to depreciation of rails. In 1850 Lardner wrote about rails as follows: 'The prevalent opinion, countenanced and supported by the most eminent practical engineers, was, until a late period, that the duration of a railway was secular, and that the wear and tear of the rails was so utterly insensible, that for all practical, financial, and economical purposes it might be totally disregarded. Thus, it was said, that the rails of a properly laid line would last for one hundred to one hundred and fifty years.'[1] It was probably for this reason that the first discussions of depreciation centred on the rolling stock and not on rails. Although the rails of the Liverpool & Manchester Railway (opened 1830) required replacing very quickly, later rails lasted longer. The consulting engineer of the London & South Western Railway reported in 1858 that on 60 miles of the line the rails were still in use after 18 to 20 years.[2] Locomotives, on the other hand, obviously needed repairs and replacements from the time a railway was opened.

In the late thirties and early forties the lines which had been authorised in the early and mid thirties were opened, and the companies were immediately faced with problems of large scale railway administration of which, so far, few people had any experience. Maintaining the rolling stock in good order was one problem which demanded attention at that time. For example, in a discussion of the payment of dividends out of capital by the Durham & Sunderland Railway, the *Railway Times* in 1841 wrote:[3]

> We hope and believe that the practice of knowingly declaring fraudulent dividends is not common with Railway Managements. At the same time care must be taken that deception of a similar kind is not incurred through incaution, or from any other cause. The declaration of a dividend without making allowance for depreciation of stock, cannot in our opinion be regarded as other than fallacious. Some Companies, we fear, are running out their perishable stock, thereby exhibiting an appearance of a low scale of expenditure, and a rate of dividend not warranted by the profit really made, and thus leaving a succeeding set of proprietors to make up from their income the replacing of the exhausted stock.

Later the same journal pointed out that a depreciation fund was more than a fund for the replacement of parts:

> The machine as a whole is gradually and certainly, though insensibly, going to decay; and a time comes at last, when the replacement of

[1] Lardner, *Railway Economy*, p 42. This was, of course, apart from repairs of faults, fractures, etc.

[2] London & South Western Railway, *Reports and Accounts*, 31 December 1857. His report is dated 1 February 1858. (BTHR, RAC 1/245A).

[3] *Railway Times*, 30 October 1841, 1142. *The American Railroad Journal* for November and December 1843, made similar comments about the practices of American railway companies: 'There is not now to be found in the country a single road which has renewed its iron out of the proceeds of transportation.' (Quoted by Perry Mason, op cit, p 212.)

> parts will not maintain its efficiency, and then it must be cast aside altogether.

It went on to note that at the moment the amount set aside each half-year could only be a guess until sufficient knowledge of the life of rolling stock was available.[1]

But although the problems of maintenance and replacement were realised to be important, the solutions adopted by the different companies varied considerably. There were some companies which did not include any provision for depreciation in their accounts. The reasons given by the chairman of the London & South Western Railway (W. J. Chaplin) were these:

> If I can show you—but I would rather go beyond showing, for I have no objection to hold myself personally responsible—that the locomotive business of this Railway may be conducted, for the next ten years, for less money than it has been conducted for the last half-year, and delivered up, at the end of that ten years at its present full value, what occasion can there be to trouble ourselves with this phantom fund for depreciation?

The permanent way was being maintained by responsible contractors, and the rolling stock was in a more efficient state than it had been three months after it was paid for; the stock had had to be altered 'entirely' soon after it was bought, and should last ten years. In any case it was better to introduce new stock 'instead of vamping up the old'[2]. A year later he explained that the 'whole expense both of repair and restoration, was entirely charged to the current revenue'.[3]

This company was basing its actions partly on a valuation of the rolling stock, and other companies valued their rolling stock at regular intervals, for example, the Grand Junction Railway, the Liverpool & Manchester Railway, and the North Union Railway. The Grand Junction Railway valued its rolling stock according to its current market value;[4] the change in value, credit or debit, was entered in the revenue account. Thus in 1839 £5,000 was debited to revenue and credited to a 'Stock Account' to reflect the previous six months' depreciation.[5] That sum, intended 'to meet depreciation in value of stock previously to that date, has enabled the Company to reduce the expenditure of Capital in the purchase of stock to that extent'.[6] In 1841 its practice of 'debiting or crediting (as the case might be) the Half-year's Receipts with the balance of a comparative valuation'[7] was

[1] *Railway Times*, 4 March 1843, 262.

[2] London & South Western Railway, *Reports and Accounts*, 31 December 1841 (BTHR, RAC 1/245A) (Report of chairman's speech).

[3] Ibid, 31 December 1842.

[4] Grand Junction Railway, *Reports and Accounts*, 30 June 1838 (BTHR, RAC 1/140) (Resolution of shareholders' meeting).

[5] Ibid, 30 June 1839.

[6] Ibid, 31 December 1839.

[7] Ibid, 30 June 1841.

challenged at a shareholders' meeting,[1] and the practice was discontinued. Instead, a depreciation fund was instituted; this was intended 'for the improvement of the stock, and to meet that insensible but sure decay which is perpetually going on, and which no care or expense can prevent'.[2] The accounts from 30 June 1842, include a 'Depreciation and renewal of Stock Fund';[3] eighteen months later it was hoped that the current allocation of £5,000 would be the last necessary to build up a fund.[4] In the meantime the accounts show various items of expenditure from this fund, 'to replace Stock worn out'.[5] In addition the company established a reserve fund to meet contingencies, primarily to avoid fluctuations in dividends.[6]

The practice of valuing rolling stock on the basis of *current market prices* was disputed by the *Railway Times* in 1841[7] and later by Lardner.[8] The *Railway Times* favoured a half-yearly valuation . . .

> provided a right principle were adopted. The market price or selling value of the articles should have nothing whatever to do with it, but the original cost of the stock being assumed as the starting point, the only consideration is the amount of depreciation from the wear and tear unrestored by repairs at the end of the period.

It was thought possible to do this in two ways: by the 'North Union plan' of taking the exact sum which the valuation each half-year showed to be required, or by the London & Birmingham Railway's method of debiting a regular percentage of cost to provide a fund to meet the occasional heavy outlays (apart from ordinary repairs) which were due to 'the gradual destruction of parts that cannot be immediately replaced'.

The London & Birmingham Railway, indeed, had established a 'Reserved Fund (for Depreciation of Stock)' in 1838, before the line was wholly open.[9] From 1839 the company regularised the depreciation at 5 per cent each half-year 'on the actual Cost'.[10] and later it was explained that the principle of the fund had been adopted 'with a view of providing the means for making the receipts of each half-year bear more equally their proper share of charge, and of maintaining the Carrying Stock on an effective and uniform footing'.[11] A year later the chairman of the company,

[1] Report of meeting in *Railway Times*, 14 August 1841, 864–5.

[2] Grand Junction Railway, *Reports and Accounts*, 31 December 1841 (BTHR, RAC 1/140).

[3] This included the sum set aside for this purpose in the previous half-year.

[4] Grand Junction Railway, *Reports and Accounts*, 31 December 1843 (BTHR, RAC 1/140).

[5] Ibid, 30 June 1843.

[6] Ibid, 31 December 1839.

[7] *Railway Times*, 6 November 1841, 1167.

[8] Lardner, op cit, pp 119–21.

[9] London & Birmingham Railway, *Reports and Accounts*, 30 June 1838 (BTHR, RAC 1/226).

[10] Ibid, 31 December 1839.

[11] Ibid, 30 June 1840. But part of the fund was used to pay the dividend.

George Carr Glyn, gave more details of the purpose of the depreciation fund:

> In making up our account we have pursued the plan . . . of setting aside a fund to meet the unavoidable depreciation of stock. . . . The plan which we in this Company follow, and the plan which is virtually followed in almost every other Company,[1] is to appropriate a portion of the profits of every half year to meet the depreciation which has taken place during that period in the value of the Company's stock—a depreciation which it is clear must be made good either from the profits of working, or defrayed from the capital of the Company. The course adopted in this Company is to set aside from the profits of every half year a certain percentage on the capital originally invested in the purchase of Stock . . . and in the 'Capital Ledger' to write off against it the amount of such per-centage.[2]

Another main line company, the Great Western, similarly preferred a fixed amount to be set aside, and accounted for depreciation by appropriating annually £20,000 for ten years 'to redeem the depreciated value in the first cost . . . the Directors do not think any benefit is derived from pretending to ascertain periodically the opinions of parties, however competent, as to the then supposed value of such property'.[3] This practice lasted until 1846 when it was suspended 'until some of the Extension Lines . . . are finished'.[4]

During the mania, and for a few years after it, accounting for depreciation seems to have been dropped by some companies, presumably in order that the revenue account should be relieved of charges so that dividend rates could be more easily maintained.[5] When the companies settled down again after the excesses of the mania they once more recognised the need to allow for depreciation in the accounts. In the report of the Select Committee on Audit of 1849 there are several references to this, and in its third report the committee stated that the idea of a depreciation fund 'seems now to be generally admitted as necessary, and in some instances, the Committee rejoice to observe, it is practically adopted'.[6] And some of those who gave evidence also stressed its desirability; for example, Sir John Easthope,

[1] In fact, as is shown, this was not the case. Many important companies did not set aside part of their profits.

[2] London & Birmingham Railway, *Reports and Accounts*, 30 June 1841 (BTHR, RAC 1/226), chairman's speech.

[3] Great Western Railway, *Reports and Accounts*, 31 December 1841 (BTHR, RAC 1/164).

[4] Ibid, 31 December 1846. Auditors' Report.

[5] Thus the London & North Western Railway, newly formed in 1846, made no allowance for depreciation. This company was an amalgamation of, amongst others, the Grand Junction and London & Birmingham companies, which had had depreciation funds. One of the reasons for dropping depreciation on the part of some companies may simply have been that their numerous activities in promoting new lines, building extensions, amalgamating with other companies, etc, led to a state of accounting indigestion.

[6] PP 1849, X, Third Report, p x.

formerly of the London & South Western Railway,[1] William Quilter,[2] a London accountant—'the practice of my firm I believe to be the most extensive in England'[3]—and Peter Blackburn (chairman of the Edinburgh & Glasgow Railway).[4]

The South Eastern Railway did not have a depreciation fund until one was recommended by a Committee of Investigation and adopted by the directors in 1849, when they referred to the fact that 'the soundness of the principle is universally admitted', and established separate accounts for the depreciation of permanent way and of rolling stock.[5] The year before the Midland Railway had adopted a 'fund for the renewal of Permanent Way' in order to avoid large, sudden payments which would result in fluctuations in dividends. (However, it did not bother with one for rolling stock on the ground that the expenditure was more stable).[6] But neither of these depreciation and renewal funds survived for long. The South Eastern's fund for rolling stock disappeared from the accounts in 1851[7] and that for rails in 1854 (when it was exhausted and overdrawn). The Midland withdrew its permanent way renewal fund in 1857 (it was then in debit).[8] It had never seen fit to provide for depreciation of its rolling stock and asserted, in a report to its shareholders, that those companies which had adopted the plan of a depreciation fund for rolling stock 'have abandoned it, and now repair and renew their Rolling Stock from Revenue each half-year as the necessity arises'.[9] The Midland may have been basing its generalisation on the London & North Western Railway. In 1847 that company had reintroduced depreciation funds for the renewal of rails and stock.[10] But the amount deducted from revenue account for the depreciation of stock was almost at once considered to be unnecessary, and in the next account was transferred to a reserve account.[11] Six months later the directors stated that 'the practice of the . . . Company is to maintain the working plant at its full

[1] Ibid, Q 2638.

[2] Ibid, Q 2255.

[3] Ibid, Q 2215. The firm was Quilter, Ball, Jay and Crosbie.

[4] Ibid, QQ 3260, 3261.

[5] South Eastern Railway, *Reports and Accounts*, 31 July 1849 (BTHR, RAC 1/1/378).

[6] Midland Railway, *Reports and Accounts*, 31 December 1848 (BTHR, RAC 1/290).

[7] The newly appointed auditors had recommended that the rolling stock be kept up out of revenue: Auditors' Report, 11 September 1850 (BTHR, RAC 1/378).

[8] In an article on 'Maintenance of the Seven Great London Railways', *Herapath* (8 March 1856, 282–3) noted that only three of them had renewal or reserve funds (viz, London & North Western, Eastern Counties, and London, Brighton & South Coast), and that these were spending an increasing amount from revenue rather than from the reserve funds. The other four companies were: South Eastern, Great Northern, Great Western, and London & South Western.

[9] Midland Railway, *Reports and Accounts*, 31 December 1849 (BTHR, RAC 1/290).

[10] London & North Western Railway, *Reports and Accounts*, 31 December 1847 (BTHR, RAC 1/233). Part of the chairman's speech explaining the need for the funds is given in Perry Mason, op cit, p 213.

[11] London & North Western Railway, *Reports and Accounts*, 30 June 1848 (BTHR, RAC, 1/233).

effective value, repairing it as required, and replacing it when worn out, from the current revenue'.[1] All this was in line with the view of *Herapath* which, in the course of an article on 'Reserve Funds' stated: 'The shareholders are entitled at the end of every half-year to divide amongst themselves *all* the profits their Companies have realised during that period.'[2]

Lardner thought that in depreciation policy a distinction had to be made between rolling stock and permanent way. Stock was being repaired continually, parts of locomotives replaced and new stock added. This did not result in large sudden demands on revenue, as did the relaying of permanent way, which therefore required a depreciation fund.[3] In 1849 the chairman of the London, Brighton & South Coast Railway (Samuel Laing) wrote a *Report on the Question of Depreciation and on the Policy of establishing a Reserve Fund* which similarly made a distinction between renewal of rolling stock and renewal of permanent way and buildings. 'The alternative evidently lies between the adoption of a reserve fund, future creations of capital, or future fluctuations of dividend.' Given a closed capital account at that date, and the undesirability of unstable dividends, the best alternative was to make appropriations from revenue. This applied to the rails. Rolling stock should be kept up out of revenue (pp 15–16). But on this there were differences of opinion. *Herapath* noted that the Lancashire & Yorkshire Railway had dropped their 'road renewal fund' and rejoiced that the directors had 'discovered the absurdity of this fund and abandoned it. . . . Keep the stock and road in repair, and away to the winds with all "road renewals" and "stock depreciation" whims'.[4] Other companies which discontinued the practice of providing for the depreciation of rails—for example the Midland and the South Eastern—have already been mentioned. But the London & North Western continued it until 1865 when, the directors explained, the amount being spent equalled the amount being credited to the fund. In future the directors would charge annually the amount actually spent.[5]

Clearly the adoption of depreciation accounts from the late forties was a reaction to the scandals of the mid forties, as well as a desire to keep dividends stable. That they did not last long was due to the increase in traffic in the fifties and sixties, when companies found that their past allocations to depreciation reserves were inadequate. Increasingly companies turned to the practice of not providing for depreciation as such but of debiting the actual expenditure on maintenance and renewals to the periodic revenue accounts.

[1] Ibid, 31 December 1848. Additions to rolling stock were charged to capital at this time.

[2] *Herapath*, 28 May 1853, 574.

[3] Lardner, op cit, pp 114–15.

[4] *Herapath*, 5 March 1853, 267.

[5] London & North Western Railway, *Reports and Accounts*, 30 June 1865 (BTHR, RAC 1/234).

CAPITAL EXTENSIONS DEBITED TO REVENUE

In the late forties, particularly after the financial disaster of 1847, the main line companies found themselves burdened with heavy programmes of capital expenditure. Their dividends were falling, their shares were no longer in favour with the investing public, and the shareholders of many companies asserted themselves and called a halt to capital expenditure. Henceforth any capital expenditure was to be specially authorised by the shareholders, which meant a stop to new promotions and an abandonment of some previously authorised branches. The list of companies which set limits to their capital expenditure in an attempt to close their capital accounts included: the London & South Western,[1] the London & North Western,[2] the London, Brighton & South Coast,[3] the Midland,[4] the Edinburgh & Glasgow,[5] and the South Eastern.[6] George Carr Glyn, the chairman of the London & North Western Railway said in 1851: 'My opinion is, that no large undertaking is firmly based and placed in a proper position until the capital account is closed.'[7] And the London, Brighton & South Coast Railway boasted that 'there is no large Railway Company which has so small an extent of works in progress or in prospect'.[8] Joseph Locke, the engineer, agreed that it was desirable to close capital accounts,[9] as did also the *Railway Times*,[10] the reformed board of the Eastern Counties Railway,[11] and the *Railway Chronicle*.[12]

By the early fifties most of the companies had slowed down if not actually stopped expenditure charged to capital account. But capital accounts could not be closed entirely if traffic increased and facilities were to be extended to satisfy the additional demands. Lardner, writing in 1850, already had pointed out that it 'would be utterly impracticable, unless it were deliberately intended in future to feed capital at the expense of revenue'.[13] In

[1] London & South Western Railway, *Reports and Accounts*, 31 December 1849 (BTHR, RAC 1/245A).
[2] London & North Western Railway, *Reports and Accounts*, 31 December 1849 (BTHR, RAC 1/233).
[3] London, Brighton & South Coast Railway, *Reports and Accounts*, 31 December 1848 (BTHR, RAC 1/248).
[4] Midland Railway, *Reports and Accounts*, 30 June 1849 (BTHR, RAC 1/290).
[5] *Railway Times*, 10 March 1849, 250.
[6] South Eastern Railway, *Reports and Accounts*, 21 June 1853 (BTHR, RAC 1/378). Special General Meeting.
[7] London & North Western Railway, *Reports and Accounts*, 31 December 1850 (BTHR, RAC 1/233). His speech was made on 21 February 1851.
[8] London, Brighton & South Coast Railway, *Reports and Accounts*, 30 June 1848 (BTHR, RAC 1/248).
[9] *SC on Railway and Canal Bills*, PP 1852–3, XXXVIII, Q 2931 et seq.
[10] *Railway Times*, 29 September 1849, 996.
[11] *SC on Audit*, PP 1849, X, p 365.
[12] *Railway Chronicle*, 23 September 1848, 675.
[13] Lardner, op cit, p 118.

fact the secular increase of traffic, the Great Exhibition traffic of 1851, together with the minor railway boom of 1852 and 1853, resulted in more capital expenditure by the old companies, partly in order to protect their territories. Thus in 1856 the auditors of the Midland Railway said that the company's capital accounts had increased by nearly £4½ million since 1849 instead of by the budgeted amount of £770,000. After giving the details they said that 'these being *additions*, are properly chargeable to Capital, so long as it shall not have been decided to pay everything from Revenue'.[1]

Nevertheless some companies decided to deal with extensions occasioned by increased traffic by charging the cost to revenue account. Sometimes the cost was spread over the revenue accounts of several successive accounting periods, the 'unrecovered' balance being accommodated in a suspense account. In 1851 the auditor of the London & North Western Railway reported that the amount spent on additions to works and stock was to be charged to revenue account over a period of five years.[2] Similarly, after the limit set by the London & South Western Railway for capital expenditure had been reached, expenditure on additional rolling stock was 'recovered' from revenue by instalments over a period of years.[3] This system was later extended to stations and sidings.[4]

It is not surprising that resolutions to close the capital account or, as an alternative, to write off the cost of extensions to revenue account over a short period, were not followed rigorously for long. Only 18 months after the London & North Western Railway had decided to charge new rolling stock to revenue over a period of five years through the medium of a suspense account, the auditors suggested a modification of the plan.[5] A year later the idea of a closed capital account was dropped. It had been assumed, the directors explained, that additions to traffic would be slow and steady; but they had been frequent and heavy and the company could no longer continue to charge revenue with additions to stock, stations and sidings. This would be unfair to those who were interested in current dividends rather than in the long term value of the railway. Further, the chairman (General George Anson, MP) was in favour of a fixed rather than a fluctuating dividend. He said:

> Why, gentlemen, it is impossible to expect that this enormous increase of traffic can be carried on, and that the charge for all the engines, car-

[1] Midland Railway, *Reports and Accounts*, 31 December 1855 (BTHR, RAC 1/290). The auditor's report is dated 12 February 1856.

[2] London & North Western Railway, *Reports and Accounts*, 31 December 1850 (BTHR, RAC 1/235). The auditors' report is dated 14 February 1851. But see below for the subsequent reversal of this policy.

[3] London & South Western Railway, *Reports and Accounts*, 30 June 1851 (BTHR, RAC 1/245A).

[4] Ibid, 31 December 1851.

[5] London & North Western Railway, *Reports and Accounts*, 30 June 1852 (BTHR, RAC 1/233). The Directors extended the period of liquidation to ten years: ibid, 31 December 1852.

> riages, and waggons that are to produce these receipts is to be debited against profits. I think it must be quite evident to everyone that it is not fair upon the present Proprietors that the whole of this sum should be charged to revenue. . . . If I had remained in the position I have now the honour to occupy,[1] my object would be to endeavour to maintain for you a fixed dividend. . . . And I would not be induced to change that decision by any temporary variation that might take place in the revenue. . . .

The directors recommended that the balance of the suspense account should be transferred to the debit of capital account; in future any proposed capital expenditure would be submitted to the shareholders for their prior approval in detail.[2] Similarly, the London & South Western Railway in 1853 decided to extend the period for the recovery from revenue of expenditure on new rolling stock.[3] However, the shareholders went further and asked that this expenditure and that on extensions to sidings and stations be charged to capital.[4] The directors agreed to charge the cost of new stock to capital because of its great amount.[5]

BETTERMENT

One of the most interesting and lengthy discussions in railway financial history has been that concerned with the treatment of the expenditures on improved and more costly replacements. This problem of betterment or improvement arose almost as soon as the early railways were opened, because in the experimental years of the 1830s and 1840s some equipment had to be replaced quickly and at higher cost on account of increased weight and other improvements. The experience of the Grand Junction Railway is interesting. The line was opened in 1837, and in a subsequent report[6] the directors stated that nearly all the locomotives had been found deficient, and some had been almost wholly rebuilt, at a heavy cost. 'It appeared unreasonable to charge the income during this period with an outlay not partaking of the character of current expenses or ordinary repairs, but occasioned by original defects in the Engines.' Part was therefore charged

[1] This was his farewell speech.

[2] London & North Western Railway, *Reports and Accounts*, 30 June 1853 (BTHR, RAC 1/233). In the meantime the General Finance Committee of the company, on examining an estimate for expenditure on new works, had 'apportioned in each case, the sums which, in their judgment should be charged to capital—to Revenue direct—or to Deferred payment'. They thought that if the suspense account were to be discontinued it would be desirable 'to substitute a depreciation Fund to accomplish to a considerable extent the same objects'. General Finance Committee Minutes, 11 February 1853 (minute 906) (BTHR, LNW 1/333).

[3] London & South Western Railway, *Reports and Accounts*, 31 December 1853 (BTHR, RAC 1/245A).

[4] Ibid, 30 June 1854. Auditors' report.

[5] Ibid. Directors' Report.

[6] Grand Junction Railway, *Reports and Accounts*, 30 June 1838 (BTHR, RAC 1/401).

to capital, 'being regarded as an addition to the capital outlay of the Company, in the increased effective value of the Engines'. This was probably the first time that betterment was charged to capital; at any rate this was the first company to make a coherent statement on the subject.

By the late forties the idea gained ground that the increased cost of replacements should be charged to capital. Captain J. M. Laws, in 1849, said that the whole cost should not be charged to capital, only the difference between original cost and replacement cost.[1] Similarly, Joseph Locke thought that this difference should be charged to capital.[2] But company practices varied on this as on other matters. Thus the auditors of the London & North Western Railway reported in 1867 that the cost of a wide range of improvements, as well as additions, had been met out of revenue. These included the 'renewal' of old by improved engines, many of the former remaining in use, additions to tools, machinery, carts and horses, additions to the permanent way, and the replacement of timber bridges by more substantial structures.[3]

CONCLUSION

It was stated at the outset that there were many differences in the accounting practices and 'principles' followed by the railway companies. This has been demonstrated by the discussion of selected topics and the illustrations presented in the preceding sections, which also make the point that companies from time to time changed their practices and the bases on which profits (net revenue) were calculated. Nevertheless, despite the diversity and variation, it is possible to offer some generalisations.

It seems clear that in general the early accounting practices and changes in the bases of profit calculations were not designed principally to produce statements drawn up in accordance with preconceived definitions or concepts of 'profits', 'income' or 'asset values'. It is possible that at first lack of experience may have been partly responsible for changes in the accounting treatment, for example, of depreciation.[4] But later changes in accounting policy cannot be explained in these terms. It is more realistic to recognise that in practice the calculation of profits was often influenced significantly by changing financial circumstances and the dictates of management policy. Thus in the mid forties some companies stopped providing for depreciation in their revenue accounts apparently simply in order to pay high

[1] *SC on Audit*, PP 1849, X, Q 2992, See also QQ 1263 and 3259.

[2] *SC on Railway & Canal Bills*, PP 1852–3, XXXVIII, Q 2877.

[3] Auditors' Report to the Shareholders' Audit Committee, 7 Jan 1867. (Printed with London & North Western Railway, *Reports and Accounts*, 31 December 1866 (BTHR, RAC 1/234), and reprinted in H. Pollins, 'Railway Auditing, a Report of 1867', *Accounting Research*, Vol 8, No I, January 1957, 14–22. See especially p 19.) Twenty years earlier, the extra cost of heavier rails had been charged to capital: *Reports and Accounts*, 31 December 1847 (BTHR, RAC 1/233), Chairman's speech.

[4] Noted by Lewin, *Railway Mania*, p 353.

dividends. On the other hand, stringency in the capital market and an attitude of caution seem to have been responsible for highly conservative treatment of important items (in the sense of understating profits) in the years following the mania. It is not possible to detect dominant aims or attitudes of railway directors in the period under review, since these were influenced by the changing economic scene as well as by the circumstances of particular companies. However, there is some evidence to suggest that many railway directors as well as shareholders wished to have regular rather than fluctuating dividends, and the entries in the final accounts may very well have been influenced by the desire for a record of stable earnings and dividends. The fact that many items appearing (or not appearing) in the revenue accounts involved personal judgments, and that there was not yet a generally accepted body of accounting doctrine, made it easy for the preparation of the final accounts of even the most conscientiously conducted company to be influenced by considerations of management policy.

The nature of the accounting practices in operation at a particular time may perhaps in part have reflected the composition of the shareholding body. Lardner, writing in 1850, divided railway shareholders into two main groups, permanent investors and temporary investors (including speculators).

> Now, the class of proprietors first mentioned have less regard to the amount of present dividends than to the permanent value of the stock, and they chiefly expect from the directors of the railway a due regard to the efficient maintenance of the permanent way and the movable stock out of revenue, before any surplus be appropriated to dividend. On the other hand, the latter class, and especially the speculators, care nothing for the permanent value of the concern, and look only to the present amount of dividend.[1]

The relative importance of these two broad groups changed from time to to time, and such changes may have affected the treatment of items bearing on the calculation of profits. Thus the widespread practice in the early fifties of charging items to revenue that would normally have been chargeable to capital may have been induced not only by the difficulties of raising capital for the railways; it is likely that there had been a reduction in the number of short term speculative holdings of the shares of railway companies in the crises of 1847 and the subsequent slump, and that the remaining shareholders were investors who were interested in the long term prosperity of the companies and willing to forgo current dividends in order to safeguard future dividends. This would help to explain the tendency at the time to substitute deliberate under-statement of current profits for the deliberate over-statement which had been prevalent during the preceding mania.

It has been shown that the basis for the allocation of certain important

[1] Lardner, op cit, pp 116 et seq.

items between capital and revenue accounts was not the same in all companies, and that the allocation was not carried out in a consistent manner by any major company. The close connection between the accounting treatment of those items and the declaration of dividends has also been noted. It will, therefore, be clear that any attempt to use the information in railway accounts before 1868 in order to assess the amount of annual investment and capital formation in railways has to contend with the difficulties and inconsistencies of the kind described in this article. But it may be added, as a qualification, that the legislation of 1868 did not work wonders at once, and complaints about railway accounting practices affecting profit calculations continued.[2]

[1] See, for example, the comments of the *Railway Times* (12 January 1878, 30) on the occasion of an increased dividend paid by the Metropolitan Railway:

> Could we divest ourselves of the idea that the dividends that Sir Edward Watkin has each succeeding half-year to dispense are pre-arranged, and depend rather upon considerations of financial policy than the result of an actual profit and loss balance, we should hail the announcement of the Metropolitan with unalloyed satisfaction.

The Accountant, in an editorial (12 November 1887, 618) went further:

> . . . when railway accounts are being discussed the question is not the profit shown, but the elements in the account by which that profit has been derived; and particular regard is paid when looking at the amount spent on renewals and maintenance to see whether the line has or has not been 'starved', and whether or not the next succeeding dividend will suffer in consequence. The style in which railway accounts are reviewed testifies to their utter uselessness and unreliability as revenue accounts in the proper and only true sense of the term.

In 1903 *The Economist*, in discussing the half-year's accounts said (15 August 1903), 1432):

> The fact that the chief increase of expenditure occurred in the maintenance of way department is not unsatisfactory, since it may be taken to imply that the companies took the opportunity of a fairly good half-year to improve their permanent way, though it will be seen that not much more was spent [in comparison with the corresponding half-year of 1902] on renewals of carriages and wagons, which is one of the departments in which the line between expenditure that ought to be met out of revenue and that charged to capital is apt to become a little shaky and difficult to distinguish.

Railways and the Growth of the Capital Market

By M. C. Reed

I

One of the most important by-products of the introduction and extension of the railway system in the second quarter of the nineteenth century was the part played by railway shares and debentures in assisting the development of a national market for company securities. Until the coming of the railway, the London Stock Exchange was almost entirely a market for government stock and the stock of the historic chartered companies, and as long as transfers of such stock could be executed only in London, the business was virtually reserved for London brokers.

The building of the canal network in the latter part of the eighteenth century, and the growth of insurance, dock, and waterworks companies in the early nineteenth century, although producing company securities in the form used by the railway companies, did not materially alter the nature of the formal capital market. Though canal shares appeared in Wetenhall's *Course of the Exchange* from 1811 onwards,[1] the total volume of capital represented by canal securities was insignificant when compared with the National Debt: in 1827 Henry English estimated that prior to 1824 £12,202,096 had been raised by canal companies, and the capital of other companies brought the total to £47,936,486.[2] But in 1824 the funded National Debt amounted to £792·9 millions,[3] while in that year alone £15,364,250 was raised for foreign loans.[4]

The joint stock company flotation boom of 1824–5, though insignificant in terms of permanent results, seems to have produced a temporary interest

I am indebted to the archivist of the British Railways Board, and his staff in London and Edinburgh, for access to material used in the preparation of this paper, and my thanks are also due to the public relations officer and the librarian of the London Stock Exchange, and to the secretaries of the Bristol, Manchester and Birmingham Stock Exchanges, for making available material relating to these stock exchanges. I am also indebted to Dr A. R. Hall, Dr R. M. Hartwell, Mr G. R. Hawke and Mr R. J. Morris for reading through and commenting on an earlier draft of this paper.

[1] E. V. Morgan and W. A. Thomas, *The Stock Exchange* (1964), p 102. Wetenhall's *Course of the Exchange* was the official Stock Exchange price list.

[2] Henry English, *A complete view of the Joint Stock Companies formed during 1824 and 1825* (1827), p 42.

[3] B. R. Mitchell and P. Deane, *Abstract of British Historical Statistics* (Cambridge, 1962), p 402.

[4] English, op cit, p 42.

in company business, and in many ways foreshadowed the far greater speculative promotion booms of 1836 and 1845. English listed 354 companies which had issued prospectuses in 1824 and 1825,[1] and, though few of them survived the collapse of December 1825, at the height of the boom a number of new company securities were quoted on the Stock Exchange. On 5 February 1825, for example, *The Times* reported dealings in Birmingham & Liverpool, London & Bristol, London Northern, and Kentish Railway shares. But apart from mining schemes, very few of the companies proposed had a long life, and greater Stock Exchange interest was shown in the parallel creation of loans for foreign governments.

By 1830, therefore, the London capital market was still largely orientated towards dealings in government stocks, and only a primitive mechanism existed for dealing with the relatively small amount of company securities. Dubois suggests that dealings in the shares of the smaller canal companies were generally arranged through individual brokers, and that officials of canal companies often acted as brokers for their company's shares.[2] If this was the case, it seems fair to assume that there was not sufficient business on the Stock Exchange to create a ready market in company securities, and a number of London sharebrokers' circulars which have survived reinforce this view. Like their provincial brethren, they seem to have carried out business in company securities by advertising shares for sale or wanted by name.[3] The auctioning of shares was an alternative to disposal through a broker which was widely used: even when railways were well-established on the Stock Exchange, the auctioning of railway shares was not unknown. In 1838 the London & Birmingham Railway disposed of some surplus shares at the Auction Mart,[4] and as late as 1845 a firm of brokers, Messrs Lamond and Co, advertised their intention to hold twice-weekly auction sales of joint-stock company shares at the Hall of Commerce.[5] But this last instance is rather a testimony to the amount of business available in company shares, than an indication of the primitive nature of the market, as by 1845 the rapid increase in railway business had geared the London Stock Exchange to handle a growing range of company securities.

[1] English, op cit, pp 12–26.

[2] A. B. Dubois, *The English Business Company after the Bubble Act, 1720–1800* (New York and London, 1938), p 409 n.

[3] See, for example, *Prices of Shares etc at the office of Charles Edmunds, Broker*, 31 August 1833. (Bound at the British Museum Newspaper Library with Wetenhall's *Course of the Exchange* and other lists.)

[4] *Select Committee on Railway Acts Enactments*, PP 1846, XIV, Q 1727.

[5] *Railway Register*, Vol II (1845), Advertising Sheet 3.

II

Before assessing the impact of railway development on the Stock Exchange, it is necessary to appreciate the character of railway and similar company securities. The almost universal practice of issuing company shares for a small deposit, and gradually calling up the remainder of the value of the share as the company's progress demanded, produced a security which at different stages appealed to different purchasers. A fully-paid railway share, earning a regular dividend, was a natural means of investment for a person wishing to earn a regular return on his capital; on the other hand, the newly-issued share, with no more than £1 called and no immediate prospect of a dividend, attracted speculators anxious to make quick capital gains as the shares fluctuated in price with external pressures.

Moreover, the position was further complicated by the uncertain state of the law relating to joint stock companies prior to 1844. The normal procedure when floating a railway company was to publish a prospectus and invite applications for shares.[1] Successful applicants would be given letters of allotment, signifying that a certain number of shares had been allotted to them. The next stage was for the allottees to pay the deposit on the shares they took up: this was acknowledged by the issue of a scrip certificate, or by the issue of a banker's receipt which could further be exchanged for a scrip certificate. The scrip certificate gave the holder a title to the appropriate number of shares when the formalities of incorporation were complete, and was an acknowledgment that the holder of the scrip had signed the subscription contract and parliamentary deed which bound him to pay instalments as demanded.

As was recognised by contemporary commentators, there was a contradiction here: although the names on the subscription contract were often incorporated in the Act authorising the company, and though the directors of the company were entitled to proceed against signatories for non-payment of calls, in fact the scrip certificates, made out to bearer, were readily transferable, and indeed it was generally understood that they would be transferred.[2] Until the company was incorporated, the original holder of the scrip could not transfer the responsibility incurred when signing the deed; a further complication was that until 1844 a railway company which was unsuccessful in its application to parliament for incorporation was in law a private partnership, and all signatories of the

[1] For a fuller discussion of this topic, see Harold Pollins, 'The marketing of railway shares in the first half of the nineteenth century,' *Economic History Review*, Second Series, Vol VII (1954–5), 230–9.

See also the evidence of John Duncan, *SC on Joint Stock Companies*, PP 1844, VII, especially QQ 2066–78.

[2] *SC on Jt Stock Cos*, PP 1844, VII, Q 2076.

parliamentary deed were liable to the full extent of their estates for any of the costs incurred by the company. Thus companies which could easily allocate all their shares, and even collect deposits, found it difficult to complete the subscription contract, or to have scrip exchanged for shares if the shares went to a discount; it was not unknown for investors to induce others to sign the subscription contract in their stead.[1]

Thus the procedure for obtaining and registering subscribers to a railway scheme, which was designed to see that schemes which came before Parliament had a responsible body of proprietors, often had the opposite effect. Letters of allotment, bankers' receipts, and scrip certificates were readily transferred,[2] and these transfers took place without any record. Although Stock Exchange rules forbade transactions in securities on which nothing had been paid, in the area round the Stock Exchange there was in times of excitement a large scale market in railway paper, and the 'stag' who wrote for letters of allotment he could not hope to take up was a familiar character in the company promotion booms of 1825, 1836, and the mid 1840s. The Select Committee on Railway Subscription Contracts in 1837 exposed in two volumes of evidence, which dealt with only seven companies, the extent to which subscription contracts were filled up with men of straw, and incidentally revealed the activities of the 'alley-men', the traffickers in letters of allotment and the like. The area round the Stock Exchange, including the Rotunda of the Bank of England,[3] the Royal Exchange, and the streets themselves, provided a closely-knit market for the paper of new companies, and was the natural breeding ground of 'bubble' companies. Even members of the Stock Exchange were sometimes obliged to do business with the alley-men to satisfy the requirements of their principals,[4] and it was frequently claimed that Stock Exchange members were deeply implicated in the promotion of 'bubble' companies.[5] As late as 1854, a pamphleteer alleged that in order to get a Stock Exchange quotation, the promoters of speculative companies would bribe members with allotments of shares which could be resold at a profit,[6] and the same writer repeated the accusation which had been made in 1837 that brokers were active in rigging the market for the paper of new companies.[7] More firmly-constituted companies endeavoured to keep their paper out of this market, using black-lists of known 'letter-writers' and the advice of brokers to weed their lists of applicants, but even these efforts sometimes

[1] *SC on Railway Subscription Contracts*, PP 1837, XVIII, QQ 7456; 14043; 19933.

[2] *SC on Jt Stock Cos*, PP 1844, VII, Q 2067.

[3] In 1838 the Rotunda was closed to dealers in securities. (See Morgan & Thomas, *The Stock Exchange*, p 54.)

[4] *SC on Railway Subscription Contracts*, PP 1837, XVIII, Q 5898.

[5] See, for example, *SC on Jt Stock Cos*, PP 1844, VII, Q 2422.

[6] *An Exposure of the Stock Exchange and Bubble Companies* (1854), p 17.

[7] Ibid, p 15, and *SC on Railway Subscription Contracts*, PP 1837, XVIII, QQ 9424; 9484.

failed.[1] As late as 1845, the suggestion that the London & York Railway had filled its subscription list with doubtful applicants was enough to produce a rigorous parliamentary inquiry, which delayed the line's progress.[2]

It is difficult to assess the role of this fringe market in railway paper in the development of the capital market. Certainly, it had unfortunate results on the development of the railway system, leading to the authorisation of purely speculative lines, but in this the railways were the victims of an existing system which encouraged gambling transactions in new securities, rather than its creators. However, the railway manias of the thirties and forties gave added scope to such activities, and involved a far wider circle in the evils of gambling in securities they could not afford to take up. It is not an over-dramatisation to say that the railway boom of 1845 reproduced all over the country the speculative excesses previously found only in a small quarter of London. On the other hand, it must be recognised that such gambling largely took place in paper of little or no value, and as such involved little capital; indeed, in so far as capital which might otherwise have been idle was eventually brought into railway schemes, the existence of this highly speculative market may well have widened the scope of the capital market proper.

Gambling in letters of allotment and scrip represented only the most extravagant form of dealing in 'light' shares, and once the initial deposit was paid on company shares, the Stock Exchange was able to play its more proper role of acting as a market for securities. It was recognised that the calling-up of instalments on shares in itself created a market for shares; investors who could not afford to pay up all their shares were forced to part with some in order to retain others,[3] and by the time the share was fully-paid and earning a regular dividend its owner was likely to be a person of substantial means, unlikely to gamble on temporary fluctuations in the value of his property.[4] A commentator in 1845 stated that most of the dealings on the Stock Exchange were 'light' new shares, and that fully-paid shares, from which the broker would derive a larger commission, were seen very infrequently.[5] James Morrison, an early advocate of government interference in railway matters, argued that this division of the holders of railway property into two classes, the speculative holder of light stock, and the long term holder of dividend-bearing shares, was essential to railway finance, as the substantial capitalist was unlikely to risk his money in the initial stages of a company's development.[6] The implication is that without an active market for the transfer of shares, capital could not have been

[1] *SC on Railway Subscription Contracts*, PP 1837, XVIII, 2nd Report, p 404, and Q 21452.

[2] C. H. Grinling, *The History of the Great Northern Railway* (2nd ed, 1903), pp 42–5.

[3] G. Cochrane, *The Way to make Railroad Shares Popular* (1846), pp 7–8.

[4] *Lords' SC on Audit of Rly Accounts*, PP 1849, X, Q 2951.

[5] *The City, or the Physiology of London Business* (1845), p 58.

[6] *Lords' SC on Audit of Rly Accounts*, PP 1849, X, Q 1427.

attracted to the railway system in a sufficient quantity to make possible its rapid advance.

It is in this connection that the progress of railway business on the Stock Exchange is especially significant, and where railway business differed from that in the securities of other companies was in the sheer volume of capital issued. By 1843, the amount of railway share capital actually paid up was over £43 million; by 1847, the figure exceeded £126 million.[1] Moreover, this figure excludes the substantial volume of loan capital, which was also dealt in to some extent on the Stock Exchange. In addition, the large capital of individual companies was a new factor: by 1848, the LNWR had a share capital of over £13,000,000.[2] Thus railway business rapidly outweighed business in all other classes of company securities on the Stock Exchange, and individual companies were large enough for there to be a ready market in their securities. In 1830 205 companies were named in the *Course of the Exchange*; only four of these were railways.[3] By 1844 755 companies had quotations, and though the 417 joint stock banks were the largest single category, their paid-up capital was only £26 million, compared with the £47 million of 66 railways.[4] These railway companies represented about a third of the joint-stock company capital quoted.

Some idea of the growth of railway business may be gained from the following table, compiled from the *Course of the Exchange*, which shows the number of railway companies whose securities were listed between 1830 and 1844. After 1844 the railway amalgamation movement reduces the number of securities of old companies, and by then most principal companies were quoted. From 1836 onwards it is possible to gather some idea of the amount of business from the prices quoted against a company; prior to that date, prices appear to have been left unchanged until a fresh dealing was reported.

While it is important not to read too much into this table, which does not reflect, for instance, the issue of a new class of security by an existing company, the pattern from 1836 onwards clearly follows the pattern of railway promotion, reflecting the absence of speculative companies after about 1837, and the increase in business in 1844.

For the period from 1830 to 1835, a more detailed index of activity can be compiled from a daily list of prices which has survived as a set from January 1830 to December 1835: this list has been used to construct a table which shows the marked increase in railway business during this

[1] H. Scrivenor, *The Railways of the United Kingdom Statistically Considered* (London, 1849), Appendix, p 40.

[2] Ibid, p 46.

[3] They were the Liverpool & Manchester, Stockton & Darlington, Cheltenham, and Peak Forest Railways.

[4] W. F. Spackman, *Statistical Tables of the United Kingdom* (1842), p 106. (Spackman's figures differ from the *Course of the Exchange*; this is probably because the latter only included active securities.)

period, despite the small number of securities quoted. The list records prices in half-daily periods, and a simple index of the number of half-days on which railway business was reported provides one column, while the other is arrived at by counting the number of half-days each company's securities had a price marked. Although some half-days have two or three prices marked for one security, implying several dealings, this factor has been ignored.

TABLE 1

RAILWAY COMPANIES QUOTED IN THE *COURSE OF THE EXCHANGE*, 1830–44

Year	*January*		*June/July*	
	Companies	*Prices Marked*	*Companies*	*Prices Marked*
1830	4	—	4	—
1831	4	—	5	—
1832	5	—	5	—
1833	6	—	8	—
1834	10	—	11	—
1835	19	—	21	—
1836	33	16	62	25
1837	54	16	54	14
1838	48	10	47	13
1839	49	15	43	10
1840	41	15	43	16
1841	42	10	41	12
1842	40	19	37	10
1843	35	13	37	19
1844	37	26	43	29

Notes: The issues from which these details are taken are in each case the first issue of each year, and the date closest to 30 June. Each issue covers dealings over half a week. The large increase in the number of companies quoted at the beginning of 1835 coincides with an increase in the size of the publication, and may be partly due to this.

It is clear from Table 2 that there was a marked increase in railway business in 1833, and it is worth tracing the progress of railway securities on the London Stock Exchange in a little more detail. On 28 days in 1830 a price was recorded for Liverpool & Manchester shares, no doubt reflecting speculative interest in the line's completion, and in 1831 dealings were again confined to the Liverpool & Manchester. However, the Southampton & London railway appeared on the list from March 1831 to September 1832, although no prices were recorded. This accords with the view of the *Circular to Bankers* that sharebrokers had taken an active interest in this line,[1] and is an early indication of City interest in railway schemes. In 1833, further companies were added, including the Clarence Railway, a Durham line which was financed largely from London, the London & Birmingham, in whose securities there were 77 dealings between June and December, and the London & Greenwich, with 32 dealings between July and December. The following year, business was most active in London & Greenwich shares, handled on 109 half-days: by comparison, Liverpool & Manchester shares were dealt in only on three occasions. By the end of 1835, the shares of 17 companies were being dealt in, with Great Western, London & Blackwall, and London & Greenwich the most active.

TABLE 2

DEALINGS IN RAILWAY SHARES, JANUARY 1830–DECEMBER 1835

Year	*1830*		*1831*		*1832*		*1833*		*1834*		*1835*	
Month	*1*	*2*	*1*	*2*	*1*	*2*	*1*	*2*	*1*	*2*	*1*	*2*
Jan	1	1	0	0	2	2	4	4	14	16	16	19
Feb	1	1	0	0	1	1	4	4	20	20	14	14
March	6	6	1	1	0	0	2	2	18	19	14	19
April	3	3	1	1	0	0	3	3	11	11	25	30
May	1	1	2	2	0	0	1	1	9	9	18	20
June	1	1	0	0	0	0	16	18	9	9	20	24
July	5	5	1	1	1	1	22	28	10	11	10	11
August	0	0	1	1	1	1	19	20	8	9	18	24
Sept	4	4	0	0	1	1	13	13	12	13	39	71
Oct	5	5	1	1	0	0	11	13	17	19	54	195
Nov	1	1	2	2	1	1	16	19	14	14	48	278
Dec	0	0	1	1	0	0	9	9	4	4	48	133
Total	28	28	10	10	7	7	120	134	146	154	324	838

Notes: Col 1: Number of half-days with dealings recorded.
Col 2: Number of security dealings monthly.

Source: Stock Exchange Reference Library. *British and Foreign Share List* (by James Wetenhall), 1830–5.

The increase in railway business in 1833, therefore, coincided with the authorisation of the first railway companies to serve London, the London & Birmingham and the London & Greenwich, and from then onwards railway securities were dealt in in increasing volume and variety. This conclusion is in marked contrast with the view of Evans, that the Stock Exchange was not involved in railway business until about 1844:[2] some rail-

[1] *Circular to Bankers*, 13 June 1834, 379. (Afterwards quoted as *C to B*).

[2] G. H. Evans, *British Corporation Finance 1775–1850* (Baltimore, 1936), p 10. (Quoted by Dr Broadbridge, below, p 184).

way business was done in 1830, and from 1833 onwards there was a considerable amount of business in the shares of railway companies. Though the companies mainly dealt in were 'local' companies in Evans' sense, in that they served the London area, the shares of more distant concerns were never absent from the *Course of the Exchange*, and by 1836 railway companies which did not serve the London area directly made up a significant proportion of the list.

One final index, albeit imperfect, of Stock Exchange activities during the period when railways were being established on the exchange is the number of members of the exchange. Printed lists are not available before 1837, but the following table shows fluctuations in membership from 1837 to 1847:

TABLE 3

Year	*Members*	*Year*	*Members*	*Year*	*Members*
1837	698	1841	660	1845	634
1838	692	1842	—	1846	681
1839	696	1843	640	1847	686
1840	678	1844	634		

Note: Numbers of members as at end of March in each year.
Source: Stock Exchange, *List of Members* (1837–47); 1842 is missing.

Obviously, figures in this form are a very crude index of stock exchange activity, but the pattern of membership shows an interesting similarity to the pattern of railway activities, with a decline from 1837, and renewed activity from 1844 onwards. The figures of new members admitted (included in the totals above) are available in 1845 and 1846, and these show that from March 1844 to March 1845, 49 new members were admitted, and in the following year no less than 148 new members were admitted: a marked testimony to the increase in business produced by the Railway Mania.

The evidence which has been presented and discussed in the three tables laid out above is far from perfect: unfortunately, it is impossible to reconstruct exact tables of Stock Exchange turnover, or even to identify the proportion of Stock Exchange members active in different markets. However, Tables 1 and 2 give a rough indication of the increase in railway business on the Stock Exchange from 1830 onwards, and these tables, together with the membership figures in Table 3, should be viewed together with the comments of contemporary observers who noted the impact of railway business on the Stock Exchange. As early as 1835 the *Circular to Bankers* spoke, with some misgivings, of 'the junction of the interest of the Stock Exchange with the solid, respectable, and substantial interest which, previous to such junction, solely maintained the railway system . . ..'[1] In 1847,

[1] *C to B*, 6 November 1835, 123.

Lewis Wolfe, a retired broker, agreed with a parliamentary committee that 'since the creation of railways and the extension of Joint Stock Companies', his was a line of business which had greatly augmented.[1] An anonymous writer in 1845 remarked that 'within the last eighteen months, the business of the Stock Exchange has been perfectly revolutionised by the Railway-share mania', and that the share market, previously occupied by four or five distinct brokers and a number of jobbers, 'whose means of business were very small', had become the 'grand focus of speculation and legitimate business'. English and foreign government securities were 'quite deserted for the superior attractions of English and foreign railway scrip'. While at first the specialists in share business 'who formerly had been of little reputation on the Exchange', had monopolised the business, dealings were gradually dispersed among other members. Accounts which could previously be settled in one or two days now took almost a week, and to cope with the extended business extra clerks had to be employed.[2]

III

At the same time as business on the Stock Exchange expanded due to the introduction of railways, public interest in investment prospects and stock exchange prices grew. By the end of 1825 *The Times* had followed the *Morning Chronicle's* lead, and included a detailed market report in addition to publishing price lists. The boom of 1835–6 produced one investment paper, the *Mining Journal*, devoted, as the title suggested, mainly to reports of mining companies, but also giving details of the activities of other companies. There was also a brief-lived *Railway Gazette*, but the *Railway Magazine*, founded in 1835 and taken over by John Herapath the following year, was the first permanent paper devoted specifically to railway matters. The *Railway Magazine* carried market reports of railway prices, accounts of meetings, and prospectuses of new companies, thus supplementing for a specialised readership the widespread advertising and reporting of railway matters in leading London and provincial papers.

The really significant development in railway journalism occurred in 1837 with the launching of the *Railway Times*, a weekly journal devoted almost entirely to the investment, rather than the engineering, side of railways. Detailed reporting of company meetings, accompanied by the publication of companies' accounts, made up the main editorial activity, and the *Railway Times* rapidly established itself as the leading railway journal, with a weekly circulation of about 27,000 copies by 1842.[3] In 1840, Herapath was obliged to copy the format and approach of the rival paper, and specifically widened the scope of the *Railway Magazine* to include details

[1] *Lords' SC on Audit of Rly Accounts*, PP 1849, X, Q 2314.
[2] *The City . . .*, pp 56–7.
[3] From figures given in the *Railway Times*, 1842, 337.

of the activities of joint-stock companies in other spheres.[1] These two journals, with their wide circulation and detailed coverage of company activities, gave investors access to detailed information about a wide range of companies, and enabled fluctuations in receipts and share prices to be compared systematically. Promoters of new companies, by advertising in the railway journals, were able to appeal to a widely scattered but informed body of potential investors, thus supplementing the localised interest which could be aroused by advertising in the provincial press.

During the early 1840s, rival journals began to appear, and as the railway boom gathered momentum, the size and frequency of publication of these journals began to increase as both news and advertising demands grew heavier.[2] As well as the many journals published in London, which had by 1845 proliferated to the extent that party loyalties to different companies could be served, railway papers were started in Edinburgh, Dublin and Liverpool,[3] and even *The Economist*, founded in 1843 as an Anti-Corn Law journal, began to carry a separate *Railway Monitor* section in 1845.[4]

Though most of the journals founded in the 1840s did not survive, they were the essential corollary to the widening of activities on the Stock Exchange, and the forerunners of a more broadly based investment press. Coupled with the increased interest shown by the London and provincial press in company matters, the railway press played an important part in making investment opportunities more widely known, and thus helped to create a more perfect market in company securities.

IV

While the growth of railway business played a significant part in enlarging the London Stock Exchange, and in creating a national investment press, it was in the provinces that the successive railway booms had the most direct effect. With the market in government securities completely dominated by London, the only business open to provincial dealers in shares before the coming of the railways was that in the relatively small number of canal and other company securities. This business was one which could easily be handled by the part-time attention of an accountant, auctioneer, banker, or solicitor, and it was not until the growth in the number of company securities in the 1820s and 1830s that sharebroking began to emerge as a separate profession in the provinces. A directory of Manchester, published in 1825, a year of commercial excitement, listed

[1] The title was changed to: *The Railway Magazine and Commercial Journal.*

[2] See D. Morier Evans, *The Commercial Crisis of 1847–8* (2nd ed, 1850), p 10. Evans estimated that the 'leading journals' were receiving £12,000–£14,000 weekly in advertising receipts at the height of the boom.

[3] For a list of railway papers, see Kelly & Co, *Post Office Railway Directory for 1847* (?1846), p 202.

[4] *The Economist 1843–1943* (Oxford 1943), pp 120–4.

seven 'Canal, Rail-Road &c Sharebrokers' in that town: of these, only two did not specify any other business besides that of sharebroker, while the remainder also acted either as accountants or as agents for insurance companies.[1] Sharebrokers were not distinguished in the Liverpool directory published in 1824, but none of the 16 founder members of the Liverpool Sharebrokers Association in 1836 who can be identified in the 1824 directory listed sharebroking among their activities. Five were accountants, five were merchants, one an attorney, two ship-brokers, one an insurance agent, one simply gave his occupation as broker, and one, Thomas Coglan, combined the trades of auctioneer, commission agent and broker with the proprietorship of a vapour and warm bath establishment.[2] Even by 1836, only three of the founder members of the Liverpool Sharebrokers' Association acted only as sharebrokers.[3] Much the same pattern was doubtless repeated over the country, as accountants and agents of various callings added sharebroking to their activities, and gradually devoted more of their business time to share dealing. In Edinburgh, 'the business of a stockbroker was unknown . . . until 1824';[4] Glasgow's first stockbroker proper commenced business in 1830,[5] while from contemporary advertisements it is obvious that even in large towns stockbroking continued to be combined with other businesses. While accountants, auctioneers, and estate agents regularly acted as stockbrokers, the Provincial Brokers' Stock Exchange contains a firm founded by a clergyman.[6]

The business of these provincial sharebrokers can only be assessed by referring to contemporary lists of prices and other advertisements, but it is obvious that by the early 1830s, railway companies were providing the brokers with a large share of their business. A Birmingham accountant, for example, advertised in 1830 for a variety of railway shares for which 'the highest premiums' were given: they included not only local concerns, such as the Birmingham & Liverpool and London, Coventry & Birmingham, but also the Stockton & Darlington and Sheffield & Manchester.[7] This indicates a speculative business, for apart from the Stockton & Darlington all the companies named were new companies, and certainly could not provide the purchaser with a dividend. An early Glasgow list which has survived shows a wider range of companies, with six banks,

[1] Edward Baines, *History, Directory and Gazetteer of the County Palatine of Lancaster* (Liverpool, 1824–5), Vol II, 304.

[2] Liverpool Stock Exchange, *The Centenary Book of the Liverpool Stock Exchange* (Liverpool, 1936), p 57, and Edward Baines, *History . . . of Lancaster*, Vol I, 204–352.

[3] Liverpool Stock Exchange, *Centenary Book*, p 20.

[4] John Anderson, *History of Edinburgh* (Edinburgh, 1856), pp 377–8.

[5] Glasgow Stock Exchange Association, *Records of the Glasgow Stock Exchange Association, 1844–1926* (Glasgow, 1927), p 1.

[6] Provincial Brokers' Stock Exchange, *Services, facilities and safeguards available to investors . . .* (York, 1954), p 5. Mention is also made of a sharebroking business run by a stationmaster.

[7] *Aris's Birmingham Gazette*, 6 September 1830. Advertisement by Mr Daniel, Accountant, Colmore Row.

five utility companies, seven insurance companies, two canals, and two railways listed.[1]

The provincial share market of the early 1830s can be regarded as being at a transitional stage: the flotation of joint-stock companies, which had reached a peak in 1824–5, had led to the emergence of a class of share dealers, more or less specialist, in the larger provincial centres. Their dealings were largely in local transport, utility, and insurance companies, with railways representing a significant proportion of the business, and providing the main sphere for speculative activity. Business was largely conducted in *ad hoc* dealings, and there are no signs of a current market in given securities. The transformation of the provincial share markets in the 1830s and 1840s was due almost entirely to the promotion of new railway companies; though the number of joint-stock companies operating in other fields, particularly banking, also increased, railway capital far outweighed the capital of other forms of company, and the increase in railway securities provided the provincial brokers with the bulk of their new business.

V

The effects of railway business were felt most markedly, and soonest, in Liverpool and Manchester, and this can easily be accounted for by the importance of Lancashire capital in the development of the railway system. Initially, Liverpool took the lead: despite a strong London interest in the financing of the Liverpool & Manchester Railway,[2] the bulk of the capital for that line came from Liverpool. The new companies promoted in the late 1820s and early 1830s were largely connected with the Liverpool & Manchester: the trunk line from Warrington to Euston via Birmingham can be regarded as an extension of the Liverpool & Manchester system. In such circumstances, when railways were little-known outside the north of England, and Liverpool investors were getting a good return from the Liverpool & Manchester line, it is not surprising that they should have been the first to invest in connecting lines. Even the London & Birmingham line, with strong City connections, one of the first lines in which 'the Stock Exchange people' evinced any great interest,[3] drew more capital from Lancashire and Cheshire than London and Birmingham combined, with Liverpool alone supplying almost half of the total capital of £2,500,000.[4]

However, by the mid 1830s, Lancashire proprietors looked further

[1] Glasgow Stock Exchange, *Records*, facsimile reproduction of 1831 sharelist at end.

[2] See Harold Pollins, 'The Finances of the Liverpool & Manchester Railway', *Economic History Review*, 2nd ser, V (1952), 90–7.

[3] *C to B*, 6 November 1835, 123.

[4] BTHR: *Statement of Distribution of Shares, London & Birmingham Railway* (February, 1836), LBM 2/1.

afield than lines in direct connection with Lancashire for their investments. The *Circular to Bankers* ascribed this not only to the success of the Liverpool & Manchester, but also to the profits made by the Lancashire cotton industry in 1834–5, and to the links which Liverpool had with the New York Stock Exchange, where railways were already the subject of speculation.[1] By 1835, apparently, Manchester had resolved to emulate Liverpool's early interest in railway schemes, and according to the *Circular*:

> Certain it is that in no part of Britain can so many opulent competitors in railway projects now be found as in that great manufacturing capital. We believe that several of its inhabitants have embarked sums so large as £50,000, £70,000 and even as high as £100,000, in Railways now in projection or in progress of completion, and which are not likely to yield revenue for several years from the present date.[2]

Railway promoters, remote from Lancashire, actively courted Lancashire investment: the interest of the investors of Manchester and Liverpool in a railway was taken as a sign that a line would be successfully completed, and enhanced the value of the line in the eyes of other investors.[3] References to the importance of Lancashire capital, and in particular Liverpool capital, in remote lines abound: the *Circular to Bankers* listed in 1836 12 schemes promoted in Liverpool and Manchester, including five distant from Lancashire.[4] Later, the London & Southampton, Eastern Counties, and Great Western were all noted as lines which had been supported by the intervention of Lancashire capital.[5] Unfortunately, it is difficult to recover direct evidence of the amounts invested by Lancashire subscribers in distant schemes, unless subscription contracts are used, but one or two examples will show the extent of such interests. In 1842 the South Eastern Railway received £100,783 from various bankers on account of instalments on shares remitted through them.[6] The largest single amount came from Glyn & Co, the company's bankers, who remitted £64,707. It is impossible to tell how much of this was paid directly to Glyn's, or how much was remitted by provincial bankers to them, but the remaining sum was forwarded by 11 named banks, five of which remitted more than £1,000. The largest single amount was remitted by Moss & Co, the Liverpool bankers, who had strong links with the railway world; they forwarded £12,709. Jones, Loyd & Co of Manchester remitted £9,613, and another Liverpool bank, Barned & Co, £5,347. Messrs Beckett & Co, a

[1] *C to B*, 10 March 1837, 273–4.
[2] *C to B*, 9 October 1835, 93.
[3] *C to B*, 13 April 1838, 324.
[4] *C to B*, 6 May 1836, 333. The Midland Counties, North Midland, Cheltenham Oxford & Tring, Dublin & Drogheda, and Edinburgh & Glasgow were the distant companies named. (This list appears to come from the *Manchester Guardian*, 30 April 1836.)
[5] *C to B*, 13 April 1838, 323.
[6] BTHR, SER 23/1.

West Riding firm,[1] sent £4,125, and the York Union Bank £1,410. The remaining amounts were sent by seven banks, mainly small Southern firms.

The three Lancashire banks thus sent a total of £27,669, over a quarter of the money received, and it is more than likely that Glyn's account included payments by other Lancashire proprietors.

Lancashire investors were also active in Scotland. The Edinburgh & Glasgow Railway, though not authorised until 1838, was under discussion as early as 1830, and it is clear from early minutes that Lancashire proprietors were influential in the company. In January 1831, two Liverpool directors, and one from London, were added to the board 'in respect of the large body of subscribers in England'.[2] In 1832, a special Liverpool committee of five members was set up, and at the end of that year the Scottish chairman found it necessary to make a visit to Liverpool to explain his board's conduct before the proprietors would agree to pay up their instalments.[3] In 1843, after the line was opened, the *Railway Times* reported a meeting of the Liverpool proprietors of the Edinburgh & Glasgow, which was attended by the holders of 1,000 shares:[4] this would represent 5 per cent of the total share capital. The Glasgow, Paisley, Kilmarnock & Ayr Railway was another railway which looked for Lancashire support; in its prospectus of 1832, six banks were named, four of them Scottish firms, and the remaining two a Manchester and a Liverpool bank.[5] Similarly, agents in five Scottish towns, and in Manchester and Liverpool, were appointed to receive applications for shares.

Thus, with the early interest of Liverpool proprietors in the Liverpool & Manchester and connecting lines, and the efforts made by promoters in the mid 1830s to tap Lancashire capital for distant schemes, a considerable proportion of railway securities must have been held in Lancashire, and an active market in railway shares, particularly at times of commercial pressure, seems to have existed. As early as 1832, the *Liverpool Times* (1833) was giving occasional quotations of sharelists;[6] by the end of the year, every issue contained such a list. The Manchester press seems to have been later in dealing with share matters, though the *Manchester and Salford Advertiser* occasionally quoted prices of shares at Liverpool.[7] Manchester sharebrokers, however, advertised actively, and the lists of shares they adver-

[1] It is not clear whether this refers to Beckett, Birks & Co of Barnsley, or Beckett, Blayds & Co of Leeds, though such an amount would almost certainly come from the Leeds firm. The two firms had family connections, however, and may have acted together.

[2] BTHR (S), EGR 1/1, 12 January 1831 (p 15).

[3] Ibid, 13 January 1832 (p 89) and 10 December 1832 (p 116).

[4] *Railway Times*, 1843, 115.

[5] BTHR (S), PROS S 1/1 f 8.

[6] *Liverpool Times*, 10 January 1832. Some of the lists bore the name 'Richard Dawson, Sharebroker', eg 14 May 1833.

[7] *Manchester and Salford Advertiser*, 2 January 1836.

tised shows that they dealt in shares of distant concerns. On 21 May 1836, for example, Joseph Eveleigh advertised 28 railways, only seven of which were North of England concerns. Three were local railways in London, and among the others were an Indian company, two Irish, and three Scottish concerns.[1]

The emergence of formal share markets at both Liverpool and Manchester was a logical outcome of the existence of an active trade in railway securities, with a growing body of sharebrokers. Indeed, the lack of advertising by Liverpool brokers, even at the height of the promotional boom of 1835–6, together with the regular publication, along with other Liverpool market reports, of a Liverpool sharelist, suggests some sort of informal association as early as 1833. That boom conditions provided the final stimulus in forming organised stock exchanges is evident from the comment of a London commercial paper:[2]

> Such is the rage for Railway Share speculations that in the large Commercial Rooms, at both Manchester and Liverpool, they are almost as current a commodity as cotton.

The chairman of the Liverpool Stock Exchange, giving evidence in 1878, was somewhat vague about the date of the formation of the exchange, but spoke of the inconvenience of transacting business in the Exchange Rooms, and the rapid growth of business in times like 1836 and 1845.[3]

The Liverpool Sharebrokers' Association was in fact formed in April 1836, and at the end of that month had 30 members;[4] 14 further members joined by the end of 1836, and thereafter new members were admitted at a somewhat slower rate. The revival of railway share business in 1843 was shown by the formation in that year of a rival exchange, the Liverpool New Stock Exchange, which was amalgamated with the existing concern at the beginning of 1844, and thus added 19 further members to the older exchange.[5]

Manchester was not far behind Liverpool in forming a Stock Exchange: on 12 May 1836 an association of sharebrokers was formed, and on 7 November 1836 their Stock Exchange was opened for business in a room in the Manchester Exchange. By the end of 1837, the Exchange had 16 members.[6]

Apart from Dublin, where there was an established Stock Exchange dealing in government securities, these two exchanges were the first in the United Kingdom to be formed outside London, and it is not too much to say that their formation was a direct result of the railway boom of the mid

[1] *Manchester Guardian*, 21 May 1836.
[2] *London Mercantile Journal*, 1 March 1836.
[3] *Royal Commission on the London Stock Exchange*, PP 1878, XIX, Q 7878.
[4] Liverpool Stock Exchange, *Centenary Book*, p 57.
[5] Ibid, p 21.
[6] Manchester Stock Exchange, minutes.

1830s. An early Liverpool share price list, dated 9 August 1836, named 71 companies whose shares were dealt in: 38 were railways, and banks, the next largest class, provided 15 companies. The remaining 18 were miscellaneous insurance, ferry, and utility companies. Significantly, no canals were named, suggesting that business was mainly confined to 'new' companies promoted in the post-war years.[1]

It is impossible now to estimate the amount of business done on the provincial exchanges, but Liverpool in particular seems to have been a major market for railway securities. A comparison of the Liverpool list referred to above with the *Course of the Exchange* for the same date[2] shows that though 24 more railway companies were listed at London than Liverpool, more of the Liverpool securities had recent prices marked, and that Liverpool's interests were at least as widespread as London's: indeed, the London list was inflated by the inclusion of defunct companies such as the Manchester & Oldham. Furthermore, Liverpool seems to have attracted capital and dealings from beyond its immediate area—in 1844, the *Circular to Bankers*, speaking of the new interest of West Riding investors in railway schemes, said that the share market of Liverpool would be 'inanimate if it were not kept alive by the bold men of Yorkshire'.[3] At times of excitement, Liverpool appears to have been a highly speculative market, after the London pattern: a parliamentary witness in 1845 spoke of persons 'of the highest rank' at Liverpool borrowing at 10, 12½ and 15 per cent on railway shares, and gave two instances of borrowing at 40 per cent to speculate in new shares expected to rise to a premium.[4] Time bargains were another characteristic of the London Stock Exchange borrowed by Liverpool.[5]

Moreover, it seems probable that the Manchester and Liverpool markets in the early 1840s provided, in addition to a regional market in a wide range of securities, the most active *national* market in some railway securities: it is likely that shares of companies largely owned in Lancashire found their way naturally to the stock exchanges there. A writer to the *Railway Times* in 1842 claimed that London speculators were responsible for fixing a false London price for Manchester & Leeds Railway shares: he asserted that three-quarters of the sales of M. & L. shares took place in Manchester, and that normally this railway was rarely quoted in London.[6] If this was the case with other northern and Midland railways, the Manchester and Liverpool Stock Exchanges, in addition to their local function, must also have challenged London as the most active market for a fair proportion of all railway securities.

[1] Liverpool Stock Exchange, *Centenary Book*, p 22.

[2] *Course of the Exchange*, 9 August 1836. It should be noted that the Liverpool list was of the day's dealings only, whereas the *Course* covered half a week.

[3] *C to B*, 18 October 1844, 134.

[4] *Lords' SC on . . . laws regulating the interest of money*, PP 1845, XII, Q 616.

[5] *SC on Jt Stock Cos*, PP 1844, VII, Q 2320.

[6] *Railway Times*, 1842, 664.

VI

In most other large provincial towns, it was the railway mania of the mid 1840s which stimulated the growth of stock exchanges, suggesting that large investment in railways outside London and Lancashire did not come until 1844–5. However, the conditions in many larger provincial towns before 1844 must have resembled those in Manchester and Liverpool before 1836 to some extent; for example, the *Midland Counties Herald*, which from 1838 onwards deliberately set out to be a commercial and investment paper for Birmingham and the Midlands, carried stock market prices from London, and also occasionally listed share prices at Birmingham, presumably supplied by a local broker.[1] In Edinburgh the transitional stage before the emergence of a formal stock exchange was interestingly illustrated by an appendix to Reid's *Manual of the Scottish Stocks* . . . published in 1841.[2] The author spoke of the difficulty of fixing prices for Scottish stocks, as brokers had to depend either on the price of their last dealing, perhaps over a year old, or on 'vague hearsay'. He suggested that a clerk in one of Edinburgh's principal banks should be appointed to receive details of share transactions, and to prepare lists once or twice a week.

By the end of 1845, the rapid growth in railway speculation had led to the emergence of more or less formally constituted markets in most large provincial towns. Glasgow's Stock Exchange was formed in July 1844, with 28 members,[3] and by 1845 two rival exchanges, composed of members whose other activities rendered them ineligible for membership of the original exchange, had been formed.[4] Leeds Stock Exchange was opened in January 1845,[5] and similarly by the end of 1845 had to meet the competition of two rival exchanges,[6] as well as a public stock exchange and an auction business in railway shares.[7] Edinburgh's Stock Exchange was formed at a meeting in December 1844, and opened for business the following year.[8] Bristol Stock Exchange began business on 16 April 1845,[9] and Birmingham on 22 October 1845.[10] At Leicester a Stock Exchange was

[1] eg *Midland Counties Herald*, 6 December 1838.

[2] John Reid, *Manual of the Scottish Stocks* (Edinburgh, 1841), Appendix.

[3] Glasgow Stock Exchange, *Records*, p 4.

[4] Ibid, pp 32–3.

[5] *Leeds Mercury*, 18 January 1845.

[6] *Railway Almanac, Directory, and Year Book for 1846* (London, Richard Groombridge & Sons, ?1845), pp 130–1.

[7] *Leeds Mercury*, 28 June 1845.

[8] David Keir, *The City of Edinburgh* (*The Third Statistical Account of Scotland*, Vol XV, 1966), p 586.

[9] I am indebted to the Secretary of the Bristol Local Association, Midlands & Western Stock Exchange, for this information.

[10] The minutes of the Birmingham Stock Exchange, from which this information is derived, suggest that there had been an earlier Sharebrokers' Association in Birmingham.

formed in October 1845 in the saloon of the theatre.[1] The *Circular to Bankers*, reviewing the progress of railway speculation, commented thus:[2]

> Another characteristic of this new river of speculation which is flowing through the fields of investment is that it has created for itself a great number of large markets. Railway speculation has created the markets for shares of Leeds, Wakefield, Bradford, Halifax, Huddersfield, Leicester, Birmingham, and many other inland towns; and in the great cities of Paris, Dublin and London it has rendered the market for government securities an object of inferior interest.

How directly dependent the provincial exchanges were on railway business may be judged from the following table, which shows the number of members admitted to the Stock Exchanges at Liverpool from 1840 to 1854, and Glasgow from 1844 to 1854:

TABLE 4

NEW MEMBERS ADMITTED, LIVERPOOL STOCK EXCHANGE 1840–54, GLASGOW STOCK EXCHANGE 1844–54

Year	*Liverpool*	*Glasgow*	*Year*	*Liverpool*	*Glasgow*
1840	2	—	1848	8	0
1841	5	—	1849	3	0
1842	0	—	1850	1	0
1843	5	—	1851	7	0
1844	51 (a)	34	1852	6	3
1845	84	32	1853	9	6
1846	34	9	1854	7	2
1847	13	6			

Sources: Liverpool Stock Exchange, *Centenary Book* . . ., pp 57–60; and Glasgow Stock Exchange, *Records*, pp 57–62.

Notes: (a) Includes 19 members of Liverpool New Stock Exchange, amalgamated January 1844.

The decline in new membership after 1845, most marked in Glasgow, was also shared by Liverpool, and only in the early 1850s did a slow recovery begin. A Glasgow stockbroker, examined before a House of Lords committee in 1849, testified to the decline in business: instead of the 300–400 transactions daily which had characterised the railway boom at its height, by 1849 the Glasgow Stock Exchange saw only about four or five daily bargains.[3] Another witness before the same committee was of opinion that once dealings in railway shares assumed a settled form, the local exchanges

[1] *Bradshaw's Railway Gazette*, 1846, 318.
[2] *C to B*, 11 July 1845, 3.
[3] *Lords' SC on Audit of Railway Accounts*, PP 1849, X, QQ 3278; 3281.

would 'to a great extent, cease to exist'.[1] Certainly, some changes mentioned at the height of the boom in 1845 were purely ephemeral,[2] and even the largest provincial exchanges, Glasgow, Liverpool and Manchester, could not have retained much of the business they attracted in the 1840s. After the 1840s, the spread of the electric telegraph (closely linked to the expansion of the railway network), and the emergence of the great amalgamated railway companies meant that railway business was increasingly concentrated on the London Stock Exchange, where specialised rail markets emerged. Glasgow retained a market in Scottish railway shares, and Dublin likewise dealt largely in Irish lines, but the wide market in railway shares which had been a feature of both Liverpool and Manchester in the formative years of local exchanges was largely lost to London, where the specialist division of jobber and broker was able to maintain a liquid market in a wide range of home and foreign railway shares,[3] and where the increasing concentration of banking and discount houses made all the resources of the money market available to the London Stock Exchange. The readiness of London brokers to share their brokerage fees with banks and solicitors who brought them business probably also helped to concentrate business on London, for only the most active of provincial investors would have been in touch with a local broker and as railway business settled down it would be natural for most small investors to do their occasional share business through a bank or solicitor. The provincial exchanges, despite, or perhaps because of, their rapid growth in the thirties and forties, never achieved the separation of function into jobber and broker,[4] and retained the system of dealing by 'calling' a list once or twice daily. Bargains were effected when each security was named, and subsequent bargains took place informally.[5] Increasingly, provincial exchanges did their business in local stocks, and, towards the end of the nineteenth century, in local government securities. The role of the provincial exchanges as local capital markets is outside the scope of this article, but this new role was undoubtedly important: *Phillips Investors Annual* in 1887 suggested that 'the Provincial Stock Exchanges were almost of greater importance in relation to home securities than London'.[6] However, the provincial ex-

[1] Ibid, Q 1408.

[2] For example, the Leicester and Wakefield exchanges do not seem to have survived the collapse of the railway mania. On the other hand, it should be noted that a number of the smaller provincial exchanges (for example, Dundee, Oldham, and Cardiff) emerged later in response to local developments.

[3] For a discussion of the railway markets of the London Stock Exchange, see *The Jubilee of the Railway News* (1914), pp 129–31.

[4] A small class of brokers prepared to deal in local shares on their own account to maintain a market emerged at Glasgow. See J. Cunnison & J. B. S. Gilfillan, *Glasgow* (*The Third Statistical Account of Scotland*, Vol V, 1958), p 402.

[5] See, for example, Glasgow Stock Exchange, *Records*, p 17, and *RC on the London Stock Exchange*, PP 1878, XIX, QQ 5152–59.

[6] Quoted from J. B. Jeffreys, 'Trends in business organisation in Britain since 1856' unpublished PhD Thesis, LSE, 1938, p 340.

changes did not entirely lose touch with the railway market, and an early achievement of the Council of Associated Stock Exchanges was its success in persuading the railway companies to adopt the Forged Transfer Acts.[1]

VII

The part played by the growth of railway business in the development of the formal capital market was, then, a complex one. In London, the arrival of a large volume of railway securities played an important part in enlarging the Stock Exchange and in placing a new emphasis on company securities at a time when the volume of British government debt was declining, and when investors were distrustful of overseas investment. The railway boom was also largely responsible for the creation of a national financial and investment press, and in creating widespread interest in new investment opportunities. At the same time, however, the involvement of railway promotion in the highly speculative market provided by the Stock Exchange and the fringe market in allotments and scrip meant that speculation, rather than permanent investment, was the motive of the promoters and supporters of many schemes, and produced the reckless extravagance which characterised the manias of 1836 and 1845. Even so, it must be recognised that railway promotion itself was a risky activity, and without speculative markets capital might not have been forthcoming for many early railway schemes.

On the other hand, the provincial origins of many schemes, and the opportunities which railways presented for provincial investment, produced for the first time a large scale participation in investment and speculation outside London, and with the growth of provincial interest in railway shares, stock exchanges gradually emerged, first in Lancashire and then in most large towns. This movement paralleled the enlargement of the Stock Exchange in London, and the provincial exchanges probably played at least as large a part as London in the mania of 1845.[2] Liverpool in particular seems to have had a highly developed railway share market.

However, the railway mania of the 1840s which had created most of the provincial exchanges was a passing phenomenon, and with the emergence of a more settled market in railway securities, and the consolidation of local companies into the national railway companies, London's dominance of the market for railway securities was quickly established. The provincial exchanges, largely divorced from the railway business which had been their making, instead took over the role of local capital markets in the new financial world of joint stock and limited liability companies. Nevertheless, despite the transitory influence of railway business on the provincial stock exchanges, this influence was vital to their creation, just as the railway

[1] Liverpool Stock Exchange, *Centenary Book*, pp 28–9, 34.

[2] For a contemporary expression of this view, see *The City* . . ., p 61.

movement gave London the mechanism to deal with company securities, and created a network of stockbrokers all over the country to serve the investing public. Railway companies were a model for the increasing number of companies which followed the liberalisation of company law, and the characteristics of railway capital issues—an unprecedented volume of securities, and the initial opportunities for speculative profits—ensured the enlargement of the formal capital market so that it was able to handle other company securities. The Secret Committee on Commercial Distress in 1848, questioning a Liverpool merchant, G. Turner, phrased their questions to suggest that the railway mania and the growth of local stock exchanges had together spread the habit of gambling in shares, and the consequent ruin, among a far larger section of the community. Admitting this, Turner defined the part played by the spread of the provincial exchanges quite simply: 'It gave facilities to persons to buy and sell shares, which they could not have done formerly, except by coming to London.'[1] The buying and selling of shares, unimportant before the coming of the railway, was an essential part of the Victorian commercial structure.

[1] *SC on Commercial Distress*, PP 1847–8, VIII, Pt 1, Q 1012.

The Sources of Railway Share Capital

By S. A. Broadbridge

I

In past discussions of the early railway capital market generalisations about the character of that market have frequently been accepted, yet the validity of the material, such as lists of subscribers and contemporary accounts of flotations, upon which these assertions must have been based, has been questioned. Perhaps the most widely used work on the nature of the financing of incorporated companies in the period up to 1850 is that of G. H. Evans[1] who states: 'The local character of the railways seems to have been dominant until about 1844. . . . Local promotion and finance . . . were the mainstays of the transportation industry until the listing of shares on the London Stock Exchange and the entry of London capitalists into this field of enterprise.'[2] Evans does not make it clear whether he dates this 'entry of London capitalists' at 1844 or earlier, although the implication is that it occurred at the later date. J. H. Clapham considered 1836 the turning point when 'Blind capital, seeking its 5 per cent' intervened[3] while John Francis noted the interest London took in the London & Birmingham Railway in 1832.[4] And H. Pollins has demonstrated the quite important role played by London in the *initial* promising of capital to the Liverpool & Manchester Railway in 1824–5 and 1825–6.[5]

This paper is an enlarged version of a paper which appeared in the *Economic History Review*, VIII (1955–6), 200–12, under the title 'The Early Capital Market: the Lancashire and Yorkshire Railway'.

My thanks are due to Mr H. Pollins; Mr H. L. Beales; Mr F. C. Mather (University of Southampton); the librarian of the House of Lords; and to officials of the British Transport Historical Records Office and the House of Lords Record Office. I am also indebted to Professor M. M. Postan for his criticisms and suggestions.

[1] *British Corporation Finance, 1775–1850* (Baltimore, 1936).

[2] Ibid, p 10. But Evans also says: 'There is no doubt that prior to this date there had been a number of departures from local promotion, finance and control.'

[3] *An Economic History of Modern Britain* (Cambridge, 1930), 1, 388. See also *Circular to Bankers*, no 397, 26 February 1836, for support for Clapham's opinion. The *Circular* had commented, in November 1835, on the absence of the London Stock Exchange from railway enterprise (no 381, 6 November 1835).

[4] *A History of the English Railway* (1851), I, 180–2.

[5] 'The Finances of the Liverpool and Manchester Railway', *Econ Hist Rev* 2nd ser v (1952), 90–7. It might be pointed out that Mr Pollins does not mention that the allocation of 1,000 shares to the Marquis of Stafford has been regarded as a softener, even as a bribe, rather than as an illustration of the company's difficulty in obtaining subscriptions. Cf James Wheeler, *Manchester . . .* (1836), p 281; Francis, op cit, 1, 116; and E. A. Pratt, *A History of Inland Transport and Communication in England* (1912), p 239.

It is apparent that only from studies of particular railway companies can a reliable picture of the railway capital market be drawn, but in the absence of a comprehensive series of shareholders' registers,[1] the principal available sources are the subscription contracts, which were, and are, often criticised. Certainly the works of contemporaries such as D. M. Evans,[2] John Francis,[3] Arthur Smith,[4] and Herbert Spencer,[5] and of more recent writers,[6] contain statements which hardly favour the use of subscription contracts for any purpose other than that of demonstrating the fever of speculation which gripped the middle classes in 1845. There is no doubt that much of this comment is justified for the mania periods. But Mr Pollins' comparison of the list of subscribers to the Liverpool & Manchester in 1825–6 with that of shareholders about 1845 shows that at least 25 per cent of those who subscribed were still holding shares some 20 years later, despite the fact that the L & M contract was entered into during a time of speculation.[7]

II

The subscription contracts of 13 of the companies that made up the Lancashire & Yorkshire Railway[8] have been analysed to show the geographical distribution of subscriptions. The location of all these companies within, roughly, south Lancashire and the West Riding, facilitates comparison of the relative contributions of 'interested' counties over a period of about ten years, from 1835 to 1845. On the whole it has been considered reasonable to take as locally interested, for the Manchester & Leeds, the Liverpool Ormskirk & Preston, and the Liverpool & Bury Railways, those subscribers residing in Lancashire, Yorkshire and Cheshire; and for the Preston & Wyre, the Ashton Stalybridge & Liverpool Junction, the Blackburn & Preston, the Manchester Bury & Rossendale, the Blackburn Burnley

[1] None at all exist for the Lancashire and Yorkshire Railway. Even though the records offices of the British Railways Board and the House of Lords have greatly increased the scope of railway and canal research, there are too many gaps in the lists of extant subscription contracts, and too few shareholders' registers, for one to be completely sanguine about the fruitfulness of consulting this raw material.

[2] *The Commercial Crisis of 1847–1848* (1848): 'The Railway Mania and its Effects', pp 1–52.

[3] Op cit, II, 132 ff.

[4] Eg *Railways As They Really Are* (1847), No VII: 'The Lancashire and Yorkshire Railway'.

[5] 'Railway Morals and Railway Policy', *Edinburgh Review*, October 1854.

[6] Eg O. Cyprian Williams, *The Historical Development of Private Bill Procedure . . .* (1948), I, 133. Dr Williams quotes J. Swift, who stated before the Select Committee of the House of Lords on Private Bills, 1858, that the 'subscription contract is illusory'.

[7] *Econ Hist Rev*, loc cit, p 93. The figure of 25 per cent is, moreover, exclusive of those who probably inherited shares, an occurrence 'suggested by the obvious family connections of several names in both lists'.

[8] The Manchester & Leeds changed its name to the Lancashire & Yorkshire in 1847: 10 & 11 Vict c 163.

Accrington & Colne, the Huddersfield & Sheffield Junction, and the Wakefield Pontefract & Goole companies, those residing in Lancashire and Yorkshire. There were no Yorkshire or Cheshire subscribers to the Bolton & Preston and the Blackburn Darwen & Bolton railways; nor were there any Cheshire subscribers to the Ashton Stalybridge & Liverpool Junction.

Table 1 sets out the geographical distribution of subscriptions. Lines IV and V are not, however, strictly comparable with the rest. Line IV, the analysis of the Manchester & Leeds 1835–6 contract, covers only those subscribers who signed for £2,000 or more: the Appendix to the Lords report does not contain the rest of the subscribers. More important, line V represents an analysis of *shareholdings* in the Manchester & Leeds on 1 February 1838.[1] It has been included in the table in order that the geographical distribution of actual holdings in 1838 might be compared with the distribution of subscriptions in 1835–6. But even a comparison of the broad geographical categories of Table 1 is not simple because the total of subscriptions submitted to the Lords committee was only £1,059,400,[2] the total of subscriptions of £2,000 and more was £628,700,[3] and the analysis of 1838 is of the full share capital of £1,300,000.[4]

The combined relative contributions of the 'interested' counties are shown in Table 2 on p. 188. With the exceptions of the contracts of the Preston & Wyre Railway of 1835, and that of the Preston & Wyre Dock Company of 1837, the consistently high proportions of the capital subscribed by 'locally interested' people are striking. The three Preston & Wyre contracts present a rather puzzling picture. In the first place, one would not expect to find a decrease in London's interest in a period when it is often assumed that the capital market was becoming wider. In the second place, it is worth noting the fact of the reversal of the usual positions of the 'interested' counties and London in the first two contracts. Although it is not possible to date them exactly, they were obviously drawn up in the prosperity phase of the mid 1830s: the 1837 list was deposited in the House of Lords in April 1837 and was, therefore, most probably made up before the boom broke. The participation of London cannot be attributed solely to the existence of the mania, since we see from the contracts of the Manchester & Leeds in 1835–6, and the Bolton & Preston in 1837, that it was still possible for a parliamentary deed to be filled up without London occupying any appreciable space in it. And it is clear, moreover, that the subscriptions to the Preston & Wyre in 1835 (or possibly 1834?) were not prompted by speculative fever, since it was not until September 1835 that the boom be-

[1] The figures in this line are based on information given in the *Circular to Bankers*, no 509, 13 April 1838.

[2] *Lords Committee Report*, loc cit, p 39.

[3] Ibid, Appendix, pp 45–8. The total is wrongly given in this Appendix as £630,000.

[4] The company's Act of incorporation authorised this sum, to be raised in £100 shares: 6 & 7 W, IV, c III, ss, 168–70.

gan to quicken into a mania,[1] and by then the Preston & Wyre Railway had obtained its Act.[2]

TABLE 1[3]

	Company, and Date of Contract	*Percentage Contributions* *Lan-cashire*	*York-shire*	*Cheshire*	*London*
I	Preston & Wyre Railway (1835)	22	5	Nil	71
II	Preston & Wyre Docks (1837)	31	Nil	Nil	67
III	Preston & Wyre Railway (1845)	66	3	(1)	30
IV	Manchester & Leeds (1835–6)	71	20	1	5
V	Manchester & Leeds (1838)	60	8	5	10
VI	Manchester & Leeds (1839–40)	66	7	5	10
VII	Ashton Stalybridge & Liverpool Junction (1844)	50	10	Nil	30
VIII	Bolton & Preston (1837)	98	Nil	Nil	—
IX	Blackburn & Preston (1844)	71	16	(1)	Nil
X	Manchester Bury & Rossendale (1844)	96	3	Nil	Nil
XI	Blackburn Burnley Accrington & Colne (1844–5)	85	10	(1)	—
XII	Liverpool Ormskirk & Preston (1845)	48	30	2	9
XIII	Liverpool & Bury (1845)	72	3	2	12
XIV	Blackburn Darwen & Bolton (1845)	96	Nil	Nil	3
XV	Wakefield Pontefract & Goole (1844–5)	56	42	Nil	—
XVI	Huddersfield & Sheffield Junction (1845)	12	83	(1)	2

NB (*a*) The bracketed figures under 'Cheshire' are not included in the totals of Table 2; (*b*) all figures are given to nearest 1 %. Thus the sign — means less than ½%; (*c*) line V is an analysis of *shareholdings*.

Practically the only definite conclusion which emerges from a detailed comparison of the three Preston & Wyre contracts is that so far as the *promising* of capital is concerned, the trend was away from the broadening of the capital market, towards a more pronounced emphasis on the local sources. The details of this comparison cannot be presented here for reasons

[1] Cf R. C. O. Matthews, *A Study in Trade-Cycle History* (Cambridge, 1954), pp 110–11.

[2] 5 & 6 W, IV, c 58 (3 July 1835). The greater part of the year was free from any sharp increases in the price of securities: cf A. D. Gayer, W. W. Rostow and A. J. Schwartz, *The Growth and Fluctuation of the British Economy, 1790–1850* (Oxford, 1953), I, 243.

[3] The sources for these calculations are: I, II, III, VII, IX and X printed or MS copies of subscription contracts, House of Lords Record Office; IV—*Report of the Lords Committee on the Manchester and Leeds Railway Bill*, PP 1836 (House of Lords, 147), XII, Appendix, pp 45–8 (House of Lords Library); V—*Circular to Bankers*, no 509, 13 April 1838; VI—three parliamentary deeds (British Transport Historical Records Office); VIII—PP 1837 (95), XLVIII; XI to XVI inclusive—PP 1845 (317, 625), XL.

The printed copies of the contracts for XI, XIV and XV have been consulted in addition to the Parliamentary Papers cited. This facilitated a quick check of those figures derived from the papers, which contain some 700 pages of names, etc, and it was found that discrepancies were small. Unfortunately there are no separate printed copies of XII, XIII and XVI in the House of Lords Record Office, and it must be emphasised that complete accuracy cannot be claimed for the figures from the 1845 papers.

of space, but the smallness of the sums which were contracted for would, in any event, make it unprofitable,[1] since it was possible for one person to contribute a high proportion of a contract.[2] For this reason the analysis of the Preston & Wyre's capital sources is not to be given as much weight as that of the Manchester & Leeds.

TABLE 2

THE CONTRIBUTIONS OF 'INTERESTED' COUNTIES[3]

Railway[4]	*Counties*	%
I	Lancashire and Yorkshire	27
II	Lancashire and Yorkshire	31
III	Lancashire and Yorkshire	69
IV	Lancashire, Yorkshire and Cheshire	92
V	Lancashire, Yorkshire and Cheshire	73
VI	Lancashire, Yorkshire and Cheshire	78
VII	Lancashire and Yorkshire	60
VIII	Lancashire	98
IX	Lancashire and Yorkshire	87
X	Lancashire and Yorkshire	99
XI	Lancashire and Yorkshire	95
XII	Lancashire, Yorkshire and Cheshire	80
XIII	Lancashire, Yorkshire and Cheshire	77
XIV	Lancashire	96
XV	Lancashire and Yorkshire	98
XVI	Lancashire and Yorkshire	95

III

The Manchester & Leeds is a much more satisfying study. In the first place, the amounts of capital involved are far greater than those of the Preston & Wyre. In the second place, the Ashton Stalybridge & Liverpool Junction contract of 1844 may, to some extent, be regarded as one of the Manchester & Leeds.[5] We thus have a series of three contracts which may

[1] They amounted to only £106,600 in 1835, £36,000 in 1837, and £37,606 6d 8d in 1845. There is the further drawback that the P & W Dock Company, sanctioned in 1837, was independent of the P & W Railway and was not absorbed by the latter until 1839—2 & 3 Vict, c 54.

[2] Thus John Abel Smith's subscription in 1845 represented 27 per cent of the total subscribed, and the same proportion of London's 30 per cent: *Copy of the Preston and Wyre Railways Branches Subscription Contract*, 8 Vict sess 1845 (House of Lords Record O).

[3] As some addresses were inadequate, it is possible that these figures very slightly underestimate the weight of the 'interested' counties.

[4] For the names of the railways, compare with Table 1.

[5] The AS & LJc's Act of 1844 referred to the new line as 'a Branch of the Manchester and Leeds Railway', which was given powers to lease or purchase it: 7 & 8 Vict, c 82, ss 221, 342, 343. For details of the purchase, see *Reports and Accounts of the Manchester and Leeds Railway*, 5 September 1844 (BTHR, RAC 1/204).

be compared, together with the very useful, if brief, analysis of the geographical distribution of shareholdings in the latter company in 1838.

Apart from the first two contracts of the P & W, the proportions of capital from the 'interested' counties were high for all the companies. But there is a noticeable increase in London's relative importance, so far as the Manchester & Leeds is concerned, between 1835–6 and 1844.[1] Table 2 shows that the relative weight of the 'interested' counties decreased by approximately 18 per cent between 1835–6 and 1838, and Table 1 that that of London increased by about 5 per cent.[2]

In view of the additional shares taken up after 1835–6 (those not subscribed for at the time of the Lords committee), we must ask whether these changes in 'relative weights' in fact reflect any absolute changes in the geographical distribution of holdings? The nominal value of these shares was £240,600. In 1836, of the £1,059,400 subscribed, £76,300 came from areas other than Lancashire and Yorkshire. In 1838 these other areas held shares to the nominal value of £411,800 and, therefore, even on the questionable assumption that Lancashire and Yorkshire absorbed none of the additional shares, they had received from those two counties shares to the value of £94,900. The capital market for this company at least had broadened since its inception, and the slump after 1836, far from causing a withdrawal of the more impersonal London investors, was accompanied by an increase in their ranks.[3] Thus the experience of the Manchester & Leeds was the reverse of that of the Preston & Wyre, so far as we are able to judge, and also of that of the Liverpool & Manchester in 1826.[4]

The very close correlation between the geographical distribution of holdings in 1838, and of subscriptions in 1839–40,[5] suggests that the shareholders of the earlier year were maintaining their interest. The offer of the new half-shares on a *pro rata* basis to existing proprietors, who were circularised, very probably helped to secure this correlation.[6] The company

[1] For reasons stated later, however, the AS & LJc analysis cannot be used in comparison with the M & L contracts of 1835–6 and 1839–50, without a major qualification.

[2] That the figure for 1835–6 represents only subscriptions of £2,000 and more, and that there is the difference between the total subscribed in that year (£1,059,400) and the total amount of shares in 1838 (£1,300,000) to be considered, does not affect this conclusion. Fortunately, the report of the Lords Committee gave the combined subscriptions from Lancashire and Yorkshire in 1835–6, which were £983,100 or 92·8 per cent of the total subscribed. Since the corresponding percentage of subscriptions of £2,000 and more is 91 (see Table 1), it is unlikely that any serious distortion will result from basing comparisons on the latter subscriptions. (There is, anyway, no alternative, as neither the House of Lords Record Office, nor the British Transport Historical Records Office has a copy of the contract.)

[3] As a group: naturally the composition of the group may have changed even more than the change caused by its mere expansion.

[4] Cf H. Pollins, *Econ Hist Rev*, loc cit.

[5] The original deeds were used. The indenture is dated 23 January 1839. Most of the entries were made in 1839, a few in 1840, one in 1841.

[6] 13,000 £50 shares were to be issued: *Directors' Report*, special general meeting, 17 January 1839 (BTHR, RAC 1/204).

did not, apparently, invite applications from the general public.[1] It is noteworthy that the new contract was entered into in a year that was not particularly favourable to such enterprise.[2] The business cycle that reached its peak in the March of 1839 'never reached full employment and was marked by chronic financial stringency, falling prices. . . .'[3] The index of railway share prices constructed by Gayer, Rostow and Schwartz shows a decline between March and December, to which the Manchester & Leeds £100 shares were no exception.[4] Yet the company's parliamentary deeds contain a considerable number of entries dated from March onwards. This, and the steadiness of the price of the new half-shares, does not suggest speculation.

The list of subscribers to the Manchester & Leeds in 1835–6 and 1839–40 enables us to see whether those who supported the company in the former year continued to do so. But a full comparison is impossible because only those subscribing £2,000 or more were listed in the appendix to the Lords report of 1836. Of the 162 names[5] of that year, 64 recur in the 1839 contract. A fairly conservative estimate of the number who subscribed £2,000 or more in 1835–6, and subscribed again in 1839–40, would be one-third. It will be remembered that the existing shareholders were given first refusal of the new shares. It may therefore be concluded that at least a third of those who were the original subscribers retained their shares until 1839, and also took up new ones. And by this time £50 per share were paid up. The Finance Committee minutes of the Manchester & Leeds afford some confirmation of the validity of the estimate that at least one-third of the original subscribers retained their shares between 1835–6 and 1839. Twenty-five of the 64 people who subscribed to both the 1835–6 and 1839–40 contracts appear in the minutes between 1838 and 1845, and almost all the entries come under such headings as 'repayment of pre-paid calls', and 'repayment of calls paid twice in mistake'.[6] And those who appeared in the minutes of such circumstances must of necessity have been only a comparatively small minority of the shareholders. It is therefore possible to say that in a year of speculation, 1835–6, many of the subscribers to the Manchester & Leeds desired to *invest*, rather than to speculate.

[1] A search of the *Railway Times* issues of 1838 did not reveal any advertisement inviting applications. This periodical was a favourite medium for railway companies, and the M & L inserted many advertisements which covered anything from loans to timetables.

[2] Compared with 1838, the proportion preference shares bore to all shares authorised more than doubled in 1839: G. H. Evans, op cit, p 48. The M & L issue was not preferential.

[3] Gayer, Rostow and Schwartz, op cit, I, 242.

[4] Cf the *Railway Times* share prices lists in 1839. The M & L £100 shares (£50 paid up) declined, irregularly, from 70½ to 60 between January and June. In December, the price stood at 67 to 68, but £60 were now paid up. The new £50 shares first appear in the lists in May, priced at 11 (£5 paid up). For three months after the week ending 1 June, the price was steady at 9 to 9½.

[5] Some were probably duplications, but none of these appeared in the 1839–40 lists.

[6] Proceedings of the finance committee of the Manchester & Leeds Railway, 1838–45 (BTHR, LY 1/475–7).

We may continue our study of the trend in the relative weights of the 'interested' counties, and of London, with the help of the Ashton Stalybridge & Liverpool Junction contract of 1844.[1] From Table 2 it will be seen that the percentage contributions of the 'interested' counties declined from 92 per cent to 77 per cent between 1835–6 and 1839–40, with that decline apparently confirmed by the figure of 74 per cent yielded by the analysis of Manchester & Leeds shareholdings in 1838. Conversely, the weight of London increased from about five to nine per cent in the same period.

At first sight it would seem that this decline continued, since the figures for the 'interested' counties of Lancashire and Yorkshire, and for London, in 1844 are 60 and 30 respectively. The Ashton Stalybridge & Liverpool Junction was, in effect, a part of the Manchester & Leeds right from the start, and it is reasonable to assume that the people who subscribed in both 1839–40 and 1844 were shareholders in the latter company in 1844. This assumption is reinforced in the case of those subscribing in 1835–6, as well as in the later years: 14 occur in all three contracts.[2] One more subscriber signed in 1835–6 and again in 1844, but not in 1839–40; while another twelve subscribed in 1839–40 and 1844, but not in 1835–6. Thus 27 of the 70 subscribers of 1844 were probably, and a fair number certainly, already investors in the Manchester & Leeds.[3] Of the 27, nine were London people, and their subscriptions represented about 9 per cent of the total subscribed —which figure does not, of itself, help us very much when it comes to deciding on the validity of the 30 per cent. The other London subscribers were well known and wealthy people like the Grenfells and the Kennards. The inclusion of John Peirse Kennard and Charles Pascoe Grenfell, both of whom had financial interests in the company,[4] brings the total of 'reliable' London subscriptions to about 17 per cent of the amount of the contract; and if we to regard the remaining three Kennards, together with St Leger Grenfell, as *bona fide* investors, we have accounted for almost the whole of the 30 per cent.

If these proportions are reliable, then the conventional view that railways were drawing their capital from ever-widening sources in the early 1840s, as compared with previous decades, is confirmed. Certainly, the figures conform to the pattern observed in the years 1835–6 to 1838–40.

[1] Unfortunately, there is no traceable list of subscribers to the M & L in 1841, when the first preference issue was authorised: 4 Vict, c 25, *An Act for enabling the Manchester and Leeds Railway Company to raise a further Sum of Money*. Clause 3 permitted the issue to be made 'in such Manner, for such Prices' as a meeting of the proprietors ordered.

[2] A number of these were directors at different times and were, therefore, bound to be shareholders.

[3] Many of them appear in the Proceedings of the Finance Committee (BTHR, LY 1/475–7.

[4] Proceedings of the Finance Committee, 1 May 1846 (BTHR, LY 1/477), and *Reports and Accounts*, 9 September 1846 (BTHR, RAC 1/204).

But the jump from 9 to 30 per cent of the total subscriptions, coming from London, is very steep,[1] and here we must introduce the major qualification mentioned above on p 189, n 1. The contract of 1844 contains the names of those who were subscribing for £25 shares in the Ashton Stalybridge & Liverpool Junction, whereas the Manchester & Leeds, after taking over the former company, offered M & L sixteenths to its own shareholders on a *pro rata basis*.[2] To this extent, therefore, the list of 1844 is not so reliable a measuring rod as that of 1839–40, and we cannot be certain that all those who subscribed for AS & LJC £25 shares in 1844 were actually shareholders in the M & L at the time. Although we have seen that it is reasonable to assume a number were, without the list of those proprietors who accepted sixteenths it cannot be decided whether the analysis of the 1844 contract gives a trustworthy indication of the trend in the Manchester & Leeds' capital market.

IV

The rest of the contracts are more unsatisfactory subjects of analysis, since, apart from the Manchester Bury & Rossendale and the Blackburn Burnley Accrington & Colne companies, they do not present a series similar to those of the Preston & Wyre and the Manchester & Leeds. And the MB & R and the BBA & C were sanctioned too close together, in conditions which were too similar, to make it worth while to conduct a detailed comparison.[3]

It has already been pointed out that the most striking characteristic of these contracts is the very high proportion of subscriptions coming from the 'interested' counties: over 90 per cent for six of the nine remaining contracts. However one regards the nature of the signatories, as either speculators or investors, it is interesting to note that Lancashire supplied 98 per cent of the subscriptions for the Bolton & Preston in 1837, and 96 per cent of those for the Blackburn Darwen & Bolton in 1845. If the contracts have any validity these results are not quite what one would expect. It has been said that the market for long term capital was becoming more perfect in the period after 1840, when the public had 'matriculated in the school of Hudson',[4] and emphasis has been placed upon the growth 'in London and other commercial centres . . . of a body of capitalists not directly engaged in trade, who were now seeking an outlet, with profit, for their accumula-

[1] It should be realised that expressing comparisons in this way does not allow any distinction between the contracts on the basis of the amounts of money involved. The total subscribed in 1844 was much smaller than in 1835–6 and 1839–40.

[2] *Reports and Accounts*, 5 September 1844 (BTHR, RAC 1/204).

[3] The BBA & C was merely an extension of the MB & R, and many of the subscribers appear in both contracts.

[4] M. M. Postan, 'Recent Trends in the Accumulation of Capital', *Econ Hist Rev*, VI (1935), 6: 'Capital very nearly became the perfect . . . factor of production . . . impersonal, divisible and capable of easy movement. . . .'

tions'.[1] Knowledge of railways was certainly increasing; there was an enormous increase in the number of books, pamphlets and periodicals devoted to them. Expectations of returns from railway investment were good,[2] and, other things being equal, if the capital market had been in any pronounced degree perfect, capital would have responded to expected differences in return.[3] It is not apparent that this happened. The percentage contributions of London were, for some railways, very low indeed, and for two were nil; they do not seem to reflect the pressure of a great amount of capital seeking investment from that city. If the high concentration of subscriptions in Lancashire and Yorkshire is to be explained, as it may well be, *partly* by the difficulties facing, say, the Londoner wishing to subscribe to a railway of those counties, then the capital market was just that much less than perfect.[4]

The above remarks are applicable whether the subscriptions were governed by speculative motives or by a desire to invest. But so far as capital sources are concerned, some attempt must be made to test the reliability of this group of contracts. Briefly, it may be said that a comparison of the contributions of particular towns to the railways seems to point to a much greater interest in the lines which were to serve those towns.[5]

This distribution of subscriptions also suggests that the motives of the subscribers were not merely speculative, and that the 'pure' investor was not dominant in the initial financing of these companies. In the absence of later shareholders' lists, these impressions can only rest on the evidence presented here. At the same time the analysis of the more abundant material for the Manchester & Leeds showed that a considerable number of the original subscribers to that company maintained their interest in it; and many of them reappear in the 1844–5 contracts. These subscribers may, of course, have become speculators by 1845, but it is important to remember that the railways we are dealing with were not products of mania. Railways XI to XVI, although the dating of their contracts in Table 1 (p 187) shows the year 1845, were, with one exception, *authorised*

[1] J. B. Jeffreys, 'Trends in Business Organization in Great Britain since 1856' (unpublished PhD thesis, London, 1938), p 9.

[2] Apart from the accumulation of capital, and the effect of low interest rates, the railway booms of 1836 and 1845 are commonly attributed to the success of the Liverpool & Manchester and other railways. See, for example, Gayer, Rostow and Schwartz, op cit, I, 436. W. T. Jackman, *The Development of Transportation in Modern England* (1916), II, 583, disputes this by pointing out that not all companies were successful at this time: 'The more probable cause (of the mania) was speculation.' This seems a little like writing that speculation caused speculation.

[3] That is, the differences that seemed to be promised by the various companies. The market was obviously perfect to the extent that there was the tremendous concentration of investment in the sector, railways generally, where good returns were expected.

[4] The railway companies were interested in showing strong local support; shares were *allocated* (with discrimination) as well as applied for.

[5] Although how far this is due to companies endeavouring to obtain local subscriptions, would be difficult to say. That there are exceptions to this explanation of the distribution of subscriptions is not doubted. But see below, p 209, n 4.

in that year and were therefore projected before the mania really got under way.[1] To comply with Standing Orders copies of subscription contracts had to be deposited in Parliament Office before the presentation of the petition for the Bills.[2] The petitions for our six 1845 Bills were presented in February (five Bills), and April (one Bill), 1845,[3] and the committee stages were as early as April and May.[4]

V

The contracts are now used to throw light upon the classes from which the companies received financial support. The usefulness of an analysis showing the functional sources of share capital depends not only upon the general validity of the subscription contracts, a question which was dealt with in the previous sections, but also upon the accuracy with which the subscribers were described. The genuine investor described as 'esquire' may well have been a landowner; on the other hand, he may have been a person of no occupation, but of independent means, who adopted what was already a courtesy title—although this type one would normally expect to be described as a 'gentleman'. Against this difficulty may be set two considerations. First, the purpose, and it was known, of requiring a description was to determine the status or occupation of the subscriber, and if a contract is regarded as reliable there is no reason to suppose that an individual would have given a false description. Second, a number of those who were described as 'esquire' possessed addresses such as '. . . Hall' and/or 'near . . .', which indicate landowning status. This, however, is far from conclusive proof of accuracy and to add to our difficulties the dividing line between a merchant and a manufacturer was, in practice, not at all rigid.

The subscribers to twelve of the contracts[5] have been grouped into eight categories, six of which are classed as 'occupational', and two as 'non-occupational'. The six occupational categories are: *Trade*, which in-

[1] See Gayer, Rostow and Schwartz, op cit, I, 380: 'The early stages of the railway boom . . . were probably a natural response to real increases in revenues enjoyed by the leading lines.'

Authorities, it is true, seem to differ in their opinion as to whether the flotations of the summer of 1844 were of the nature of speculative—in the more restricted sense—undertakings. W. T. Jackson, op cit, II, 584, would appear to lump them with the 1845 projects, and by October 1844, the editors of the *Morning Chronicle* were 'deeply concerned over the headlong rush of capital into railways'. Cf B. C. Hunt, op cit, p 103. What is certain is that the real speculative mania dates from the spring of 1845.

[2] T. Erskine May, *A Treatise Upon the Law, Privileges, Proceedings and Usage of Parliament* (1844), p 394.

[3] *The Railway Register*, II (1845), 225–31.

[4] PP 1845 (659), XXXVI, 113, 116, 118.

[5] The three Preston & Wyre contracts are omitted from this functional analysis because their inclusion would mean continual—and—tedious—qualification of the results. Since they were for very small sums of capital, constant reference to them would give a distorted picture.

cludes merchants, carriers, brokers, grocers, innkeepers, shopkeepers, and similar tradesmen; *Industry*, which includes all types of manufacturers, and a very few coal-proprietors; *Land*, which includes esquires (and, therefore, probably the most unsatisfactory category), yeoman, and farmers; *Banking*, consisting of bankers only; *Law*, which includes solicitors, attorneys, barristers, and a few agents; and *Miscellaneous*, which includes all types of clerks, clergymen not excepted, professional people, other than those grouped under *Law*, members of the armed services, and certain other groups. The two non-occupational categories are: Gentlemen; and gentlewomen, which includes gentlewomen, spinsters, and widows. There will be anomalies in any grouping that has to be limited to a fairly small number of categories if it is to be manageable, and the inclusion of shopkeepers and innkeepers in *Trade* tends to make it rather heterogeneous. But a 'grocer', for instance, might well perform wholesale as well as retail functions, and the category includes those whose interests were broadly similar in that they were all traders of a sort.

TABLE 3

OCCUPATIONAL AND NON-OCCUPATIONAL DISTRIBUTION OF SUBSCRIPTIONS

Company	*Date of Contract*	*Occupational* %	*Non-Occupational* %
Manchester & Leeds	1835–6	90	10
Manchester & Leeds	1839–40	83	17
Ashton, Stalybridge & Liverpool Junction	1844	96	4
Bolton & Preston	1837	89	12
Blackburn & Preston	1844	93	7
Manchester, Bury & Rossendale	1844	89	11
Blackburn, Burnley, Accrington & Colne	1844–5	91	9
Liverpool, Ormskirk & Preston	1845	85	15
Liverpool & Bury	1845	83	17
Blackburn, Darwen & Bolton	1845	94	6
Wakefield, Pontefract & Goole	1844–5	86	14
Huddersfield & Sheffield Junction	1845	91	9

For the sources from which this and subsequent tables are derived see footnote 3 to p 157. Figures are to the nearest per cent.

Table 3 on p 195 gives the percentage contributions of the two main groups of occupational and non-occupational categories. The occupied classes naturally subscribed by far the greater proportion of the capital, and the maximum variation in the relative proportions is not very great. But if Table 3 is compared with Tables 1 and 2 on pp 187 and 188, it may seem that a number of the contracts show an inverse relation (admittedly not very consistent) between the proportions of capital coming from 'interested' counties, and the proportions of non-occupational capital.[1] It is not suggested that this inverse relation is so close that a low relative contribution from the 'interested' counties must necessarily be accompanied by a relatively high proportion of subscriptions from subscribers described as gentlemen and gentlewomen. While the interested counties subscribed a *comparatively* small proportion to the Ashton, Stalybridge & Liverpool Junction, the non-occupational group contributed only 4 per cent of the total amount, the lowest proportion of any contract.

On the other hand, it will be seen that the highest percentages of subscriptions derived from the non-occupied classes most often occur in those contracts in which the relative weight of the 'interested' counties is 80 per cent or under. The most important contracts, the ones about which we know the most, were those of the Manchester & Leeds, and those lists of 1835–6 and 1839–40 showed a clear trend towards a wider geographical dispersion of the company's shares between the two dates. In the same period the increase in the relative weight of the non-occupational group in the Manchester & Leeds is very noticeable. There is some indication, here at least, of the growth of the rentier class, but the proportion of the 'local', more personally concerned, interest remained high.

VI

Table 4, p 197, shows the relative contributions of the six categories of the occupied classes. The steady preponderance, as a single group, of *Trade* is obvious: with only one exception their subscriptions totalled between one-third and one-half of the contracts. This is not, of course, an unexpected result. The merchant class was more than any other interested in improved transport communications, and its role in promoting and financing railways has been rightly emphasised. Newmarch may have been exaggerating when he said 'that the Railway Excitement of 1844–5 . . . enabled this country to pass almost at one step, and by a single sharp and effectual effort of self-denial on the part of the Middle Classes, into the possession of the most complete system of railway possessed by any

[1] In Table 3, and in subsequent tabulations of the functional distribution of subscriptions there is no set of figures which can be compared with the analysis of shareholdings in the Manchester & Leeds in 1838, Line V in Tables 1 and 2.

country[1] but it is true that the basic network of railways was projected and constructed in the short space of 20 years, from 1830 to 1850, and the merchant class played a crucial role in the process.

TABLE 4

ANALYSIS OF THE OCCUPATIONAL GROUP

Company	*Date of Contract*	*Trade* %	*Industry* %	*Law* %	*Land* %	*Banking* %	*Miscellaneous* %
Manchester & Leeds	1835–6	54	25	3	1	5	4
Manchester & Leeds	1839–40	34	10	5	17	5	11
Ashton, Stalybridge & Liverpool Junction	1844	42	9	4	23	12	7
Bolton & Preston	1837	39	32	9	Nil	3	6
Blackburn & Preston	1844	38	16	5	18	2	14
Manchester, Bury & Rossendale	1844	47	30	6	4	—	3
Blackburn, Burnley, Accrington & Colne	1844–5	33	41	4	5	1	7
Liverpool, Ormskirk & Preston	1845	42	15	6	7	3	11
Liverpool & Bury	1845	41	16	10	10	1	5
Blackburn, Darwen & Bolton	1845	26	30	8	16	1	13
Wakefield, Pontefract & Goole	1844–5	43	4	4	18	2	15
Huddersfield & Sheffield Junction	1845	43	29	5	1	2	12

Figures are to the nearest per cent; a — means less than half a per cent; rounding has resulted in slight discrepancies between Tables 3 and 4.

The role of the manufacturer is, however, equally obvious from Table 4, and it is not so often stressed. The category *Industry*, consists almost entirely of manufacturers of various kinds. In two of the contracts the subscriptions from *Industry* were more important than those of *Trade*, which, moreover, is a very broad category. Manufacturers certainly received attention from contemporaries such as Tooke and the contributors to the *Circular to Bankers* for the part their surplus capital played in financing railway development, and, generally speaking, the railways in which they displayed the greatest relative interest were those which were to run through the most highly industrialised regions. Their share of the subscriptions to the Manchester & Leeds in 1835–6 was 25 per cent, although it had declined considerably by 1839–40, as had that of *Trade*. The other examples are clearer. The Bolton & Preston, the Manchester, Bury & Rossendale; the Blackburn, Burnley, Accrington & Colne; the Blackburn,

[1] T. Tooke and W. Newmarch, *A History of Prices . . .* (1857), V, p 389.

Darwen & Bolton; and the Huddersfield & Sheffield Junction, to which *Industry* made percentage contributions of 32, 30, 41, 30 and 29 respectively, were all to serve more highly industrialised areas than the other railways.

If we combine the percentages subscribed by *Trade* and *Industry*, we find that their interest varies from between 44 per cent in the Manchester & Leeds in 1839–40, to 77 per cent in the Manchester, Bury & Rossendale in 1844, and 79 per cent in the Manchester & Leeds in 1835–6. The average for the combined categories is 63 per cent (41 for *Trade* and 22 for *Industry*) of the total of known subscriptions to the 12 contracts.[1] Thus these two classes supplied easily the greater proportion of the promised capital. It is argued later that it is the role of Lancashire in the national railway capital market, and not 'local finance' that should be stressed. In view of its extensive participation in financing of railways in all parts of Britain, it is interesting to find, especially, that manufacturers directed surpluses into railways.[2] It remains to be seen whether they participated to anything like the same extent in non-Lancashire and non-Yorkshire lines, but it is worth noting that in an age when 'ploughing back' was necessary for the expansion of business,[3] and when this factor, and the low productivity of labour, are generally regarded as being among the causes of the low level wages, mercantile capital certainly, and industrial capital possibly, should have been so widespread an influence in railway financing.

The desire for improved communications, and the wish to break the costly monopoly of the canals, two motives which are seen to perfection in the rise of the Manchester & Leeds, are well known and probably adequate explanations of the interest in the lines of Lancashire and Yorkshire. But participation in the financing of companies farther afield is sometimes not attributable to these motives. It is, of course, possible that individuals in these two classes subscribed to take advantage of premiums, and that shares, once on the market, flowed to a different type of investor, who supplied the bulk of the calls. This must have happened to some extent, and some such flow is suggested by the comparison of the geographical and functional distribution of the subscriptions to the Manchester & Leeds in 1835–6 and 1839–40 and of shareholdings in the intermediate year 1838. But the constant preponderance of *Trade* and *Industry* in the great majority of our contracts, over a period of ten years, and what we know of industrial

[1] Two points must be noted here. First, the averages are weighted, and not simple, averages of the figures in Table 4 that is, averages of the total amount of the contracts. Second, the subscriptions signed for by a number of the subscribers to the Wakefield, Pontefract & Goole are not included in the calculations for that company's contract: see footnote to p 199.

[2] Even if they were all mere speculators, buying for a rise, they still had to risk the 5 or 10 per cent deposit on the shares; and it cannot be supposed that many of the pre-mania subscribers were paid, as were some in 1845, to sign contracts.

[3] Cf A. K. Cairncross, *Home and Foreign Investment, 1870–1913* (Cambridge, 1953), p 98.

and social development at the time, render it unlikely that this flow was on a large scale. Moreover, most of those who subscribed to the Manchester & Leeds in both 1835–6 and 1839–40 and who, therefore, held shares at the later date, and had paid up £50 per share, were merchants and manufacturers. At all events, it seems certain that the view that there was a great amount of capital seeking investment in this period should be broadened to include industrial capital, capital held by still active industrialists.[1]

VII

With the exception of the Ashton, Stalybridge & Liverpool Junction, the *Land* category did not figure very prominently in the contracts, even when the unsatisfactory description of 'esquire' was taken to indicate a landowner.[2] Generally speaking, one finds that, as with gentlemen, 'esquires' were more frequently found in places other than Lancashire and Yorkshire. It is known that in Lancashire the large landowner, with the substantial and prosperous tenant farmer, was not so common as in other parts of the country. In 1815 it was reported that more than half the cultivated land of the county was divided into farms of from 8 or 10 to 100 customary acres.[3] Do the percentages given in Table 4 under *Land* conform to this picture of the agriculture of Lancashire? The figures for the Manchester, Bury & Rossendale and the Blackburn, Burnley, Accrington & Colne are very small. But the Blackburn, Darwen & Bolton received 16 per cent of its subscriptions from *Land*, and it is obvious that this capital could not have come from outside Lancashire, since its inhabitants promised 96 per cent of the amount of the contract. Some of the subscribers describing themselves as 'esquire' were: Joseph Feilden of Wilton House, and William Feilden of Feniscowles, near Blackburn; J. F. Hindle of Woodford Park, near Blackburn; Daniel Hornby of Raikes Hall, Blackpool; John Hornby, MP; the Kays of Turton Tower, near Bolton; James Simpson of Foxhill Bank, near Blackburn, and investor in, and director of, the Manchester & Leeds from 1835—all very substantial people who account for about 13 of the 16 per cent. But Simpson was a merchant when

[1] This view is supported by some remarks made by Tooke, and by the contemporary *Circular to Bankers*.

[2] The total of subscriptions for the Wakefield, Pontefract & Goole was first calculated from PP 1845 (317, 625), XL. The percentage contribution from *Land* was 62. But it was found, from the printed copy of the Wakefield, Pontefract & Goole contract in the House of Lords Record Office, that there were two schedules. Schedule B was signed by nine prominent people connected with the Manchester & Leeds, who described themselves as 'esquires', presumably because they regarded the description, in the circumstances, a neutral one. They were signing on behalf of the Manchester & Leeds, to which they were to hand over the shares. Elsewhere they put down their correct descriptions.

[3] R. W. Dickson, *General View of the Agriculture of Lancashire* (1815), p 116. G. H. Tupling, *The Economic History of Rossendale* (Manchester, 1927), p 228.

he signed the 1835–6 contract of the Manchester & Leeds, and had obviously retired by the time of the Blackburn, Darwen & Bolton contract of 1845,[1] and there are other examples of subscribers changing their descriptions upon retirement. This complicates the analysis but the very fact that we are able to trace these changes means that their connections with our companies were continuous.

It is clear from Table 4 that no judgment is possible on the accepted view that landowners gradually changed from opponents to avid supporters of railways. Herbert Spencer, when writing of the 'illegitimate agencies' in railway promotion, maintained that[2]

> Conspicuous amongst these is the self interest of landowners. Once the greatest obstacles to railway enterprise, owners of estates have of late years been amongst its chief promoters.

The landed interest dominated Parliament, hence the change in the attitude of the legislature from one of opposition to one of support.[3] But David Spring's statement:[4]

> In spite of the approval and even the promotion of the early railroads by some of the gentry, the evidence would suggest that landed gentlemen did not figure conspicuously as investors in railway stock. . . . (They) took slowly to investment in railways, as the Parliamentary Returns of 1845 and 1846 might suggest.

is confirmed by the results of an analysis of the Lancashire & Yorkshire companies' contracts. Only 1 per cent of the Manchester & Leeds contract of 1835–6 was taken up by the *Land* group, while it subscribed 17 per cent to the Manchester & Leeds in 1839–40. In 1844–5 the category is responsible for 18 per cent of the Wakefield, Pontefract & Goole's contract, and a mere 1 per cent of the Huddersfield & Sheffield Junction's in 1845.

It is not, therefore, possible to say whether there was increasing support from landowners as the railway system was extended in the 1840s. The high contribution from landowners to the Wakefield, Pontefract & Goole may be explained by the nature of the country through which the railway was to pass. Much more than any of the other lines, this company was to serve an agricultural area, since Wakefield was a noted wheat market at the time, and was the centre of an extensive wheat growing district. According to Lewis's *Topographical Dictionary*, published in 1840, corn and wool were the staple commodities of Wakefield, and the trade in corn had greatly increased, while a considerable number of warehouses had been

[1] Simpson was also described as 'esquire' in the 1839–40 contract of the Manchester & Leeds.

[2] *Edinburgh Review*, loc cit, p 428.

[3] Ibid, pp 429–30.

[4] 'The English Landed Estate in the Age of Coal and Iron: 1830–1880', *Journal of Economic History*, Vol IX, No 1 (1951), pp 6–7.

built, in addition to a new corn exchange.[1] Associated with the local malting establishments was the cultivation of barley. Pontefract and its surrounding districts were essentially an agricultural area, which was also noted for its manufacture of Pontefract cakes. A more extensive participation of landowners is reasonable, therefore, especially when we remember that well over 90 per cent of the *individual* subscriptions to this company came from Yorkshire. The comparative absence of manufacturers, who subscribed only 4 per cent of the contract, is very noticeable against the higher proportion from the landowners.

The remaining contracts to which the *Land* group subscribed more than 10 per cent were those of the Manchester & Leeds in 1839–40, the Ashton, Stalybridge & Liverpool Junction, the Blackburn & Preston, and the Liverpool & Bury. The geographical dispersion of the Manchester & Leeds £100 shares in 1835–6 and 1839–40 might be associated with the very steep jump in the *Land* percentage from 1 to 17 per cent. The proportion of scrip held by residents of Lancashire and Yorkshire was 91 per cent in 1835–6, but by 1839–40 London and areas other than Lancashire, Yorkshire and Cheshire accounted for 23 per cent of the subscriptions. In addition to London and places outside England and Wales, there were subscriptions from people in 27 English and Welsh counties, who were placed in the *Land* group much more frequently than were subscribers in Lancashire, Yorkshire and Cheshire.

Those bearing the vague description of 'esquire' must obviously be treated with great care. But whatever the validity of the *Land* category, the agricultural interest was comparatively unimportant in the initial financing of these railways. Included in this group are farmers and yeomen who were not, of course, necessarily landowners, but of whom there were very few indeed. And when a yeoman or a farmer subscribed, it was usually for a small amount, and very often for the minimum, depending upon the denomination of the shares. It is likely that this paucity of farmers reflects the state of agriculture rather than the farming community's lack of knowledge of the possibilities of investment and speculation in railway shares.

Since some of the 'gentlemen' might have been landowners it is advisable to consider the contributions of this class of subscribers in this connection. Even combining the 'gentlemen' with the 'esquires', the farmers and the yeoman, does not, generally speaking, greatly enhance their relative importance. The percentages they subscribed are tabulated in Table 5, on p 202. *Land* supplied 8 per cent, and gentlemen 10 per cent of the total amount of all contracts. Thus *Land* was responsible for less than a tenth of the total amount promised to our companies, while the combination promised less than a fifth. This figure, which certainly exaggerates the influence

[1] The Wakefield wheat market was important enough in the 1830s to be quoted by the *Circular to Bankers*, No 479, 15 September 1837.

of the landed interest, nevertheless contrasts with the three-fifths and more promised by *Trade* and *Industry*.

TABLE 5

TOTAL SUBSCRIPTIONS OF 'GENTLEMEN' AND LAND

Company	*Gentlemen* %	*Land* %	*Total* %
Manchester & Leeds	9	1	10
Manchester & Leeds	13	17	30
Ashton, Stalybridge & Liverpool Junction	2	23	25
Bolton & Preston	7	Nil	7
Blackburn & Preston	4	18	22
Manchester, Bury & Rossendale	10	4	14
Blackburn, Burnley, Accrington & Colne	8	5	13
Liverpool, Ormskirk & Preston	14	7	21
Liverpool & Bury	15	10	25
Blackburn, Darwen & Bolton	3	16	19
Wakefield, Pontefract & Goole	12	18	30
Huddersfield & Sheffield Junction	8	1	9
Averages	10	8	18

The averages are of the absolute totals.

VIII

The rest of the categories serve to emphasise the paramount importance of the merchants and manufacturers in the financing of the railways. The category *Law* was separated partly for the reason that its activities in the the railway sphere have received considerable emphasis. While its percentage contributions were not very high they do compare very favourably with those of *Banking* which, one would have thought, was a more wealthy class. The 10 per cent subscribed by *Law* to the Liverpool & Bury is perhaps the most noteworthy figure. It represents £59,000, which was easily the highest total subscribed by the group to any contract, and was substantial for such a limited category. Since the number of solicitors and attorneys would not be anything like the number of merchants and grocers, their subscriptions may be regarded as relatively quite important. It would not be true to say that people like solicitors were necessarily the speculative London type. Almost without exception the subscribers in this category who signed, for instance, the Liverpool & Bury contract, were residents of Lancashire or Yorkshire. Some, like Henry Bury and Samuel Darbishire, were closely associated with the Manchester & Leeds.

Linked with the solicitors in the descriptions of the flotation of railways, and especially in the accounts of the railway manias, are engineers and surveyors. Their importance is undoubted. Most of the comment on the Stephensons is eulogy. R. M. Martin, for instance, spoke of 'the bold and comprehensive genius of George Stephenson', who was 'backed by the capital of our Lancashire merchants and manufacturers. . . .'[1] But few writers failed to castigate the 'pettifogging attorneys and rejected engineers' who were 'the true authors, . . . of three-fourths of the railway schemes before the world at this moment (1845)'.[2] Morier Evans, Herbert Spencer, James Loch writing to Huskisson, John Francis—all burst out against this breed from 1829 onwards. But in our contracts, the engineers and surveyors were few in number.

Bankers were never prominent numerically in the contracts, although the Ashton, Stalybridge & Liverpool Junction managed to attract 12 per cent of its subscriptions from this class. On the whole it was the same few bankers who appeared in the contracts of our companies, and some of them were very wealthy men. Samuel Brooks, of Cunliffes, Brooks & Company, a director of the Manchester & Leeds, and one of the original promoters of the line, was evidently most fortunate in that 'Everything he touched brought him revenue.'[3] According to Grindon, he disposed of the greater part of his real and personal estate before he made his will, but still left an estimated £2½ millions when he died in 1864.[4] Like Brooks, Edward Loyd, the head of the Manchester section of Jones, Loyd & Company, was a director of, and a prominent subscriber and lender to, the Manchester & Leeds and various other companies of the Lancashire & Yorkshire network. He had, it was said, not 'the slightest taint of avarice', and was 'indifferent to speculation, the desire to get rich by leaps, which, being a disorderly thing, he constantly discouraged'.[5] Others of these firms, notably Roger and James Cunliffe (London), and Lewis Loyd were constant subscribers. It is the continual reappearance of these men as subscribers that largely makes up the contribution of the banking class, although other Lancashire bankers were not entirely absent, and we find steadfast subscribers from farther afield—Timothy Rhodes Cobb of Banbury is one example. The proceedings of the Finance Committee of the Manchester & Leeds show, moreover, that they were more than mere subscribers: for many years they appear not only as payers of money in advance of calls, but also as substantial lenders on mortgage.[6]

The *Miscellaneous* group is a fairly wide category, and what is surprising, therefore, is not that occasionally it subscribed about 15 per cent of a contract, as with the Wakefield, Pontefract & Goole, but that more often

[1] *Railways—Past, Present, & Prospective* (1849, 2nd ed), pp 6–7.
[2] D. M. Evans, *City Men and City Manners, . . .* (1852), p 77.
[3] Leo H. Grindon, *Manchester Banks and Bankers* (Manchester, 1878), p 208.
[4] Ibid, pp 199, 214.
[5] Ibid, p 151.
[6] Proceedings of the Finance Committee of the Manchester & Leeds, *passim* (BTHR, LY 1/475–7).

its weight was really insignificant. Surprising, that is, only when we bear in mind what has been said of the activities in railway finance of those who comprise the group. The majority of the subscriptions in this category came from surgeons, physicians, accountants, book-keepers, clergymen, engineers, surveyors, clerks, teachers, and army and navy officers. It follows that the impecunious clerk, whose speculative participation in the manias of 1836 and 1845 has probably been legitimately emphasised, was comparatively unimportant even in the 'mania' contract of 1835–6. The percentages are not very large for such a broad category and the mere clerk was certainly not very conspicuous, either for the frequency with which he appeared or for the amounts which he subscribed, although the group did increase somewhat in relative importance in 1844 and 1845.

In addition, it should be mentioned that the 'clerk' was often a clergyman. While many describing themselves as clerks prefixed the explanatory 'Reverend' to their names, there are examples of so-called 'clerks' being entered in a contract with no indication that they were in holy orders. The entry 'Richard Bassnett, clerk, Gorton', occurred twice in the Manchester & Leeds contract of 1839–40. The Reverend Richard Bassnett figured in a resolution at the special general meeting of the company's proprietors in January 1839, that is, before the contract was drawn up.[1] Other examples of what are almost certainly misleading entries in the same contract are the following: Thomas Butt, clerk, Trentham, Staffordshire—the Reverend Thomas Butt is mentioned several times in the Manchester & Leeds finance committee minutes;[2] Miles Formby, clerk, Melling, near Liverpool —the Reverend Miles Formby is entered in the finance committee minutes for the meeting of 1 April 1842; James Balfour, clerk, Cheltenham—the Reverend James Balfour had produced, in 1845, a dividend cheque for October 1841, to the finance committee.[3]

The clergy themselves have received considerable attention for their speculative activities in the mania periods. In 1845 *The Times* coined the amusing phrase, that the clergy were almost 'forsaking scripture for script'.[4] But the four mentioned above were all *bona fide* investors. To these may be added further clergymen who signed the 1839–40 contract, who put themselves down as reverends, and who are mentioned in the finance committee minutes in connection with shareholdings: James Cawley, Samuel Best, and James Edwards.[5] The majority of the clergymen who subscribed in 1839–40 were investors to the extent that they kept their

[1] *Reports and Accounts*, 17 January 1839 (BTHR, RAC 1/204).

[2] Proceedings of the Finance Committee of the Manchester & Leeds, eg 16 August 1838, and 10 July 1840 (BTHR, LY 1/475; 476).

[3] Ibid, 5 September 1845 (BTHR, LY 1/477).

[4] Cf B. C. Hunt, *The Development of the Business Corporation in England: 1800–1867* (Cambridge, Mass, 1936), p 106.

[5] Proceedings of the Finance Committee, eg 23 November 1838, 10 July 1839, and 5 February 1842 (BTHR, LY 1/475; 476).

shares for a sufficiently long period for them to receive dividends, or for them to pay calls.

1839 was a depressed year and there was consequently no speculative fever in railway shares. We are unable to tell whether these clergy subscribed in the speculative year of 1835–6 since they all received shares to the value of less than £1,000 in 1839–40 and, assuming that they took on the *pro rata* basis, they would therefore have held less than £2,000 of the original stock. (The 1839 issue was of £50 shares.) We have only the list of those who subscribed £2,000 or more in the earlier year, and it contains none of the clergy mentioned. But while it cannot be proved that clergymen-subscribers of a mania year were not mere speculators, genuine investment motives lay behind the acquisition of shares by most of the clergy who supported the Manchester & Leeds. Several of them paid considerable sums in advance of calls, as the finance committee minutes show.[1]

There is one other point which may be mentioned in this context of clerks' subscriptions. It must be true that their salaries could not in general have been very large. Morier Evans, speaking of London, said:[2] 'Most of the private bankers employ between forty and fifty clerks each, and the fair average of salary they receive is £200 a year.' But if we are to believe the evidence put forward by Grindon, the Manchester banker's clerk, for example, was often far from mediocre or impecunious, and some of them later became successful bankers themselves. According to Grindon, the salary of one of the clerks (William Morton, who died in 1839) of Jones Loyd & Company, was said to be £2,000 per annum.[3] Thomas Barlow Jervis, who subscribed £1,150 to the Manchester & Leeds in 1839, and also subscribed to the Ashton, Stalybridge & Liverpool Junction in 1844, was chief clerk at Jones Loyd at the time. In 1848 he became a partner upon the reorganisation of the bank that followed the retirement of Edward Loyd.[4] These clerks would have been able to invest in railways. It is possible that Jervis and others like him were merely signing contracts on behalf of clients of their banks, without stating power of attorney, but this is unlikely, because the Manchester & Leeds was against such practices.[5] Whether such people signed contracts on their own or on others' behalf, they still did not constitute a substantial body of subscribers.

Finally, it may be of some interest to consider the part played by the proverbial widow. This is, of course, the pathetic figure brought into so many controversies over railways, from their early history to nationalisa-

[1] Ibid, 28 December 1838, 21 June 1839, and 24 June 1841 (BTHR, LY 1/475; 476).

[2] D. M. Evans, *The City*, p 8.

[3] Grindon, *Manchester Banks and Bankers*, for this, and similar information, see especially, pp 179–82.

[4] Ibid, pp 159–63. Edward Loyd was the uncle of Samuel Jones Loyd, later Lord Overstone.

[5] Cf Proceedings of the Directors of the Manchester & Leeds Railway, eg 26 January 1836, and 14 April 1836 (BTHR, LY 1/2).

tion. Joseph Pease, the Quaker and member of the famous Darlington family, wrote to another company shareholder in 1842 on the proposed establishment of the Manchester & Leeds reserve fund.[1]

> The widows, the trust-money of orphans. . . . Should the interests of these be sacrificed to satisfy the rapacious shareholders? If this is the way to support the prosperity of railways, then permit me to say, perish railways, and live justice and truth immutable. . . . Allow me, my friend, to guard thee against putting thy money and thy conscience in the same pocket, for gold is in reality so much harder than conscience that it often wears conscience out.

For Samuel Salt, the 'heaviest, because the most helpless, sufferers' from the railway depression, were the poor widows and orphans.[2] Lardner maintained that 'the fortunes of the widow and orphan, . . . are fraudulently transferred to . . . directors. . . .'[3] These accusations were no doubt to the point after speculative mania such as the 1845 boom, but this, and so many other similar features of railway finance, have been stressed at the expense of a balanced view of railway development. The widows have been included in the gentlewomen category, and in fact the number of gentlewomen and spinsters in a contract was usually larger than that of widows. But the contributions of the whole group were not very significant, as the figures show: 1 and 4 per cent for the Manchester & Leeds in 1835–6 and 1839–40; 5 per cent for the Bolton & Preston in 1837; 2, 3, and 1 per cent in 1844 for the Ashton, Stalybridge & Liverpool Junction, the Blackburn & Preston, and the Manchester, Bury & Rossendale; and 1, 1, 2, 3, 2 and 1 per cent in 1844–45 for the Blackburn, Burnley, Accrington & Colne, the Liverpool, Ormskirk & Preston, the Liverpool & Bury, the Blackburn, Darwen & Bolton, the Wakefield, Pontefract & Goole, and the Huddersfield & Sheffield Junction respectively.

The figures for 1844–5 are particularly low, yet this was a year of rapidly increasing railway activity, in which this type of investor, or speculator, might have appeared in greater relative strength. Since the widows formed only a small section of the group to which the figures relate, their role in the promising of capital was small, and even absolutely their number was insignificant.[4] Many of the female subscribers to the Manchester & Leeds can, moreover, be shown to have had a more than speculative interest in the company. There are, it is true, only three names of women to be found in the 1835–6 contract—the reason is no doubt that the average subscription of a female was less than £2,000—but all three subscribed again in 1839–40, and two of them are mentioned more than once in the Finance Committee minutes as payers of calls in advance. The list of 1839–40 is,

[1] By means of a letter to the *Railway Times*, 26 March 1842.
[2] *Railway and Commercial Information* (1850), p iii.
[3] Dionysius Lardner, *Railway Economy* (1850), p 514.
[4] Women and clergymen were accused of causing 'bubble' subscription lists—G. H. Evans, op cit, p 35.

however, a full one, and of the 51 female subscribers 13 are shown by the Finance minutes to have paid calls in advance between 1839–40 and 1841.[1] As for the rest—failure to pay calls in advance does not, of course, mean that a person's subscription cannot be regarded as a reliable indication of a source of capital.

In the light of this evidence, and on general grounds, it would be unreasonable to reject as sources all subscription contracts because it was possible for them to contain the names of speculators and fictitious characters. The contracts used here were those of companies whose Bills were, with only one exception,[2] successful in the sessions for which they were prepared; of companies which built the lines which were sanctioned. The nucleus of the Lancashire & Yorkshire, the Manchester & Leeds, experienced little difficulty in raising money in the unfavourable years between 1837 and 1843.[3] Further, Henry Ayres showed that, in comparison with many other companies, the Lancashire & Yorkshire continued to display the financial soundness of its parent company. He noted the correlation between the low proportions of ordinary paid-up capital, and the poor financial results of many companies,[4] and the level of dividend on ordinary stock was highest in companies such as the London & North Western and the Lancashire & Yorkshire, which had the highest proportion of such stock.[5]

There is one other factor which is thought to have a most important bearing on this discussion: the role of Lancashire in the early railway capital market. This factor, it is believed, places the high percentages of subscriptions coming from Lancashire in a rather new perspective. G. H. Evans's remark to the effect that local promotion and finance were the mainstays of railways until about 1844 has already been quoted. We are here concerned only with finance, and it is suggested that it is not local finance that should be emphasised for this period, but rather the part played by Lancashire in the financing of the principal railways. The importance of Liverpool in this sphere has often been recognised,[6] and Evans allowed that there had been 'a number of departures from local promotion,

[1] Proceedings of the Finance Committee, *passim* (BTHR, LY 1/475; 476).

[2] The Liverpool Ormskirk & Preston, which was thrown out on Standing Orders (cf PP 1845 (659), XXXVI, 118) but which was successful in 1846.

[3] *Reports and Accounts*, particularly 17 September 1838 and 17 March 1842 (BTHR, RAC 1/204), at which it was proudly announced that not a single call had been unpaid. Many calls were paid in advance throughout the same period, although by 1847, along with most other companies, the M & L was having trouble over the arrears of calls caused by the great expansion of 1845 and 1846.

[4] Henry Ayres, *The Financial Position of Railways* (1868), p x.

[5] Ibid, pp xi and xxxiv. It is, perhaps, only fair to Mr Ayres to point out that he did not mention the L & Y in his text. Only his general view of railway finance, and his figures, have been used.

[6] See, for example, H. G. Lewin, *Early British Railways* (1925), p 71. Many early railways looked to the Liverpool area for 'a substantial part of their money'. Also J. H. Clapham, op cit, I, 387, 393.

financing and control'. But the impression gained from various sources is that these departures, at least so far as financing and, probably, control were concerned, were in fact most of the principal companies of the 1830s.

Of the London & Birmingham and Grand Junction Railways Tooke said: 'It has been computed that the Lancashire proprietors form seven-eighths of the whole in amount.'[1] Stretton's description of Stephenson's efforts in Liverpool on behalf of the Leicester & Swannington is classic,[2] and the Midland Counties and the North Midland are further examples of Liverpool's pervasive influence.[3] As late as 1850, at a meeting of the Midland proprietors, it was stated that there were 1,200 shareholders in the Liverpool district, who held £1,623,000 worth of shares.[4] Southern railways appear to have needed, and received, strong Lancashire backing. The London & Southampton was, according to Francis, dominated by the Lancashire interest,[5] while it was said that, 'The Stock of the Great Western, held in Liverpool alone', amounted, 'to very nearly £500,000, if it do not exceed that sum.'[6] MacDermot's monumental work on the GW contains several references to the pressure the 'Liverpool party' exerted on the company's board.[7] But it is in the east of England that we have the classic example of the Lancashire, and particularly the Liverpool interest. The Eastern Counties, which was the largest line sanctioned in 1836, derived less than a third of its capital subscribed in that year from local sources,[8] and it seems certain that most of the rest was supplied by Lancashire and north Cheshire.[9]

In addition to specific references to the participation of Lancastrians in the financing of particular companies, there is a wealth of contemporary comment on what was felt to be the paramount influence of Lancashire in this sphere. Some of the comment was laudatory, some uneasy. Lalor was worried indeed about the growth of a society typified by Lancashire,[10] whose 'remarkable population' impressed no less the editors of the *Circular*

[1] T. Tooke, *A History of Prices . . .* (1838), II, 275 n.

[2] C. E. Stretton, *The History of the Midland Railway* (1901), p 8. C. R. Clinker, *The Leicester and Swannington Railway* (Leicester, 1954), disputes the accuracy of Stretton's account of the Liverpool interest in this railway.

[3] Ibid, pp 32, 33, 34, 47.

[4] Ibid, p 144.

[5] Francis, op cit, I, 228, 230.

[6] *Circular to Bankers*, No 522, 13 July 1838. There is also a reference to the large proportion of London & Southampton stock held in Lancashire.

[7] E. T. MacDermot, *History of the Great Western Railway* (1927), 1, 59, 72, 73, for examples.

[8] E. Doble, 'History of the Eastern Counties Railway . . .' (unpublished PhD thesis, London, 1939), p 35.

[9] *Select Committee on Railways*, PP 1839 (517), X, minutes of evidence to the second Report, QQ 2152–64. See also the account of the fifth general meeting of the proprietors of this company in the *Railway Times*, 2 March 1839. It was stated at the meeting that 'Lancashire and Cheshire held . . . nearly two-thirds of the entire number of shares', and that 'taxation and representation' should be brought together.

[10] John Lalor, *Money and Morals* (1852), especially Ch IX 'The New Gold'

to Bankers. The latter was a London periodical, and it was by no means uncritical of some of the methods by which railways were promoted. It often gave warnings of the dangers of speculation,[1] and in fact, on several occasions, it obviously thought it necessary to deny any particular antipathy towards the new system of communication.[2] Its sustained praise of Lancashire enterprise and wealth is therefore all the more noteworthy. One issue carried a long article which contained passages such as: 'It is notorious that the largest proprietors of the Liverpool & Manchester, the Grand Junction, the London & Birmingham, the Southampton, and the Great Western live' in and around Lancashire.[3]

To return to the Lancashire & Yorkshire Railway, it will now be seen that the high 'local' concentration of the subscriptions to its constituent companies carries a different emphasis. In view of the extensive participation of Lancashire in the financing of companies in other parts of the country, it is not surprising that it, and to a less extent the West Riding, should figure so largely in the contracts we have used and which, after all, were those of mainly Lancashire companies.[4] Nor is it surprising that an area which was undergoing the most rapid industrialisation, and which supplied the bulk of Britain's exports, should have had large reserves of capital. The rate of industrial growth reached its peak in the three decades up to 1851,[5] and Schlote has shown that the 'rate of expansion' of exports in the period from 1845 to 1855 was the greatest seen in the nineteenth century.[6] And according to Imlah, cottons and woollens alone constituted about 55 per cent of the country's exports in 1850.[7] It is impossible to ignore the evidence of Lancashire's great importance as a source of railway capital.[8] It suggests that the emphasis placed on the local nature of railway

[1] *Circular to Bankers*, No 309, 20 June 1834.

[2] Ibid, eg No 483, 13 October 1837.

[3] Ibid, No 509, 13 April 1838. See also, No 485, 27 October 1837.

[4] The *Reports of the Select Committee on Railway Subscription Lists* of 1837 are often quoted on the subject of invalid subscriptions. The briefest study of them will show that almost all the companies investigated were either metropolitan or the London-South Coast type. Even here there are encouraging remarks, eg most lists of subscribers were the result of a 'cautious selection from among the mass of applicants'. *First Report*, 1837 (226), XVIII, Pt I, p 23. Also, one of the principal grounds for invalidating subscriptions was failure to state power of attorney.

[5] Cf P. Deane and W. A. Cole, *British Economic Growth 1688–1959* (Cambridge, 1962), p 297; also Brinley Thomas, *Migration and Economic Growth* (Cambridge, 1954), p 124.

[6] Werner Schlote, *British Overseas Trade from 1700 to the 1930's* (Oxford, 1952), p 41 and Table on p 42.

[7] A. H. Imlah, 'The Terms of Trade of the United Kingdom, 1798–1913', *Journal of Economic History*, November 1950, p 184.

[8] The examples quoted by no means exhaust the list of railways in the financing of which Lancashire participated. W. H. Marwick, *Economic Developments in Victorian Scotland* (1936), p 138, mentioned that the stock of the Edinburgh & Glasgow (1838) 'was held largely in England—over a third by Lancashire merchants'.

We must, it is true, await a comprehensive investigation of the capital sources of the companies dealt with—if, indeed, this is possible—before we may accept without reserve the evidence presented here.

finance up to 1844, at least, has been to a large extent misplaced. It is very probably true that many of the smaller local lines were locally financed, but the statement made in 1836 that 'no considerable Railway can be completed that depends upon local money power for its outlay'[1] seems, on the whole, to be correct. Moreover, if it is accepted that Lancashire was a primary source of capital for non-Lancashire companies, the importance given by G. H. Evans to the 'remoteness (of transport undertakings) from the large capital centres' as one of the causes of local financing, is not really justified.[2] Lancashire, not London, was the main reservoir of capital, the area with the surpluses which as Tooke said, 'could (not) be profitably reinvested in the same business, great and expanding as that business'—the cotton trade—was.[3]

X

Where there is sufficient material available, investigation of the sources from which railway companies derived their capital in the period up to 1845 will, it is believed, support the various points made in this article. These may be summarised as follows. The capital market for railways appears to have undergone no really substantial change up to 1845. There is some evidence that the market was becoming something like the perfect market of the traditional story. But the tables depicting the percentage distribution of subscriptions, contract by contract, show that even in 1845 there was not a wider geographical spread. As a tentative suggestion based, perhaps unwisely, on the study of the Manchester & Leeds, I should say that the market was to a certain extent perfect in the sense that once shares were put on the market they flowed over the country. But serious imperfections remained, and for the Manchester & Leeds the 'local interest' remained high. The practice of this, and many other companies, in making new share issues on a *pro rata* basis would alone impart a certain rigidity to the capital market, even if it is assumed that some of the shareholders did not retain their shares. The imperfections were still great enough in the mid 1840s and, for this group of companies particularly, the position of Lancashire was still so dominant, for the analysis of the late 1844 and early

[1] *Circular to Bankers*, No 422, 19 August 1836. Obviously 'local' is used here in a narrower sense that I have used it in calling counties 'local'.

[2] G. H. Evans, op cit, p 6. It is, however, sometimes difficult to decide whether Professor Evans intends his statements to refer to both canals and railways throughout his period.

[3] It may be thought that there is a contradiction between this argument, and the emphasis on the concentration of subscriptions on 'local' lines. But it was most probably the surpluses of Liverpudlians, Mancunians, and of the residents of a few other large towns, which flowed over the country. Lancashire railways alone could not absorb the excess of capital. For the smaller centres, the 'home' lines probably provided opportunity enough.

1845 contracts to yield results similar to those yielded by the analysis of the contracts entered into between 1835 and early 1844.

It is, further, believed that it was the pressure of Lancashire capital, and not that of London, which was the important influence in the early railway capital market. One hesitates to criticise so excellent a thesis as that of J. B. Jeffreys, but one wonders just who were the 'capitalists not directly engaged in trade', to whom he refers. As long as 1849, Locock Webb was wondering the same thing:[1]

> . . . it is unintelligible, why that class (the commercial class) of persons to whom we are indebted for the prompt development of Railways, whose spirit, energy, and business habits have overcome all difficulties, should give way to a non-commercial class. . . . But where shall we turn in Great Britain to find the non-commercial portion of the community to invest some £300,000,000 of capital in Railways? . . . A 'non-commercial' class, in England at least, requires some translation of its meaning. . . . Who is the stockholder, but the trading class?

[1] C. Locock Webb, *A Letter . . . on Railways, their Accounts and Dividends* . . . (1849), pp 41–2.

Railway Contractors and the Finance of Railway Development in Britain

By HAROLD POLLINS

I

The contractor is an elusive figure in the history of British railways. There is the important study of his activities by Jenks[1] and several useful biographical works,[2] but those who write on railway history are not usually concerned with the company as a business unit and the constructional side of the story is seldom discussed in financial terms.[3] Yet the contractor was an imposing and well-known figure. Charles Thomas Lucas was described as 'one of the foremost men of the nineteenth century'; the firm of Lucas & Aird is said to have been 'one of the largest employers of labour in the country'.[4] William Dargan was regarded as 'a gentleman who has constructed Irish railways and employed Irish labour to a larger extent than any other Irishman ever did, and who has thus acquired a noble and well-earned fortune'.[5] Contemporary railway periodicals, not noted for their inhibitions or selectivity, attacked contractors constantly—often more than directors or officials. In the mid Victorian period the contractor moved up the social scale easily and quickly, and the prototype career (portrayed by Trollope in *Dr Thorne*) of a fortune, knighthood, election to

This article was first published in the *Journal of Transport History*, Vol III (1957–8), 41–51, 103–10, and appears in this volume in a slightly revised form.

I should like to thank the following for their criticism and advice: Dr Charles Feinstein, Professor W. E. Minchinton, Dr E. A. Course, Mr E. W. Cooney, Mr Charles E. Lee.

[1] L. H. Jenks, *The Migration of British Capital to 1875* (London & New York, 1927). He is mainly concerned with overseas railways, but has a great deal to say on British railway development.

[2] A. Helps, *Life and Labours of Mr Brassey* (1872); F. MacDermott, *The Life and Work of Joseph Firbank* (1887); Henry Peto, *Sir Morton Peto* (1893); G. A. Hobson, *The Life of Sir James Falshaw* (1905); J. A. Spender, *Weetman Pearson* (1930); I. Thomas, *Top Sawyer; a biography of David Davies of Llandinam* (1938); R. K. Middlemas, *The Master Builders* (1963); D. Young, *The Member for Mexico* (1966).

[3] This is the case too of *The British Civil Engineering Contracting Industry* (Federation of Civil Engineering Contractors, 1956), but it has some useful points on finance.

[4] *Proceedings* of the *Institution of Civil Engineers*, Vol 124 (1895–6), 439–40.

[5] *Illustrated London News*, 21 May 1853, 393. His contracting life began in the early 1830s on the Dublin & Kingstown Railway (O. J. Vignoles, *Life of Charles Blacker Vignoles* (1889), p 182). Another important, and now forgotten, contractor was Peter Thompson, 'for several years . . . known as one of the largest railway and general contractors in the country', *Herapath*, 20 May 1876, 563.

Parliament, and fall from grace was no mere caricature.[1] Even sober bodies, such as the Institution of Civil Engineers, could find room in their publications for caustic remarks on some of the earlier contractors:

> The nature of the relation which subsisted between the engineer of a public company and the contractors who undertook the execution of the works was, at the commencement of Mr Brassey's career, very different from that which subsequently obtained. The early contractors were, for the most part, men of strong natural abilities, insight into the cost and method of executing work amounting to instinct, low tastes, violent habits, and grasping tenacity of purpose. A contract being once made, it seemed to be regarded as natural that the contractor should set his wits to work to make the most of it. This was to be done, on the one hand, by grinding his labourers under the pressure of the truck system and the 'tommy shop', and on the other hand by 'scamping' his work. . . . As a rule, vexatiously minute inspectors were open to bribes. They gave trouble unless they were bought off.

Brassey, it noticed, did a great deal to ameliorate these conditions, as did other large contractors, notably Peto.[2] It was not common for the *Railway Times* to say anything laudatory about anybody in the railway world, but in a discussion on the East London Railway in 1865 it stated that 'the contract with Messrs Brassey fully assures completion of the works within the capital defined in the act of Parliament'.[3] In railway history that is high praise.

It would be absurd to suggest that the contractors were the most important figures in the railway world, but in the period after the great mania of the 1840s any history of railway construction which ignored them would be ludicrously incomplete.[4] There were well-known 'railway politicians' (concerned with negotiations between companies about working arrangements and also construction) and railway operators—James Allport of the Midland Railway, for example. But there is no doubt that in the period between the fall of George Hudson, the 'Railway King', in 1849, and the emergence of Sir Edward Watkin (who came into prominence in the late 1860s) it was the contractors who were the centre of attraction.

Their activities after 1850 are usually associated with the overseas railways. As the *Railway Times* put it:

[1] There is a short description of the kind of rich, vulgar contractor who started as a navvy in J. Francis, *A History of the English Railway* (1851), Vol I, 271–2.

[2] *Proc Inst Civ Eng*, Vol 33 (1871–2), 248–9 (Brassey). For complementary remarks on Peto, see *Select Committee on Railway Labourers*, PP 1846, XIII, Report, p iv; also J. Francis, op cit, I, 266–73.

[3] *Railway Times*, 17 June 1865, 790. See also Joseph Devey, *Life of Joseph Locke* (1862). Chapter XI, 'The Railway Contractor', is largely in praise of Brassey.

[4] A virtue of such books as Charles E. Lee, *Metropolitan District Railway* (South Godstone, 1956); C. P. Gasquoine, *Story of the Cambrian* (Wrexham, 1922); and C. G. Maggs, *The Midland & South Western Junction Railway* (Newton Abbot, 1967) is that the activities of the contractors are given due place.

> No one can have failed to observe the active movements of our wealthy and enterprising contractors, gentlemen who have made large fortunes within a short time, and who now seem bent on losing them as quickly. Having completed as they consider their work at home, and having given us an almost perfect system of railways here, they have started on a kind of knight-errantry to supply railway deficiencies all over the world.[1]

Herapath's Railway Journal, which often took a less jaundiced view of railway events than did the *Railway Times*, could be more sympathetic. During the Crimean War it praised the railway contractors in these terms:

> Our great railway contractors will figure in history as having performed a conspicuous part in the destruction of the Russian enemy, as well as in the construction of railways all over the world—both operations being most beneficial to the interests of society at large.[2]

Their work in Britain was also important. They were associated with numerous public works, and their financial guarantee made possible the Great Exhibition of 1851.[3] In particular the 'contractors' lines' are worth investigating; these were the railway companies in which the contractors' activities amounted to a great deal more than merely building the line.

The railway contractors were not new in the 1850s; railways had almost always been built by them from the earliest days, as had, indeed, the canals before them. Railway companies might resort to direct construction in an emergency—the most famous example being the Kilsby tunnel on the London & Birmingham Railway in the 1830s, when the engineering difficulties proved too great for the contractor.[4] And the great contractors emerged early; Peto and Brassey were engaged in extensive overseas contracts in the 1840s.[5] Nevertheless their greatest significance in railway finance came after the period of the great mania of the 1840s.

By the end of the mania just over one-third of the total route-mileage ever built had been constructed; by 1870 the figure was about three-quarters, and in the succeeding fifty years another 5,000 miles were built. A great deal was obviously accomplished in the 1850s and 1860s—about 8,000 route miles were opened[6]—and it was done in a period of acute diffi-

[1] *Railway Times*, 27 November 1852, 1257.

[2] *Herapath*, 2 December 1854, 1239. Also M. Robbins, 'The Balaklava Railway', *Journal of Transport History*, Vol I (1953).

[3] C. R. Fay, *Palace of Industry, 1851* (1951), p 7. William Dargan virtually financed the Dublin Industrial Exhibition of 1853: *Illustrated London News*, 21 May 1853, 393.

[4] S. Smiles, *Life of George Stephenson* (3rd ed, 1857), pp 329–31. There is a useful description of early contracting methods in *Railway Times*, 20 January 1844, 63–4, and 23 February 1844, 228. Much information is contained in *SC on Railway Labourers*, PP 1846, XIII, and Jenks, op cit, pp 134–6.

[5] In May 1846, at the peak of railway construction, Peto was employing, directly or indirectly, 9,000 men. (*SC on Railway Labourers*, PP 1846, XIII, QQ 1228; 30).

[6] There is a useful analysis of the growth of railway mileage in G. A. Wade, 'Twenty-two thousand miles of railway', *Railway Magazine*, October 1904, 290–7.

culty for the railways. Broadly, for a generation after the mania British railway companies, old or newly established, found it hard to raise money.

Some of the reasons were peculiar to the railways: the excesses of the 1840s, and the low rate of dividend with share prices below par for much of the 1850s, even in the case of the major companies, did not endear them to the investing public, despite the continuing expansion of traffic. The high proportion of capital with fixed interest and fixed dividends reduced the amount of net profit available to holders of ordinary shares. Nor was confidence enhanced by the continued depredations of railway servants—most companies at some stage or other had to report absconding officials. Some companies exhibited peculiar finances and committees of investigation were appointed from time to time. The affairs of at least one company—the West Hartlepool Harbour & Railway Company—were the subject of a parliamentary inquiry.[1]

Particularly noteworthy was the prohibition in 1847 of the payment of interest on calls. This may well have been a major cause of the shortage of capital, even though it was evaded by, amongst other methods, contractors paying interest.[2] The long period between the promotion of a railway company and the first dividend paid meant that shareholders might wait for years before any net profit was divided. (Existing shareholders often insisted that the capital of extensions and branches should be separate and should not participate at once in the general profits of the company.) Finally, the most profitable routes had already been built.[3]

The unpopularity of British railways to investors came just as other opportunities became available. The extension of limited liability to industry and commerce, and, more especially, the growth of overseas investment, notably in railways, provided important competitors in the money market.[4] In the 1850s and 1860s the railway journals commented continually on the slowness with which investors took up shares in British railway companies. The older companies were particularly affected. In 1863, a year of improving trade in the upswing of the trade cycle, the chairman of the London & North Western Railway, Richard Moon, said:

> You will find that capital is going out to India, and all over the world seeking for employment in railways. What is the state of things in England? There is not one of the great companies in this country who can raise sixpence without preference or guaranteed shares. There are no proprietors willing to come forward to make a railway. They are

[1] *SC on the West Hartlepool Harbour and Railway Company*, PP (Lords) 1863, XXXIV (113).

[2] *SC on Standing Order 167*, PP 1882, XIII (196), Report, p iii, Q 263.

[3] A useful study of the financial problems of railway promotion and construction in the 1850s is contained in J. R. T. Hughes, *Fluctuations in Trade, Industry and Finance; a study of British Economic Development, 1850–1860* (Oxford, 1960), Chapter 7.

[4] *Railway Times*, 19 April 1856, 491,' French and English Investments'.

made by contractors, engineers, and speculators, who live on the fears of the companies.[1]

Capital was needed in the first instance to meet the needs of growing traffic (thereby defeating the brave attempts to close capital accounts).[2] In any event they were forced to engage in new capital works. For the promotion of new lines was bound to affect the 'territory' of an existing company; if it ignored them or opposed them in Parliament, a competing company might take them up. Thus 'the fears of the companies' were real enough, for though new lines might be promoted in the 'traditional' manner, with local meetings at which subscriptions might be obtained,[3] it became normal practice for new companies to try to get the support of a main line company. A proposed line, strategically placed between two existing routes, would have no difficulty in either getting assistance from one of them or being taken over.

As well as these ways of financing new construction—old companies building to meet the demands of traffic or for self-preservation; new companies assisted by old companies—there was a third way: new companies associated with contractors.[4] It is not easy to find examples of new companies obtaining their funds entirely from the public;[5] nor of the major, established companies being concerned in these contractors' lines.[6]

II

The normal arrangement between company and contractor was that the contractor was paid monthly on the certificate of the railway company's engineer. Usually 10 per cent of the amount would be retained by the company as a guarantee fund. A contract between the London & North Western Railway and Thomas Brassey and Alexander Ogilvie stated:

[1] London & North Western Railway, *Reports and Accounts*, year ending 31 December 1862 (BTHR, RAC 1/234), Chairman's speech.

[2] H. Pollins, 'Aspects of Railway Accounting before 1868', in A. C. Littleton and B. S. Yamey (eds), *Studies in the History of Accounting* (1956). (Reprinted in this volume, p 138 ff.)

[3] G. H. Evans, *British Corporation Finance, 1775–1850* (Baltimore, 1936); H. Pollins, 'The Marketing of Railway Shares in the first half of the Nineteenth Century', *Economic History Review*, 2nd ser, VII (1954).

[4] T. Coates, *Railway Deposits Discussed* (1864), p 8. This is one of the few contemporary publications to praise the contractors' lines.

[5] Studies of some of the small railway companies bear this out: D. S. Barrie & C. R. Clinker, *The Somerset & Dorset Railway* (South Godstone, 1948); J. G. Spence, *The Caterham Railway* (South Godstone, 1952); D. S. Barrie, *The Rhymney Railway* (South Godstone, 1952).

[6] A minor, isolated example in 1851. The old-established Eastern Counties Railway discussed building a line by paying the contractor in bonds: ECR Board Minutes, 25 September 1851 (BTHR, EC 1/10, p 74).

> The Company shall and will pay to the Contractors for and in respect of the said Railway and Works . . . the sum of Three hundred and sixty nine thousand five hundred and ninety one pounds sixteen shillings. The said sum shall be paid monthly in such proportions as shall be certified by the Engineer as being in his judgment the proportionate value of the works executed during each month subject to a deduction of Ten pounds per cent to be held and retained in hand by the Company as a guarantee . . . against any default or neglect of the Contractors.[1]

In the case of the contractors' lines this was changed. A deduction was still made but the method of payment was different: the company's securities were taken by the contractor instead of cash. An abortive contract between the Swindon, Marlborough & Andover Railway and William Wright stated that the contract price of £399,045 was to be paid as to one-third in debentures and two-thirds in shares. (This was modified later to £100,000 in debentures and the remainder in shares.)[2]

It is true that even before 1850 contractors and other creditors would take shares and bonds instead of cash. In 1848 the Great Northern Railway paid Thomas Brassey £22,000 by a mortgage bond, and in the same year the North Staffordshire Railway paid him £45,000 in bonds.[3] But the records of the companies show that these methods were irregular and infrequent, and companies would as soon rely on promissory notes, if they were short of money, or temporary loans.[4] A hint of the future was the offer by the contracting firm of Charles Fox & Co to invest £150,000 in a proposed Cornwall Railway;[5] and the tendency of contractors to lend money or to be owed large sums, in the late 1840s, was another indication of things to come.[6]

When a contractor was paid in securities the railway company was obviously solving its financial problems. For the contractors a possible motive was the need to keep their permanent staff and equipment occupied. By the 1850s some had large organisations; in 1860 Peto, Brassey & Betts were described as 'the largest contractors in Europe'.[7] Of Thomas Brassey it was said:

> The capital that Mr Brassey dealt with was never idle. As soon as any part of it ceased to be wanted for any one great work, it was required for another, which either had to be commenced or was entering into a

[1] Contract for the Runcorn & Aston branch, 1 May 1863, cl 36 (BTHR, LNW 3/28).

[2] Contracts dated 27 July 1875 (cl 18); 19 October 1875 (BTHR, MPR 34/7).

[3] Great Northern Railway Finance Committee, 2 August 1848 (Minute 108) (BTHR, GN 1/219); North Staffordshire Railway, Board Minutes, 25 November 1848 (Minute 349) (BTHR, NS 1/4).

[4] G. H. Evans, op cit, *passim.*

[5] Devon & Cornwall Railway, Provisional Committee, 30 October 1843 (BTHR, COR 1/1). This is the company referred to in E. T. MacDermot, *History of the Great Western Railway* (2 vols, 1931), II, 261–2.

[6] H.P., *Peto*, pp 20–1; *Bradshaw's Railway Shareholders' Manual*, 1854, 109.

[7] *Engineer*, 20 January 1860, 35.

> phase of full activity. It must be recollected, that a main object with Mr Brassey was to furnish sufficient work for all that staff of skilled agents and for those large bodies of workmen whom he had collected around him.[1]

With railway companies and investors not keen to go in for new works, contractors had to participate in the promotion of schemes if their capital equipment was to continue to be fully employed. It is difficult, however, to decide who exactly were the promoters of many of these lines. In the boom of the 1860s there was a great deal of talk about lawyers' and engineers' lines,[2] as there had been in the mania of the 1840s. And, as ever, there were numerous schemes which began in provincial towns, with local notabilities trying to get railway accommodation. But although the evidence is not very clear—the minutes of companies are often silent on these matters—it seems likely that contractors at least helped to promote. Matthew Sheild and G. F. Bruce, two contractors who became bankrupt in the late 1860s, were described as promoters of railway schemes.[3] It is not always clear, however, because there was a great deal of talk of contractors' nominees sitting on railway boards,[4] the absence of a contractor's name in the early proceedings of a company does not, therefore, preclude the possibility of his inspiring it. And although it was said on several occasions that they did not promote lines,[5] the fact that the subscription contracts of two Irish companies were signed only by contractors provides strong, if not conclusive, evidence of promotion.[6]

Railway companies were statutory companies, obtaining their powers and legal status from Parliament. Part of the necessary procedure was the submission of a subscription contract containing the names and other details of potential shareholders who had paid a deposit and agreed to take shares if the company obtained its Act. The House of Commons abolished this requirement in 1858 on the grounds that such subscription contracts

[1] Helps, *Brassey*, p 154. However, another view refers to 'the habit of contractors to wind up the services of the entire staff at the end of a contract, and to engage new staffs for each contract as it came along'. Spender, *Pearson*, p 38.

[2] *The Economist*, 14 January 1865, 36.

[3] *Railway Times*, 26 January 1867, 89.

[4] Richard Samuel France, the contractor for the Mold & Denbigh Junction Railway, stated this quite explicitly:

> It is usual, that when a Contractor undertakes the entire responsibility of finding the whole of the money, and carrying out the works, he has the option of putting some of his own friends on the Board in order to take care of his own interests.

Letters and correspondence between Lord Redesdale and Mr France upon the subject of the Mold and Denbigh Junction Railway, PP (Lords) 1867, XIX (20), p 8.

For an attack on R. S. France and the Welsh contractors' lines, see *Railway Times*, 23 February 1867, 203–4.

[5] *SC on Railway and Canal Legislation*, PP 1857–8, XIV, Q 1294. *SC on Standing Orders (Parliamentary Deposits)*, PP 1864, X, Q 666 ff. *SC on Standing Order 167*, PP 1882, XIII, Q 170.

[6] The companies were the Cork, Midleton & Youghal, and Dublin & Wexford, both in 1853 (BTHR, SUB 3/1).

were not very reliable in providing a guarantee that the company had a solid body of financial support. Doubts as to their validity had been common for many years before they were discontinued,[1] but while they continued to be required the companies had to take seriously the question of 'filling up' the contract. In addition a deposit was submitted—usually in government stock—as a security, while the Bill was being considered and the line being built. Thus a company's initial financial and administrative needs might be sufficiently acute for its progress to be held up. The nature of the parliamentary timetable was such that a delay was disastrous. The documents and funds had to be submitted by a certain date, otherwise the Bill might not be examined that year and the company would have to wait 12 months, by which time the shareholders might well have lost heart or another company might have got in first. This all accounts for the feverish activity in October and November each year on the part of companies preparing to go to Parliament (or watching for possible competing schemes).

In the 1840s it had been common for directors of existing companies to sign the subscription contract on behalf of their own branches or for nominally independent lines.[2] This continued to be done in the 1850s; but in the case of new companies the contractors played a large part too. The largest individual subscriber to the West End & Crystal Palace Railway in 1853 was Edward Ladd Betts (£60,000 out of a total of £223,750). William Dargan subscribed over one-third to an Irish line. And Brassey, Peto & Betts subscribed to others. Four contractors subscribed £33,500 out of £72,070 to a Mid-Kent extension line in 1857,[3] and there are numerous other examples.[4] Contractors, too, supplied money for the parliamentary deposit. In 1861 one-half of the deposit for the Bill of the Metropolitan Railway's extension to Moorgate Street was provided in this way.[5]

The fact that contractors signed the subscription contract and financed the deposit is not in itself important—the records of many companies show that the deposit was in fact often borrowed.[6] What is significant is that the signing of the subscription contract became part of the negotia-

[1] O. C. Williams, *Historical Development of Private Bill Procedure and Standing Orders in the House of Commons* (2 Vols, 1948–9).

[2] Pollins, 'Marketing of Railway Shares', loc cit, 235.

[3] *Railway Times*, 11 June 1853, 601–2; 7 May 1853, 481; 10 January 1857, 32–3. This journal printed many subscriptions, or extracts from them, in the 1850s, as did *Bradshaw's Railway Shareholders' Manual.*

[4] See, for example, the two volumes of subscription contracts, BTHR, SUB 3/1 and 3/2.

[5] *Railway Times*, 31 August 1861, 1098. This journal argued that the contractors in their turn borrowed money for the deposit: ibid, 26 March 1864, 469.

[6] Robert Baxter, a parliamentary agent, said the deposit was invariably borrowed. *SC on Standing Order 184, Section 2*, PP (Lords) 1866, XXVIII (168), Q 775.

Many of the deposits for the London tube railway Bills in the early twentieth century were borrowed: Underground Electric Railways, Board Minutes, 5 August 1902 (Minute 71); 29 March 1904 (346); 10 January 1905 (432); 12 September 1905 (493) (BTHR, UER 1/1).

tions between company and contractor. Examples are to be found in the case of two companies, which may be regarded as case-studies.

The Rhymney Railway was formed during the boom of the early 1850s. The board had the support of the neighbouring Taff Vale Railway, the Rhymney Iron Company, and the trustees of the Marquess of Bute. Nevertheless the company found itself compelled to approach George Wythes, the contractor, 'to fill up the Subscription list in case of need'. He agreed to take the contract for the line and also 2,500 shares, but in the end he signed the subscription contract for £15,000. A year later an extension line was proposed and again Wythes signed the contract for £15,000, paid the deposit, and obtained the contract.[1]

The East Kent Railway (the name was changed in 1859 to the London, Chatham & Dover) was also a result of the boom in the early fifties. The minutes of the Provisional Committee, which begin in October 1852, show quite clearly that the Railway was leaning quite heavily on Sir Charles Fox (of Fox, Henderson & Co). After some vague references to negotiations the company agreed that out of the 30,000 £25 shares[2] Fox and his friends should take 14,500 and pay the deposit of £2 10s 0d on them, provided that 5,000 were subscribed by individuals on application to the company and the deposit paid. In return Fox would have the contract. Fox agreed to find £36,250 for the parliamentary deposit. And out of the authorised capital of £700,000 the subscription contract was signed to the amount of £544,375, of which only £135,375 was subscribed locally (by 334 local shareholders). Fox himself signed for £31,875.[3]

It follows from all this that such competition as there was between contractors was not over the price of the tender, but rather over the ability of the contractors to provide funds in some way.[4] There were contemporary allegations of a price ring among contractors;[5] there was certainly an association of railway contractors which held quarterly meetings.[6] In this situation the likelihood of capital accounts being inflated was clearly very great.

[1] Barry, *Rhymney Railway*, pp 52–3. Rhymney Railway, Board Minutes, 14, 22, 27, 31 December 1853, and correspondence with Wythes in BTHR, RHY 1/1, p 393. He also signed the subscription contract for a later branch line: ibid, 30 December 1856.

[2] After various amendments to the prospectus—detailed in the minutes—the capital was fixed at £700,000 (ie 28,000 shares): *Railway Record*, 4 December 1852, 786.

[3] Provisional Committee, 22 November 1852 (BTHR, LCD 1/5). See also *Railway Record*, 11 December 1852, 790, where it was stated that two thirds of the capital had been taken by 'capitalists'; *Reports & Accounts*, 31 December 1854 (speech by Fox); *Railway & Travel Monthly*, November 1919, 295; *Railway Times*, 15 January 1853, 62–3.

[4] Swindon, Marlborough & Andover Railway, Letters etc relating to tenders . . . (BTHR, MPR 34/2). In this file there is a list of tenders from various contractors. Those which made no offer about finance were rejected.

[5] *Herapath*, 17 June 1848, 644; 4 November 1848, 1161; 25 May 1850, 508–9; 18 September 1852, 1017. These news items also refer generally to the absence of competition and to the tendency to tender for the whole of a line.

[6] *Railway Times*, 6 April 1839, 295.

III

It is not possible to give a comprehensive list of contractors' lines. It is apparent that many were promoted in the 1850s and 1860s, especially in the boom of 1864–6; many of the lines promoted in East Anglia, associated with the name of Peto, were of this character.[1] Some of the companies which were analysed in a series of articles in the *Railway Times* in 1869 under the heading of 'Insolvencies' and 'Abortions' were contractors' lines, and it is interesting to observe that *The Economist* estimated that two-thirds of the capital authorised in the session 1864–6 was for schemes which could be characterised as contractors' lines.[2] Robert Baxter, a parliamentary agent, said in 1864 that 'nine railways out of ten are made with the aid of contractors'.[3] Not all of them were small; some of the most important ones were the London, Chatham & Dover, the Metropolitan District and the various companies that made up the Cambrian Railways.

While contractors might have promoted companies, and have taken part in the parliamentary proceedings, the essential characteristic of contractors' lines was that payment for construction was in the railway company's securities. The activities of the contractors would often go beyond construction. It was not uncommon for contractors to arrange to buy the land, pay the railway company's engineer and solicitors, and guarantee the interest on the shares during construction. The contract[4] between the Swansea Vale & Neath & Brecon Junction Railway and John Dickson of 1864 had these clauses:

> The Contractor as the Agent of the Company will as soon as can be enter into and carry into effect the requisite Contracts for the purchase by the Company of all Lands Buildings and other property which shall be requisite either temporarily or permanently for the Railway and the Sidings Stations and other works and conveniences thereof. (clause 9)
>
> The amount of the purchase money or compensation in every case of voluntary agreement shall be determined exclusively by the Contractor and in all cases of reference to Arbitration or to a Jury the lawful and reasonable requirements or directions of the Contractor as to the proceedings thereof shall be observed by the Company and their Solicitor. (clause 11)

Similarly in the case of Thomas Savin and the Brecon & Merthyr Railway. In 1860 Savin made a proposition about the construction of the line.

> Mr Savin undertook to construct their lines for so much a mile, out of which he was to provide for all incidental expenses such as the payment

[1] See the account in *PETO VIA, being a review of the scheme for a railway from Pitsea to Colchester . . . by a tooth of the dragon* (1857).

[2] *Economist* Commercial History and Review of 1866, 9 March 1867, p 31.

[3] *SC on Standing Orders* (*Parliamentary Deposits*), PP 1864, X, Q 645.

[4] Contract dated 29 September 1864 (BTHR, MPR 261).

of the Company's Engineer and Solicitor, and all charges for land, or parliamentary expenses, he also undertook to lease the line for 5 per cent for ten years after opening and to pay the same rate of interest during construction.[1]

The paying of interest during construction was a fairly normal feature of contractors' lines. In 1853, for example, Sir Charles Fox agreed to pay interest at 4 per cent during construction,[2] and a great deal of evidence testifies to the continuance of this practice into the eighties and nineties.

It may seem strange, after the discussion so far about contractors taking shares, that they should have agreed to pay interest on them. The point is that in many cases shares were issued to the public in order that the more normal relation between company and contractor should supervene. And when the contractor took shares his prospects of getting rid of them, or borrowing on their security, were correspondingly improved by the offer of guaranteed interest. Indeed one contract, between the Swindon, Marlborough & Andover Railway, and Watson, Smith & Watson stated explicitly that the contractors should take the contract for shares and debentures, or cash if it were available. That some cash would be forthcoming was guaranteed in the contract, because the directors and solicitors arranged to take a certain number of shares. The eventual result was that a large proportion of the contract was paid in cash, promissory notes, and Lloyd's bonds.[3] Similarly, the Central London Railway arranged to pay its contractors partly in bonds; the company had 1,911 shareholders, and the shares were paid up.[4]

Nevertheless there is no doubt that in many cases contractors were paid wholly or largely in shares and debentures. The shares were usually taken at a discount; this was well known at the time. In 1863 the secretary of the London & North Western Railway gave evidence before a select committee of the Lords:

> Earl of Airlie: You know, as a matter of fact, that the contractor does take shares in the case of small Companies who are in difficulties at a lower rate than their nominal amount?
>
> Charles Stewart: Yes; but those shares must be considered as paid up in full.[5]

In one case, it is true, the contract specified that the shares were to be taken

[1] 'Conybeare and the Brecon & Merthyr Railway' (BTHR, MPR 4/32). Conybeare was the engineer to the company.

[2] East Kent Railway, Provisional Committee, 24 August 1853. Also *Railway Record*, 27 August 1853, 580.

[3] The contract is dated 15 September 1879. It is in a file of papers (BTHR, MPR 34/1) which contains a list of payments made to the contractors specifying the various methods of payment.

[4] *Railway News*, 24 February 1900, 307.

[5] *SC on Railway Companies' Borrowing Powers*, PP (Lords) 1863, XXXIV (175), Q 361.

by the contractor at par. But since the contractor increased his prices the eventual result came to the same thing as an issue at a discount. The contract was between the Swindon, Marlborough & Andover Railway and William Wright. The contractor at first offered to take the contract for £344,797 if he were paid in cash, or £407,828 if paid in shares and debentures. The contract price was eventually fixed at £399,045, to be taken in shares and debentures. The specification shows that the contract price was increased by a flat 17½ per cent to bring it up to £399,045.[1] This seems to be a different situation from that described by the engineer to the Brecon & Merthyr Railway in 1866. In the course of a letter to the company's solicitors, the engineer, H. Conybeare, wrote:

> In the case of Contract lines for a lump sum per mile, it is not usual that anything should be paid to the Contractor, except on the Engineer's certificates, and out of the paper given by the Board on such certificates, the Contractor finds money to pay all charges whatsoever, law, land, Parliamentary, and engineering; it is so on the Irish Contractors' lines, to which I am engineer; it is so on the London, Chatham, and Dover, where the price certified for earthwork is 2s 11½d per cubic yard, instead of the usual rate (for earthwork 'pur et simple)' of 1s per yard; the reason being that all other expenses, land, law, Parliamentary, and engineering are charged on works and paid for by Contractors, out of proceeds of Engineer's certificates.[2]

John Fowler, the engineer, generalising on this matter said: 'I think the Committee may take it as a broad fact, that in most cases where the contractors find the greater part of the capital, and takes (*sic*) payment in shares, the contract price will be higher than if the company could go into the open market, and pay for the works in cash.'[3]

These details provide further evidence of the difficulties involved in examining railway accounts to try to establish capital expenditure. But more important is the question: how did the system work? The contractors needed money for their men and for their material. They often had to pay for the land in cash. To some extent, no doubt, contractors obtained long credits from their suppliers. But they still required a certain amount of cash for their work. As has been shown, some companies were able to issue shares and so obtain money from the public; some contractors were engaged in many different works (some of which would be paid for in cash) and one contract might well have assisted another. In addition, the contractors often had large investments in other industries—George Wythes, for example, invested heavily in mining and blast furnaces.[4] The income

[1] William Wright to Swindon, Marlborough & Andover Railway, 2 June 1875. (BTHR, MPR 34/2 and 34/7). See Maggs, *M & SWJR*, for a detailed history of this company.

[2] 'Memorandum on Engineers Certificates', BTHR, MPR 4/32.

[3] *SC on Standing Order 184*, PP (Lords) 1866, XVIII, Q 218.

[4] *Proc Inst Civ Eng*, Vol 74 (1882–3), 294–7.

from these activities could be used to tide them over difficult periods.[1] But it is noteworthy that in the case of William Wright, in 1875, a backer was obtained, Raisbeck Robinson (Temple Chambers, 32 Fleet Street), who wrote to Wright that he was 'prepared to finance this Railway for you on your obtaining the Contract'.[2] But Wright was a small man, who gets into this narrative through the accidental survival of some documents, and he may not be a typical case.

The shares and debentures issued to contractors could be used as security for borrowing, or be sold to the public. In fact contractors often held on to the shares, perhaps because they could not get a reasonable price for them; the reports of bankruptcy proceedings (there are many of them) in the journals invariably refer to the fact that the contractor had in his possession large numbers of worthless shares. And John Dickson, the contractor for the Neath & Brecon Railway, said in 1867, a few months before he became bankrupt, that he was the largest shareholder in the railway.[3] But it is not easy to decide how much of the contractors' shareholding was held as *bona fide* investment, and how much they were simply unable to dispose of.

The great expansion of contractors' lines in the 1860s required sources of finance greater than could be arranged in this *ad hoc* way. These came with the emergence of credit and finance companies. Their history has been traced by Mr King,[4] and it is sufficient to say here that it was those companies above all which permitted the great expansion in the number of contractors' lines in the boom of the 1860s. Lord Redesdale, who (as chairman of committees in the House of Lords) was an acute observer of railway matters and a participant in them, stated: 'It was in 1864 that the difficulties began to arise, the railway contractors then experiencing pressing difficulty in obtaining money for their undertaking, and certain "finance companies" were formed for the avowed purpose of providing the capital which would enable contractors to carry out their schemes.' He even went so far as to say: 'Last year all the schemes which were brought before Parliament by Bills more or less looked to these finance companies for assistance.' He argued that the fall of Overend, Gurney & Co in 1866 (which precipitated the crisis of that year) was occasioned to a large extent by the 'advances made by them to railway companies or to contractors on railway securities'.[5] Little enough is known about the detailed workings of these

[1] Noted by John Fowler, *SC on Standing Order 184*, Q 85.

[2] Robinson to Wright, 1 July 1875 (BTHR, MPR 34/2).

[3] Minutes of Evidence on the Neath & Brecon Railway Bill (Lords, 28 May 1883), QQ 2–3 (BTHR, MPR 261). But George Wythes did not remain a shareholder in the Rhymney Railway. See Rhymney Railway Share Registers (BTHR, RHY 2/1).

[4] W. T. C. King, *History of the London Discount Market* (1936), especially Chapter 7. Also Jenks, op cit, Chapter 8.

[5] *Hansard*, CLXXXIII (1866), col 858. See for example the prospectus of the Contract Corporation Ltd. (*Herapath*, 19 December 1863, 1345) which refers to the onerous terms on which contractors had to raise money.

finance companies, but there is no doubt of the extent of their activities. Even such an important contractor as Peto came into contact with them.[1]

Another innovation, which had particular reference to the contractors' lines, was the use of Lloyd's bonds, which were invented 'to meet the cases of young companies struggling with monetary difficulties'.[2] They were not necessarily initiated with a view to their use by contractors' lines; any railway company which had difficulties in getting funds to continue work could use them. It might be that the capital powers were exhausted, the bankers would not advance funds and the directors could not, or would not, give their personal security for a loan. In this situation a Lloyd's bond would be issued. They were, however, taken up to a great extent by contractors, who received them from the railway companies instead of cash or shares.

The Railway Act of 1844 (s 19) had made illegal the issue of loan notes—a commonly-used instrument of the late 1830s and early 1840s to secure debts; they were little more than IOUs, with no mention of security or maturity date on the document.[3] Loan notes had provided a useful method, adopted by many railway companies, to tide them over a period when it was impossible, for some reason, to issue more capital (their powers may have been exhausted, for example). The way to get round this prohibition on loan notes was to make use of Lloyd's bonds. They were not a debenture or loan note but 'in the form of an acknowledgment, under the seal of the company, of a debt incurred and actually due by the company to a contractor or other person for work done, goods supplied (or otherwise, as the case may be) with a covenant for payment of principal and interest at a future date'.[4] That is to say the companies did not raise money on these bonds; they merely secured a debt.

They were named after the barrister with whom they originated, John Horatio Lloyd, who gave a detailed account of them to the Select Committee of the House of Lords on Railway Companies' Borrowing Powers (1864). Lloyd explained that the bonds were useful in a situation where a railway company had exhausted its funds. The contractor in such a situation would be able to continue work if the company gave him 'an acknowledgment, under seal'. This the contractor would take to a banker 'or some capitalist' and obtain an advance, providing him with the funds to continue the work. The rate of interest on them was higher than that on a debenture—usually 5 or 6 per cent; they were issued by small, new companies, not

[1] *Railway Times*, 9 June 1866, 708; *Herapath*, 16 June 1866, 670. *Railway Times*, 16 November 1867, 1158. Further discussion of railways and finance companies is in *Railway Times*, 18 September 1875, 904–5.

[2] *Railway News*, 9 January 1864, 33.

[3] G. H. Evans, op cit, p 72; F. Clifford, *History of Private Bill Legislation* (2 Vols, 1885–7), I, 127–8; *Railway News*, 9 January 1864, 33; *Stock Exchange Official Intelligence*, Vol 20 (1902), 1935.

[4] H. Godefroi and J. Shortt, *Law of Railway Companies* (1869), p 39.

the large ones such as the London & North Western or the Great Western. And they were eventually discharged by applying to Parliament for powers to issue capital or were paid out of revenue.[1] The advantages of these instruments were summarised by a contemporary writer.[2] The contractor was enabled to go into the market and obtain cash upon the bond 'at a much better rate than he would be able to procure the same upon his bare personal security' and it allowed him 'where the work was paid for in this way by sections, to undertake considerably more extensive contracts than his capital would otherwise justify him in doing. The railway company also would be able to carry on their works with a reduced capital, having time to pay cash for its construction until profits came in'. And of course companies could use them without bothering about the statutory one-half of the share capital being paid up before exercising their borrowing powers.[3]

Lloyd thought there were several millions in Lloyd's bonds in circulation, and the Select Committee agreed that there was no limit to the gross amount that could be used. Their most important advantage was that they were not illegal. (This did not stop the *Railway Times* from describing them as 'a peculiar but inevitable fraud'.)[4] Lloyd's bonds were not a feature of the 1860s and 1870s only. In 1900, during the negotiations about the electrification of the Metropolitan and Metropolitan District Railways, one method of payment being considered was by these bonds.[5]

It is not surprising that this kind of financial dealing often led into difficulties.[6] While it would be too gross an exaggeration to say that the history of contracting is a history of bankruptcy, it would be reasonable to suggest that most contractors found themselves embarrassed at one time or another. The most spectacular case was that of Peto in 1866—associated with the fall of Overend, Gurney, and with the London, Chatham & Dover Railway. At that period Thomas Brassey is said to have lost £1 million[7] and, as well as a host of minor people, John Watson & Co, Smith Knight & Co, and Thomas Savin were affected even before the crisis of May 1866.[8] The typical reason was that their railway shares, which they held in great numbers, were worth very little; their value was often insufficient to cover their debts. This is in addition to the more usual kind of problem. Peto in the 1830s had to borrow to carry on the work of the Hanwell Viaduct be-

[1] *SC on Railway Companies' Borrowing Powers*, PP (Lords), 1864, XXVII (127); reprinted in PP 1864, XI; QQ 117; 180–1; 207; 235.

[2] H. J. Tarrant, *Lloyd's Bonds; their nature and uses* (1867), p 8.

[3] *SC on Borrowing Powers*, PP 1864, XI, Q 117.

[4] Ibid, Q 117; Report, p iv; *Railway Times*, 12 August 1865, 1039.

[5] *Railway News*, 24 November 1900, 746.

[6] Jenks, op cit, p 259, refers to the 'many railways, within the British Isles and without, that contractors had built upon the credit of their smiles'.

[7] *Engineering*, 16 December 1870, 443. But he was able to offer Peto half a million pounds in that year and take over his contracts: *Railway News*, 17 December 1870, 714; *Railway Gazette*, 4 February 1938, 215.

[8] *Railway Times*, 26 March 1864, 464; 28 October 1865, 1391; *Herapath*, 23 December 1865, 1429; 31 March 1866, 383–4.

cause of a dispute with the Great Western Railway over the contract price.[1] And in the 1870s Peto was in trouble again with the Cornwall Minerals Railway. The private diary of William Pease, steward to George Fortescue, Boconnoc, Lostwithiel, gives an interesting sidelight on this.

> *13 February 1875.* Sir Morton Peto came this day and gave me particulars as to the state of his affairs. The Minerals Ry contract has ruined him. He has not a shilling of his own and owes thousands of pounds to those who lent him money to enable him to proceed with the contract. The Railway Compy has taken all his plant and he owes a large sum for rail iron. He does not know what course his creditors will take, but there is nothing more for them. In order to make the payments which has been made, his plate was sold and also his wife's jewels. He said the estimates for his contract were far too little in consequence of the great rise in wages and in the price of material. The land cost *three* times as much as was calculated on, and rail iron £5 per ton beyond what it can now be had for and many of the labourers had 7/6d. per day.[2]

IV

This article has been concerned with only one aspect of the contractors' activities in the construction of British railways in the second half of the nineteenth century. It has shown their transformation from a prime concern with engineering to an equal if not greater interest in finance. It is not surprising to find Peto, in the early 1860s, helping the London, Chatham & Dover Railway to liquidate over £1¼ million of Lloyd's bonds.[3]

In the course of this article I have not referred to the contractors' activities as railway operators; that would be worthy of a separate study, as would a discussion of their organisation (including the significance of subcontracting and truck). Nor must it be thought that the railways were the only industry in which contractors were financially important. Some of the urban horse-tramways were built with the financial aid of contractors.[4] Without their financial aid railway building would have been on a smaller

[1] *Proc Inst Civ Eng*, Vol 99 (1889–90), 401.

[2] I am grateful to Mr C. R. Clinker for providing me with this extract. It should be pointed out that the crisis of 1866 had already virtually finished Peto's career; compared with the London, Chatham & Dover Railway, with which Peto's downfall in 1866 was associated, the Cornwall Minerals Railway was a small affair.

[3] *Herapath*, 27 October 1866, 1181–2. This was explained in the course of a long speech to his constituents at Bristol (Peto was an MP) in which he defended himself against the attacks made on him by a Committee of Investigation of the LCDR. Similarly, William Dargan was a director of the International Financial Society Ltd, formed to make advances on landed estates: *Railway News*, 23 January 1864, 96. Jenks, op cit, p 252, generalises about 'the readiness with which railway contractors . . . lent the prestige of their names to the directorates of finance companies'.

[4] William Jaques, the manager of the South London Tramways Company, said that the contractors paid the dividends on his company's shares during construction: Minutes of Evidence on the South London Tramways Bill (6 June 1883, Commons), QQ 1693–6 (BTHR, PYB 1/1078).

scale—if, that is, it had been left to the existing companies or to new companies financed by the public, or to landowners. Not only did the contractors build new lines but they probably stimulated older companies to build in order to protect their territories. How desirable it all was is difficult to decide. Obviously many of the lines were necessary and would have been built at some time or other—some of the London Transport railways for example. But many had an unhappy history, which included the payment of small dividends or none at all, and even bankruptcy. A full assessment would need to go beyond the profit and loss of the particular line, and take in any net additions to the profits of the company or of the network, as well as general social and economic benefits.[1]

The history of railway construction, as it is provided in many standard works, peters out at about 1850, despite the impressive mileage built after that date. Whatever the reasons for this—and there is a crying need for the work done by H. G. Lewin to be continued after 1852—this article has shown some of the financial questions involved. Clearly the 1850s were a watershed in constructional finance; the problems were new and so were the solutions. To that extent the traditional story of railway finance in Britain needs modification.

[1] See G. J. Ponsonby, 'The Closing of Branch Lines and Intermediate Stations', *British Transport Review*, Vol I, 1951, and the recent applications of cost-benefit analysis.

Index